D0889988

Reading Athena's Dance Card

Reading Athena's Dance Card

Men against Fire in Vietnam

Russell W. Glenn

Naval Institute Press
Annapolis, Maryland

Naval Institute Press
291 Wood Road
Annapolis, MD 21402

Library of Congress Cataloging-in-Publication Data
Glenn, Russell W.
   Reading Athena's dance card : men against fire in Vietnam / Russell W. Glenn.
     p. cm.
   Includes bibliographical references and index.
   ISBN 1-55750-316-8 (alk. paper)
     1. Vietnamese Conflict, 1961–1975—United States. 2. Vietnamese Conflict,
1961–1975—Campaigns. I. Title.
DS558.G6 2000
959.704'3373—dc21
                                                                                    00-24977

Printed in the United States of America on acid-free paper ♾
07   06   05   04   03   02   01   00   9   8   7   6   5   4   3   2
First printing

To our men and women who died in Vietnam and those more fortunate who served in and lived through that war, especially my father, Russell A. Glenn, a soldier who in his over thirty years of active duty never forgot that service is about the good of the nation, not the promotion of oneself.

Contents

Foreword

Anyone who was ever in a firefight in Vietnam would have excellent cause to doubt the findings of S. L. A. Marshall in *Men Against Fire,* his study of American soldiers in combat during World War II. Marshall wrote that his research showed that only 15 to 25 percent of frontline soldiers actually fired their weapons at the enemy. Marshall's thesis was that American soldiers, by their very upbringing, had deep-rooted moral objections to the taking of lives, even of enemies who were trying to take theirs.

Russ Glenn, a combat veteran and retired army officer with over twenty-two years of active service, has done us all a favor by demonstrating that Marshall's findings, whether valid or not for World War II, certainly did not represent the American fighting man's performance in Vietnam. In fact, in Southeast Asia the evidence of one's own eyes and ears was to the contrary. There the problem was often the reverse: A good deal of effort on the part of officers and NCOs went into preventing soldiers from switching their M16 rifles to "rock 'n' roll," or automatic, and pouring fire on anything remotely threatening, including green bushes at night.

This was especially true of new arrivals, who were inclined to shoot first and ask questions later. A case in point: One brigade of a famous infantry division, fresh off the boat in 1965, settled itself into a perimeter that sat squarely above the spider holes of two or three local guerrillas. Each evening at dark the VC would take turns popping up, squeezing off a round, and then settling back into their holes to watch a spectacular firefight of the brigade's soldiers against each other. The casualties of that first tumultuous week were not inconsiderable, and included one U.S. soldier who launched a grenade straight up and was killed when it came straight back down. As American soldiers became experienced in the ways of the bush they were more careful, more wily, but certainly no more reluctant to fire when fired upon.

Did every single man in a unit return fire? No. Moving in formation through dense jungle imposes commonsense restrictions on the infantryman: If he cannot see the enemy and he cannot see his friends, he cannot shoot, or should not, for fear of killing his friends.

The soldier's or marine's ability to exercise common sense, to bring seasoned judgment to the violently unpredictable circumstances of jungle warfare and live to benefit from experience, depended on other factors that Russ explores, including equipment, training, the length of command tours, and the rotation system. He has gone a step further by polling veterans on what worked best in precombat training and what more could be done to better prepare tomorrow's fighting men for the reality of any battlefield and to make them more effective at their job, which is to take the enemy under fire and eradicate the threat he poses.

We owe him no small debt for this undertaking and the light it sheds on soldiers and marines at the cutting edge of combat.

Joseph L. Galloway

Acknowledgments

This book would have been unachievable without the help of those 1st Cavalry Division and other Vietnam veterans who responded to a stranger's call for information with no offering of compensation in return. Tim Millar's assistance while heading the division association was invaluable. To him, to all who responded to either of the surveys that supported this work, and to the members of the 1st Cavalry Division Association staff, my thanks.

Many veterans included their names when responding despite having not been asked to sacrifice their anonymity. I have nevertheless made every effort to insure that no respondent's name appeared in the following text unless subsequent permission was granted. The following men granted that permission. They represent the many who, because of death, illness, choice, changed address, or simply not having originally identified themselves on a survey, cannot be personally recognized. Their names appear in alphabetical order; service to one's country is such that military rank should have no meaning after an individual completes his tour of active duty: David Bowman, David M. Bray, Gerhard Brostrom, Billy D. Burns, J. D. Coleman, Douglas A. Fields, Sherman Flanders, Bobby G. Franklin, Leroy Emit Harrison, Jr., David A. Hart, William J. Jones, Walter L. Kudlacik, Thomas D. Lent, Ronald H. Martin, Jack Walter Pellington, Jay H. Phillips, Bruce W. Rehmer, and John M. Steele.

A second group that provided invaluable assistance was the superb staff of the Combined Arms Research Library (CARL) at Fort Leavenworth, Kansas. Rusty Rafferty was extraordinary in providing unceasing assistance to the author during his pursuit of many documents on which this work relied. Rusty was not alone; the following are only some of the members who over the years have been members of one of the finest library staffs in the world and to whom I am most grateful: Kathy Berveiler, Betty Bohanon, Bernie Brose, Charlene Buduo, Dan Dorris, Susan Fowler, Diane Karis, Alice King, Joanne Knight, Pam Kontowicz, Carol Morrison, Elaine

McConnell, Ginny Navarro, Mary Jo Nelson, Mary Otto, Carol Ramkey, Dorothy Rogers, John Rogers, Helen Rutledge, Pamala S. Tijerina, and Pat Wells.

Six gentlemen who selflessly shared their knowledge comprise a third group deserving special thanks. Each possesses extraordinary skills both as a scholar and teacher. To describe the help provided over the past several years by Ted Wilson and Phil Schrodt of the University of Kansas, Roger Spiller of the Command and General Staff College, Jim Schneider of the School of Advanced Military Studies, Jake Kipp of the Foreign Military Studies Office, and Peter Maslowski of the University of Nebraska would itself take a book.

Others who helped in finding and confirming facts, uncovering valuable resources, or reviewing portions of the completed manuscript include Curt Bowers; Lionel Galway; Larry Gavin; Hal Moore; John Wayne Raines; Australians Bob Breen, Garth Pratten, and Nick Welch; Vincent Demma and Steve Everett of the United States Army Center of Military History; Richard Sommers at that service's Military History Institute; and Robert J. T. Joy, formerly Head of the Department of Medical History, Uniformed Services University of the Health Sciences.

I have been fortunate in having unceasingly had a loving and supportive family since the day I was born. My parents, Priscilla Beardsley Glenn and Russell Alger Glenn, raised three sons who were made to realize that there is more to life than personal gain. The sons' successes are their parents' successes. Nor did my extraordinary fortune falter after I left my childhood home. Years of travel, separation, and writing have been hard on my wife and two young men; encouraging words and young sons' hugs meant more than I perhaps let be known at the time. Dee, Russell, and Drew, this work is as much yours as mine. Drew, my particular thanks to you for your assistance as we selected the title for this book.

Reading Athena's Dance Card

1

Introduction

Your presence is requested . . .

The history of a battle is not unlike the history of a ball. Some individuals may recollect all the little events of which the great result is the battle won or lost; but no individual can recollect the exact order in which, or the exact moment at which, they occurred, which makes all the difference as to their value or importance.

The Duke of Wellington, in a letter dated 8 August 1815 to
John Wilson Broker, quoted in Wellington at War, 1794–1815,
ed. Antony Brett-James

In 1947, S. L. A. Marshall wrote that only 15 to 25 percent of American World War II combat soldiers engaged the enemy with their weapons. He believed that their failure to fire was due to a combination of factors, the most significant of which had its roots in the moral upbringing of the American fighting man. The soldier was

> what his home, his religion, his schooling, and the moral code and ideals of his society have made him. The Army cannot unmake him. It must reckon with the fact that he comes from a civilization in which aggression, connected with the taking of life, is prohibited and unacceptable. . . . It stays his trigger finger even though he is hardly conscious that it is a restraint upon him.[1]

Marshall's ratio of fire values and related conclusions won widespread acceptance. Notable historians cited his statistics as fact in respected analyses.[2]

I found Marshall's observations surprising when I first read them as a young captain. Nothing in my years with soldiers had led me to doubt their willingness to perform the unfortunate but essential act of killing human adversaries. My father, who had seen combat in both Korea and Vietnam, answered my questions with conviction: He had never seen men fail to engage the enemy when the situation demanded their fire. Readings of first-person wartime accounts by soldiers and marines revealed scant mention of any hesitation to engage, providing little evidence that a staying of the trigger finger was characteristic of World War II or more recent combat. Nor did Marshall's findings go unchallenged. Harry W. O. Kinnard (who was with the 101st Airborne Division during the Second World War and who later commanded the 1st Cavalry Division in Vietnam) and Gen. James M. Gavin, commander of the 82nd Airborne Division during World War II, were among those who disputed the low values. Gen. Bruce Clarke, commander of the forces defending St.Vith during the Battle of the Bulge, flatly discounted Marshall, finding his estimates "ridiculous and dangerous assertions—absolute nonsense."[3] British author George MacDonald Fraser recognized that moral upbringing influenced soldiers' views on killing, but his firsthand experience as a young British soldier during operations in World War II Burma offered a counter to Marshall's views: Fraser had found combat "exciting. . . . We all have kindly impulses, fostered by two thousand years of Christian teaching, gentle Jesus, and love thy neighbor, but we have the killer instinct, too, the murderous impulse of the hunter."[4]

This is not to say that evidence of soldiers' failure to fire was nonexistent. Combat veteran Roy Moore wrote of American men hesitating to engage the enemy in his 1945 *Infantry Journal* article "Shoot, Soldier"; another cited similar experiences undergone by both himself and a relative who had served with the American army during World War I.[5] Autobiographies by high-ranking World War II officers on rare occasion cited similar observations.[6] These, however, were generally written after publication of Marshall's findings in 1947 and could have been influenced by his work.[7] Further, the perspective of these general officers, while extremely valuable in understanding the decisions and actions of those at the highest echelons, hardly reflected the combat experiences of men whose lives were dominated by frontline fighting. Questions therefore arose regarding the problems cited in *Men Against Fire;* pens and voices rallied to both sides of the controversy.

The importance of the issue fueled these debates. Leaders and men could rely on the fire of only two or three in an infantry squad if but 15 to 20 percent of a unit used their weapons. Squads frequently fought at less than full strength because of losses to sickness, rotation, leaves, passes, schooling, casualties, or the many other causes of organizations going into combat with less than their full complement of warriors. If only two or three men per squad could be counted on to engage the adversary, future conflicts would be longer and the vulnerability of American soldiers would thus be prolonged. Artillery and mortar shells, mines, booby traps, and enemy soldiers perhaps less hesitant to kill than their American counterparts posed deadly threats.

I continued to observe soldiers during training, better aware of their possible unwillingness to engage after having read *Men Against Fire.* Soldiers relished employing MILES (Multiple Integrated Laser Engagement System) weapons with their mounted laser transmitters that emitted a pulse when a blank round was fired, thereby allowing them to "kill" a mock adversary wearing a harness and helmet band containing laser sensors. All realized that the "adversaries" so engaged would not actually die, but none seemed bothered by the short leap to that final, vital element. Importantly, however, this training lacked the sudden blast of noise and dust that accompanies many contacts with the enemy, the sights and sounds associated with comrades wounded and killed, and the danger of incoming fire, any of which might better explain a failure to use a weapon in combat than would the constraints imposed by moral upbringing.

Later in my career, an assignment to the School of Advanced Military Studies in Fort Leavenworth, Kansas, provided the opportunity to further study the subject of American fighting men during combat and their willingness to engage their enemy.[8] Early research revealed that Marshall had visited both Korea and Vietnam. He wrote that roughly half of American soldiers fired their weapons in the former and nearly all in the latter war.[9] At this point of apparent impasse, I was fortunate in meeting Dr. Roger Spiller at the United States Army Command and General Staff College. Dr. Spiller was in the process of thoroughly analyzing the procedures S. L. A. Marshall had used in determining the percentage of men who fired their weapons in combat during World War II. He found that Marshall's work had shortcomings that spawned serious reservations regarding the validity of the 15- to 25-percent values.[10] As the approach used by Marshall in Korea and Vietnam had been similar to that used in World War II, these findings cast doubt on his conclusions regarding all three conflicts.

MEN IN BATTLE

The difficulty of understanding soldiers' behavior in combat has made it as inexact an undertaking as any in historical study. Each man's wartime performance, experiences, and perceptions are unique, different even from those of the man with whom he shares a foxhole for months on end. Any attempt to portray a typical life in combat through the creation of an "average" soldier is a demographer's phantom. Nor would building such a composite provide a more accurate description of wartime experiences than a personal memoir. The memoir would, in fact, always be far superior. It would relate an actual experience; the events experienced by a constructed "average" soldier would be fiction. The unfortunate shortcoming of a personal memoir, however, is similar to that of a tale told by an attendee at Wellington's ball: It consists of but a single interpretation of events. Further, any one man's memory is selective: Some events are consistently and accurately remembered with extraordinary clarity even after decades; recall of others may be triggered by a word or conversation; many are forever lost. An episode that included an exceptionally dangerous moment tends to be retained, whereas specifics are less likely to survive the passage of years if a particular event occurred during an extended period of extreme danger.[11]

The reader interested in a particular war can attempt to overcome a single memoir's limitations by reading several of the numerous autobiographies written after virtually any conflict. Nevertheless, the perspective gained is a limited one; such undertakings are frequently accounts of men with literary abilities or positions of authority that make them unrepresentative of most soldiers. Considering their works as reflections of the whole would be like portraying the daily lives of a metropolis's residents by collecting the thoughts only of arts council and city commission members. Oral histories provide a broader but often too select range of perspectives rather than comprising comprehensive studies.

The student of men at war can alternatively refer to historians' reconstructions and analyses. Generally lacking the angst of first-person accounts, their works nonetheless provide a scope that memoirs and oral histories cannot. If the reader is fortunate, the historians' efforts are both honest attempts at objectivity and demonstrations of familiarity with the topic of combat. These labors offer much in their descriptions and interpretations, to the extent that access to records, availability of personal correspondence, language skills, and the many other hurdles to historical analysis allow.

It becomes obvious that the Duke of Wellington's observation applies to wars as a whole much as it does to single battles. Memoirs provide individual histories, flawed in recall of "exact order" and "exact moment" but rich in the insights that only a participant can provide. Oral histories and archival historians' compilations help to fix the details, the order, and the moments, but they unavoidably confront contradictions, lapses in coverage, and even fabrications often impossible to completely resolve.

Even official records may be a poor reflection of the truth. Paul Fussell, author of *Wartime* and *The Great War and Modern Memory* among other works, derided both official unit after action reports and medal citations as sources of historical fact. He felt that the former would necessarily be "justifications, and are therefore useless." As for medal citations, Fussell told of his platoon sergeant, killed by his side during an artillery attack during World War II in Europe. A shell fragment struck the sergeant, killing him "within a half second." Fussell was wounded by the same round and had to be evacuated. He returned to his unit to find the sergeant had been awarded the Silver Star. Fussell by no means begrudged him the award, but he was surprised to find that the citation spoke of completely fabricated and extraordinary actions on the part of the noncommissioned officer, to include calling headquarters with critical information and performing a number of heroic acts between the time he was wounded and his death.

The analysis on the following pages relies to some extent on these traditional historical sources, but it also draws on the survey responses of 302 men who themselves drew on their combat experiences to address a variety of issues important to personal survival and unit effectiveness. These critical elements include: (1) men's willingness to engage the enemy, (2) the relationship an individual had with his weapon, the primary implement with which he was to kill his adversary, (3) the training that was to prepare him for this climactic act and the environment in which it would take place, and (4) the influences of fixed tour lengths and frequent loss of experienced leaders. This book, then, is a look into selected elements that fundamentally influenced the daily lives of America's fighting men in Vietnam, their combat effectiveness, and the likelihood that they would return home alive.

Men at war and the factors influencing their performance have been subjects of investigations for centuries. Sun Tzu, Carl von Clausewitz, Ardant Du Picq, Lord Moran, and J. C. Dunn are but a few of the many more recently joined by Richard Holmes, John Keegan, Charles Moskos, John Baynes, Samuel Stouffer, and others who have expanded our understanding of one of history's greatest enigmas. Paul Fussell, himself both a participant in and philosopher of armed conflict, warned that anyone undertaking an analysis of war, regardless of the specific focus, had "to specialize in a given war, not wars. There are too few significant similarities between them."[12]

That Vietnam was unlike any other American war is a given, but the differences should not be exaggerated. Only twenty years passed between the end of World War II and the major buildup of U.S. forces in Vietnam. Men who had seen their first combat in the earlier conflict were among those who went to Southeast Asia in 1965. Though jets rather than propeller-driven aircraft flew overhead, though the world entered its third decade in the shadow of nuclear standoff, though soldiers spent twelve months instead of the war's duration in the combat theater, the mud, terror, weapons, and arbitrariness of death were much the same for the infantrymen in Vietnam as for the generations before in World War II and Korea. Father and son talking of their service experiences would have found much in common. The men who educate us regarding these and other historic conflicts help us to understand the Wellington's ball of American combat in Vietnam as well. So, too, do the observations of the 302 respondents who collectively offered insights on seven years of fighting in Southeast Asia between 1965 and 1972.

THE SURVEYS

Given interest, cause, and opportunity, I set out to determine if failure to fire had been a problem during the Vietnam War and what factors influenced a man's readiness to engage his enemy. There were no records available on which to base such a study; original data had to be mined, and it was obvious that a survey of Vietnam veterans was the appropriate tool. Many of the army and marine division veteran organizations contacted were unable to help for various reasons. The notable exception was the 1st Cavalry Division Association.

The first step was to conduct a survey of the unit's Vietnam combat veterans, those whose job it had been to find, close with, and kill the enemy, or whose task it had been to accompany these men into combat and support their efforts. The two groups consisted primarily of infantrymen, helicopter crewmen, medics, artillery forward observers, radiomen, aviators, door gunners, combat engineers, or chaplains.[13] The infantrymen themselves were no homogeneous group. That status applied to riflemen, machine gunners, grenadiers, mortar men, and those in infantry unit leadership positions. It could also apply to men in reconnaissance units, mechanized vehicle crew members, and others in organizations that might or might not include "infantry" in the title. The survey used was the same regardless of a soldier's duty position; each veteran respondent was asked to provide relevant demographic information and to reflect on his own combat performance.[14] Veterans who had never fired their weapons or had not fired during one or more combat engagements were asked to explain their reasons for not engaging. Each man was also questioned regarding his fellow soldiers' willingness to fire on the enemy. Additional questions addressed factors that could have otherwise influenced weapons participation and combat performance: the terrain in which the soldier fought, his duty position, the weapons he carried, and training. Finally, veterans were provided an opportunity to make any general observations they thought appropriate.

There were imperfections in the process, not the least of which was the span of fifteen to twenty-two years between the veterans' service in Vietnam and their autumn 1987 consideration of the survey questions. Memory is an imperfect recorder of the past; its quality diminishes with time. Historian Richard M. Swain, a 1st Cavalry Division veteran who twice served in Vietnam, concluded an interview with the telling observation: "That, of course, is how I remember it, not necessarily how it was."[15] Another historian, Anne Firor Scott, similarly noted her imperfect memory as she wrote of inconsistencies between entries in her diary and events in World War II America as she remembered them some years later:

> There is much of great immediacy in my journal, but there are also mysterious silences—events that I remember vividly and thought were very important were never recorded at all, while some of the record has no place in memory. Even more puzzling are the places where memory and record do not jibe. I am chastened to find that over the years I have rewritten a good deal of the past in my mind.[16]

Two steps were taken to help compensate for the considerable span of time that passed between the events of concern and the conduct of the survey. First, the survey included a large number of veterans, so that one individual's lapses in memory might be compensated for by another's recall. Additionally, a second survey was conducted to provide a basis for comparison.

Even given the vagaries of memory, it should be remembered that the passage of time is not without its benefits. Official records that were unavailable shortly after the war were later declassified or catalogued in archives. Though the years may dim a veteran's memory, they provide an opportunity for objective retrospection. The respondents' willingness to offer additional comments and the nature of those comments demonstrated that the intervening years had done little to dampen their dedication to the nation and to those who had assumed the responsibility for its defense.

THE VETERANS

The primary survey went to five hundred 1st Cavalry Division Vietnam combat veterans.[17] Responses were notable for their objective self-evaluation and desire to pass on costly lessons learned. Comments regarding their own performances, that of fellow soldiers, and army experiences were frank and frequently biting. Descriptions of specific events were often very detailed. The nature of combat is such that it includes events that forever remain with the person who experiences them. The emotional shock of loss, the surge of adrenaline brought on by a sudden ambush, the heightened sense of reality that can accompany combat: these tend to make key episodes unforgettable. Chances that respondents remembered events addressed by the survey were increased by the nature of those events: they were asked to recall episodes that conflicted with their expectations, namely, cases in which soldiers did not fire their weapons during a fight.

A second survey was mailed to sixty-three officer veterans of Vietnam combat who were serving at Fort Leavenworth in the autumn of 1987.[18] The forty-four officers who responded to this second survey had seen combat in the same time period, on the same types of terrain, and against the same enemy as had the veterans who responded to the 1st Cavalry Division survey. They represented not one division, however, but fourteen divisions, separate brigades, or battalions. Their comments, like those of the 1st Cavalry Division, were sharply frank at times. Responses regarding soldiers' willingness to engage the enemy were similar in both surveys, lending considerable assurance that the results are likely not too far off the mark.

Of the 258 men who responded to the 1st Cavalry Division survey, just over half had enlisted as volunteers for military service.[19] Comparison with the percentage of volunteers and draftees army-wide in Vietnam (see table 1.1) reflects that draftees constituted a larger percentage of this division than of the service as a whole during the years of greatest American involvement (1968 and 1969). Further, fifty-one of the men who responded to the 1st Cavalry Division survey had more than one combat tour in Vietnam; of these, only one had originally entered the service as a draftee. (It should also be noted that 1st Cavalry Division respondents may not have served their Vietnam tours with that organization.) Removing the numbers of volun-

Table 1.1   Volunteers and Draftees, U.S. Army and 1st Cavalry in Vietnam

Time periods account for tours spanning both years.

% Vol/ % Draftee (NA = Not Available)	Pre-1965	1965 or 1965–66	1966 or 1966–67	1967 or 1967–68	1968 or 1968–69	1969 or 1969–70	1970 or 1970–71	1971 or 1971–72
U.S. Army, Vietnam-wide	NA	NA	NA	NA	58/42	61/39	61/39	NA
1st Cav Division—All respondents	100/0	86/14	70/30	54/46	51/49	54/46	62/38	75/25
1st Cav Division— 1st tour soldiers only	100/0	86/14	67/33	48/52	49/51	44/56	39/61	33/67
Draftees as percent of U.S. casualties	NA	NA	NA	NA	58	62	65	NA

Note: "U.S. Army, Vietnam-wide" and "Draftees as percent of U.S. casualties" data are from *A Study of Strategic Lessons Learned in Vietnam: Volume VII—The Soldier*, prepared by the BDM Corporation, 11 April 1980, 4-68.

teers on their second, third, or fourth tours reveals the striking predominance of draftees among 1st Cavalrymen on their first tours. Draftee ranks were dominated by men new to the army. New men tended to be of lower rank (not yet having had the opportunity to earn promotion). Headquarters or rear-area units, where experience was often deemed essential to job demands, had a greater percentage of senior soldiers or marines. Those having recently entered the military were therefore more likely to be assigned as infantry squad members or as engineers, medics, and artillerymen supporting those infantrymen in the field to "line" units in divisions and to positions involving greater exposure to combat. This helps to explain Paul Savage and Richard Gabriel's conclusion that "both absolutely and proportionately, army draftees in Vietnam became casualties in greater numbers than did volunteers."[20]

Seven out of every ten 1st Cavalry Division veterans surveyed had been infantrymen in Vietnam. Nearly nine of ten were enlisted men. They fought in virtually every type of terrain found in the combat theater. By tour's end the majority had battled in jungles, rice paddies or other open areas, and on military installations or fire bases. Nearly a third also had seen combat in civilian villages or cities. Eighty-five percent had only one tour in Vietnam. One in ten had two tours; four in one hundred had three tours. For the vast majority, then, the firsthand experiences with the war were contained within their single tour of duty.[21]

As was the case with the 1st Cavalry Division respondents, 70 percent of Fort Leavenworth respondents were infantrymen. Sixty-one percent had only a single Vietnam tour; the remainder had two assignments in the war zone. Fifty-nine percent had served as platoon leaders in Vietnam and 71 percent as company commanders.[22] Their experiences with various terrain types were comparable to those of the men in the 1st Cavalry Division survey. They, too, had seen combat in much of Vietnam and its environs.

HISTORICAL BACKGROUND:
THE 1ST CAVALRY DIVISION IN VIETNAM

The United States Army tested a new concept early in the 1960s: a division that used helicopters as its primary means of moving soldiers and equipment.[23] The 11th Air Assault Division, a test unit, was created in January 1963 to evaluate this innovative approach. Two and one-half years later, personnel of that organization were directed to prepare for deployment to Vietnam. The orders came after months of training, exercises, and testing, yet well before all phases of scheduled evaluations had been completed. The soon-to-be-deployed 11th Air Assault Division then acquired a combat-proven moniker; it became the 1st Cavalry Division (Airmobile), continuing a history reaching back to operations on the U.S.–Mexican border in the 1920s, in the Pacific during the World War II, and in blunting North Korea's attack in 1950. Helicopter-borne, the 1st Cav's newest reincarnation would soon appear in Vietnam.

Only 9,489 of its 15,890 authorized personnel were on hand when the division was formally activated on the first of July 1965, and only half of those soldiers were eligible for the movement to Vietnam that would come in the following months.[24] Helicopter pilots and airborne (parachute-qualified) personnel were specialties that had been in particularly short supply during the early years of the war; thus, many with these skills had already been to Vietnam and were not immediately subject to another combat assignment. The shortage of pilots was especially difficult to overcome in a division that had a fundamental operational concept based on helicopter transport.[25] This lack of men with particular skills was one problem. A second was a sudden influx of inexperienced soldiers; nearly two-thirds of the organization was new to both the unit and the airmobile concept as the division deployed to Vietnam.[26]

The rush to get the organization overseas also ensured that very few in the division received sufficient predeployment training on their recently issued M16 rifles, the replacement for the heavier M14 that had been found wanting in the terrain and weather of Southeast Asia.[27] Despite this shortcoming, 1st Cavalry Division soldiers would see their first Vietnam combat on 18 September 1965, only ninety-five days after the division's activation at Fort Benning.[28]

The bulk of the division's ground combat strength was organized into three maneuver brigades with a total of eight cavalry (infantry) battalions (see table 1.2).[29] The 1st Squadron, 9th Cavalry (hereafter referred to as the 1/9 Cavalry; other unit designations are similarly abbreviated throughout the text) was designed primarily for reconnaissance and to gain initial contact with enemy forces. It was generally controlled directly by the divisional headquarters. Other battalions were moved between the brigades to meet the demands of specific missions. During the Ia Drang campaign in early November 1966, for example, 3rd Brigade had the 2/5 Cavalry assigned in addition to the 1/7 and 2/7 Cavalry, as shown in table 1.2, below. Other units assisted the brigades and 1/9 Cavalry as missions demanded. At any given moment, several of the division's units might be in support of organizations outside the 1st Cavalry Division, while it in turn often had other American, Army of the Republic of Vietnam (ARVN), or allied organizations working with it.

In late October 1965, Gen. William C. Westmoreland ordered the 1st Cavalry Division to find and destroy enemy forces withdrawing toward Cambodia after a failed attack on the Plei Me Special Forces Camp in Pleiku Province (see map 1 on page twelve). On the morning of 14 November 1965, after two weeks of sporadic contact with the enemy, Lt. Col.

Table 1.2   First Cavalry Division Organization, 3 July 1965

Source: Harold G. Moore and Joseph L. Galloway, *We Were Soldiers Once . . . And Young* (New York: Random House, 1992), 30

Headquarters and Headquarters Company (HHC)

HHC, 1st Brigade	HHB, Division Artillery[2]
1st Battalion, 8th Cavalry (Airborne)	2nd Battalion, 19th Artillery (105mm)
2nd Battalion, 8th Cavalry (Airborne)	(Airborne)
1st Battalion, 12th Cavalry (Airborne)	2nd Battalion, 20th Artillery (Aerial
HHC, 2nd Brigade	Rocket)
1st Battalion, 5th Cavalry	1st Battalion, 21st Artillery (105mm)
2nd Battalion, 5th Cavalry	1st Battalion, 77th Artillery (105mm)
2nd Battalion, 12th Cavalry	Division Support
HHC, 3rd Brigade[1]	8th Engineer Battalion
1st Battalion, 7th Cavalry	13th Signal Battalion
2nd Battalion, 7th Cavalry	15th Medical Battalion
1st Squadron, 9th Cavalry	15th Supply and Service Battalion
	15th Transportation Battalion (Aircraft)
HHC, 11th Aviation Group	27th Maintenance Battalion
HHC, 227th Assault Helicopter Battalion	15th Administrative Company
HHC, 228th Assault Helicopter Battalion	545th Military Police Company
HHC, 229th Assault Helicopter Battalion	191st Military Intelligence Detachment
11th Aviation Company	371st Army Security Agency Company
	HHC and Band

[1]A ninth cavalry (infantry) battalion, the 5th Battalion, 7th Cavalry, joined the division in the spring of 1966.
[2]HHB: Headquarters and Headquarters Battery. Artillery units designated their company-sized elements as batteries. An additional battalion (1st Battalion, 30th Artillery) was assigned to the division 1 June 1968–6 April 1971.

Hal Moore led the men of the 1/7 Cavalry into Landing Zone X-Ray (LZ X-Ray). The landing zone sat at the base of Pleiku Province's Chu Pong Massif, just east of the Cambodian border. It was suspected that enemy forces were in the area, but the 457 men of the 1/7 Cavalry did not expect to confront the over one thousand North Vietnamese Army (NVA) regulars of the 33rd and 66th People's Army Regiments located in the immediate vicinity.[30] The Americans were not ignorant of their enemy's close proximity for long. An NVA prisoner captured less than an hour after the initial landings told them that there were "three battalions on the mountain who want very much to kill Americans but have not been able to find any."[31]

The ensuing battle for LZ X-Ray was a brutal struggle that raged for three days and two nights. Moore's warriors fought to hold their ground and defeat an enemy determined to destroy the recently arrived Americans.

North Vietnamese Army (NVA) forces broke contact only as two additional 1st Cavalry Division battalions approached LZ X-Ray on November 16th. The three battalions subsequently left the area so that American bombers could attack the remaining enemy forces.[32] The cavalrymen of Moore's 1/7 Cavalry were lifted out by helicopter while the other two battalions marched to nearby clearings for extraction. One, the 2/7 Cavalry, was ambushed by the 8th Battalion, 66th People's Army of Vietnam (PAVN) Regiment in the jungle as it approached a clearing designated as LZ Albany. One hundred and fifty-one American soldiers were killed in the ensuing melee, bringing the total American losses to 230 killed and 242 wounded in the four days of fighting on LZs X-Ray and Albany. The unit had been in Vietnam less than three months; its last units would not depart for another six years.

During each of those six years the division would suffer an annual turnover of soldiers often exceeding its authorized strength. Combat casualties accounted for no small part of these losses, but it was the expiration of a soldier's year-long tour that cost the organization greater attrition than enemy action. This turnover necessitated a continuous remolding of unit cohesion and fighting expertise as veterans were replaced by new, inexperienced soldiers. Replacements required training beyond what they had received in the United States. Instruction addressing requirements unique to the division, lessons learned during recent operations, and corrections of shortcomings found in stateside training were at first provided to soldiers after they had gone to their brigades, battalions, or other units.

Having to conduct such preparations over-tasked the smaller organizations' capabilities; the division therefore consolidated replacement training at division level during the autumn of 1966. All new soldiers through the rank of major attended a four-day course that included basic orientations, weapons demonstrations, air mobility instruction, completion of a quick-fire reaction course, briefings on both friendly and enemy tactics, and M16 zeroing, which involved setting the front and rear sights so that the weapon

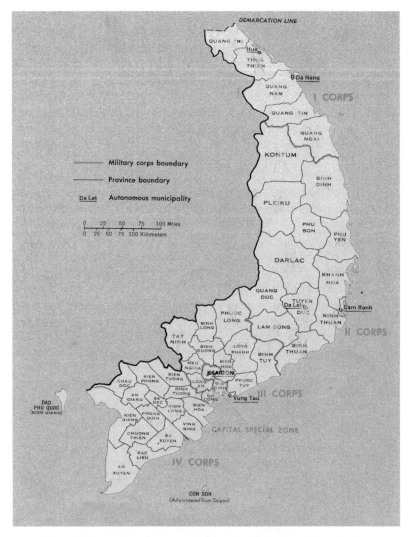

Republic of Vietnam Provinces and Corps Tactical Zone Boundaries

Adapted from "South Vietnam Provincial Maps," Office of Basic and Geographic Intelligence, Directorate of Intelligence, Central Intelligence Agency, September 1967.

was properly aligned when its user took aim at a target. (The number of positions in a soldier's front and rear sights were offset from a designated starting point to put them in alignment was the rifleman's "zero." Without a proper zero, a few inches offset from the aiming point at short range translated to many feet at greater distances, causing a soldier to completely miss his target.) A one-week orientation for senior officers (lieutenant colonel and above) was conducted separately.[33]

Actions in the months subsequent to the fighting on LZs X-Ray and Albany took the division's soldiers to all four of Vietnam's Corps Tactical Zones and into the neighboring nation of Cambodia. For much of 1968 the division was assigned to the U.S. Marine Corps III Marine Amphibious Force in the northern reaches of the Republic of Vietnam.34 First Cavalry Division soldiers were therefore fortuitously positioned to assist in the retaking of Hue during the aftermath of the 1968 Tet offensive. Just weeks later the division received orders to aid in relieving besieged American marines at Khe Sanh airfield. It was the 1st Cavalry Division that led the main effort after President Nixon authorized attacks into Cambodia on 28 April 1970.35

These changes in mission and location challenged the unit's leaders and forced adaptation to new terrain and enemy tactics. The adversary's adroitness at camouflaging positions and employing booby traps varied in nuance and detail over time and by region. Sniper tactics in the south differed from those the division's soldiers had come to know in northern provinces. An enemy fighting near Saigon tended to position himself higher in trees and employ grenade launchers in addition to rifles as sniper weapons. NVA and Vietcong (VC) soldiers in the south also made greater use of infiltration tactics in order to give the impression of inflated enemy presence in the rear of 1st Cavalry Division units.[36] The impact of changes in areas of operations thus went beyond differences in terrain and a corresponding lack of familiarity with the ground. Experience gained in other regions was at times of limited use. Combat became the classroom in which new lessons were learned—lessons that were later passed on to newcomers during their weeks in the division's replacement school.[37]

The 1st Cavalry Division's return home began with initial units' redeployment to the United States on 1 March 1971. The division colors formally left Vietnam for Fort Hood, Texas, on April 29th of that year.[38] The 3rd Brigade remained, however, with four infantry battalions (1/7 Cavalry, 2/5 Cavalry, 2/8 Cavalry, and 1/12 Cavalry), the 229th Aviation Battalion, B Troop of the 1/9 Cavalry, support units, and Brig. Gen. Jonathan R. Burton assigned as its commander.[39] A squadron (battalion) of the 11th Armored Cavalry Regiment, not customarily a 1st Cavalry Division unit, was also assigned to the brigade. Rifle squad strength in infantry units was reduced by one man (from ten to nine) so that the U.S. military could meet limits on the number of U.S. personnel allowed to remain in Vietnam.[40]

The 3rd Brigade itself left Vietnam on 26 June 1972.[41] By that time, 1st Cavalry Division units had operated from the far northern reaches of the Republic of South Vietnam to its southern environs, from Cambodia and the Laotian border in the west to the South China Sea in the east. Over

150,000 soldiers had served in the unit during those years. Sixteen of every one hundred of its soldiers—over 24,000 young men—were wounded or killed in action. In World War II and eighteen months of Korean War service combined, the division had lost 3,546 killed and 15,685 wounded.[42] Vietnam had indeed been costly for the men serving in the ranks of the "First Team."

THE SOLDIER'S LIFE

On average, two 1st Cavalry Division soldiers awoke to their last sunrise every day of the six and a half years the unit was in Vietnam.[43] Their chances of being killed were greater if they were riflemen, helicopter door gunners, or men who served in other positions that routinely required them confront the enemy in the field.

There were factors that made a given mission more or less ominous. Some of these were obvious: a soldier met the day knowing that his chances of seeing it to its conclusion were better or worse than the norm. Others became apparent only in retrospect. Some days would pass in which no soldier fell to enemy action. Others would keep chaplains at home busy with visits to the freshly widowed.

A primary factor influencing a given day's cost in lives was the Southeast Asian climate. The northern portion of what was the Republic of Vietnam (South Vietnam) normally had its rainy season from September through January. The rains came from May to September for the southern parts of the nation, leaving much of the region under water. Infiltration routes for bringing men and supplies from the north were therefore difficult to travel in all but the February-to-May period. This cycle influenced soldiers' chances of survival for nearly twenty-five years; both the French and Americans suffered their greatest combat losses during these months.[44]

An American soldier preparing for a mission knew the enemy was more active during these periods, just as he sensed the increased threat as his helicopter flew him into a known enemy stronghold. He was also aware that some regions were more dangerous than others. Three of South Vietnam's provinces accounted for forty percent of American combat deaths between January 1967 and the end of 1972 (Quang Tri [16 percent], Quang Nam [15 percent], and Thus Thien [9 percent]). Ten of the nation's provinces were the sites of over three-quarters of American deaths; seven of these ten were among the eleven provinces in which the 1st Cavalry Division was most heavily committed during the war (Quang Tri, Thua Thien, Tay Ninh, Bin Duong, Binh Dinh, Kontum, and Hau Nghia).[45]

While the soldier or marine might know that a given province or time of year was notably dangerous, whether fate had put him in Vietnam during a twelve-month span that would prove to be relatively peaceful or especially vicious was indiscernible except in retrospect. The total number of casualties in a particular time frame was a function of many factors, to include the number of one's own soldiers committed to combat, the quantity and quality of the enemy's forces, and the intensity and duration of fighting during the period.[46] United States Army personnel strength in Vietnam increased over the 1964 to early 1969 period, thereafter decreasing from its February 1969 peak of 365,497. The tours of 1st Cavalry Division respondents reflected this waxing and waning (with minor variances), as did those of the officers responding to the Fort Leavenworth survey (see table 1.3).

Even accounting for the greater number of Americans in Vietnam in 1968 does not alter its status as the most dangerous year to have served in the war. Nearly fifteen thousand American soldiers were killed in action in 1968 alone; no other year accounted for over ten thousand Americans lost in hostile action. Twenty-eight of every one thousand army personnel in the combat theater died in combat that year, the most of any such period in the conflict.[47] It was likewise the most costly year of the war for the United States Marine Corps; III Marine Amphibious Force lost nearly three thousand marines killed and over twenty thousand wounded.[48] This peak was largely due to the coincidence of very high numbers of Americans in the combat theater during 1968 and the enemy's conduct of the Tet offensive in its opening months. The rapid decline in United States combat casualties beginning in 1970 was attributable to the initiation of troop withdrawals. Twenty-five percent of American forces redeployed from Vietnam that year, resulting in the lowest U.S. force strength in the country in three and a half years. The earliest redeployments disproportionately consisted of combat units; those forces remaining in Vietnam were thus less likely to have contact with the enemy.

Table 1.3   U.S. Vietnam Combat Deaths by Year

Source: Thomas C. Thayer, *War Without Fronts: The American Experience in Vietnam* (Boulder, Colo.: Westview, 1985), 34, 37, and 119, and "Study of the 12-Month Tour," Office of the Deputy Chief for Personnel, Washington, D.C., 7 June 1974, 2

	Year								
	1964	1965	1966	1967	1968	1969	1970	1971	1972
U.S. total combat deaths	—	—	5,008	9,368	14,592	9,414	4,221	1,380	300
U.S. deaths/1,000	—	—	18	21	28	20	11	6	5
US Army (end of year strength in thousands)	15	117	239	320	360	331	251	120	14
1st Cav respondents with tour in year[1]	4	35	44	52	60	64	37	12	2
Fort Leavenworth respondents with tour in year[1]	0	3	6	9	10	13	12	10	0

[1]Numbers of responses include multiple tours by some veterans. Not all tours were with the 1st Cavalry Division. (Some 1st Cavalry Division veterans also had combat tours with other units.)

The character of the force confronting the American soldier also varied over time. The Vietcong outnumbered their North Vietnamese army (NVA) counterparts in the years before 1968; the reverse was true in later years.[49] This meant that after 1967 the American soldier's opponent was more likely to be better equipped and trained than the Vietcong had been.[50]

The nature of enemy tactics evolved with the passage of time. Battalion attacks comprised more than one in every ten ground offensive actions against U.S. or allied forces in 1965. NVA and VC casualties in such actions were high, in no small part due to the attractive targets that high enemy concentrations offered to American aircraft and artillery. In later years the Vietcong and NVA reduced the number of these larger-unit offensive actions (the Tet offensive made 1968 the exception). Vietcong and NVA units also increased their use of artillery and mortars in lieu of force-on-force engagements to lessen the exposure of their soldiers to U.S. firepower. Small target size and a related ability to fire and move before counterfire could be brought to bear made a single mortar or gun an effective method for the harassment and demoralization of American soldiers and their allies.[51]

Although a soldier or marine arriving in Vietnam in 1965 or 1966 might have characterized his contacts with the enemy as attacks by groups of enemy infantrymen ranging up to several hundred in strength, his successors would rarely see such concentrations. Far more numerous were terrifying and infuriating attacks during which they huddled in foxholes as mortar or artillery shells rained on their positions: terrifying because they killed as effectively as an enemy bullet; infuriating because infantrymen had little means of directly retaliating against the unseen but deadly foe. Equally trying were the dangers and losses related to the enemy's use of booby traps and mines. Men who died in action during these later years of the war were more likely victims of enemy artillery, mortars, rockets, mines, or booby traps than direct engagement by another rifleman.[52] Mines and booby traps alone killed or wounded more than triple the number of men similarly injured in either World War II or Korea.[53]

Whether it was the Americans or the enemy who initiated infantry engagements also affected a fighting man's chances of survival. Several Vietnam War analysts have concluded that American and allied forces were tactically on the defensive at the onset of most engagements. Frequently these contacts were quickly broken off by the enemy. One study stated that in the earlier years of the war, the NVA or Vietcong initiated the firing in up to eight of every ten engagements; the study concluded that American army and marine casualties therefore increased or decreased far more as a function of the enemy's willingness to fight than U.S. efforts to take the fight to their adversaries.[54] The British counterinsurgency expert Sir Robert Thompson wrote that "the pace of the fighting" during 1965 and 1966 "was dictated by the North Vietnamese and the Vietcong, not by the United States."[55] In 1969, the Department of State admitted that while it did not have the data to permit a detailed analysis of this question, we believe that to a considerable extent, the Communists are able to control the rate of attrition of their forces. First, they have retained a surprising degree of tactical initiative, even during periods of intense fighting. . . . In addition to choosing the timing of the engagements, the enemy is able to determine the type of attack, ranging from a costly assault on a major urban center to a relatively inexpensive harassment of a village or hamlet. . . . Studies of combat statistics show little relationship between the number and scale of Allied operations and the rate of estimated enemy combat deaths.[56]

After suffering dramatically higher numbers of marines killed and wounded in 1968 than in previous years, the U.S. Marine Corps took a number of steps to remedy the situation. Nonetheless, their official history concluded that "the casualty picture improved markedly, due not to Marine Corps action, but to the inaction of the North Vietnamese Army."[57]

Each man's chances of surviving were also affected by more individual factors. The chances that a replacement would die in his first three months in Vietnam were nearly the same as those for the last three-quarters of a tour.[58] Perhaps no factor so influenced the character of a man's experience and likelihood of his returning home as his duty position. As has been noted, soldiers whose jobs required them to seek out the enemy were more likely to be killed in action than others more removed from the sharp end. These men also had a view of daily life that was different from that of soldiers in the "rear." What was critical to a combat soldier's daily survival was often of little concern to others; the fighting man's waking thoughts each day were unlike those of men who stood little chance of meeting an adversary in combat.

The veterans of the 1st Cavalry Division remain justifiably proud of their accomplishments in Vietnam. Members of other army and marine units can similarly look back with the knowledge that they served their nation and comrades well. While the experiences of each were unique, the following pages will demonstrate that they shared much with warriors of earlier American wars, with other soldiers and marines fighting in Vietnam, and with each other, despite differences in time, location, or organization. As did those who went into battle before them, these men have much to teach the nation's soldiers and marines who follow.

SUMMARY

The combat soldier knows the agony of personal loss, the stupor of fatigue, and the obscenity that fragments inflict on flesh, but he often has a grasp of little more than the part he and his comrades play in an engagement. Surveys provide a means of piecing the experiences of many into a whole. The fit is admittedly imperfect: the pieces overlap; one contradicts another, and it is possible that none are entirely correct. Yet the potential is unmatchable scope and detail; the contradictions stimulate further investigation and themselves tell us something of the men who fought.

What follows is an attempt to describe and understand selected aspects of American soldiers' combat performance in Vietnam. Memoirs, histories, and archival materials played their part in this analysis, but its foundation was the responses of 302 men whose experiences together offered an otherwise unattainable view of the American soldier in that Southeast Asian war. To have been on Athena's dance card was to have experienced heart-pounding anticipation, the excitement of stiletto-sharp senses, and the incomparable ravishment of life-threatening combat survived. The 302 are among the more fortunate of those who danced with Athena.[59]

2

Soldiers and Their Weapons
Choose Your Partners

Weapons are like a woman; they have to be loved and understood.

1st Cavalry Division respondent 115

The Vietnam soldier or marine found his weapon a basis for comfort, a means of defense, and a source of both confidence and trust as well as the instrument with which he accomplished his assigned task of killing. The man at war slept with his weapon. He woke at night to touch it, ensuring it was within reach. It was with him at every moment. The warrior was nagged by a sense of absence when he departed the war zone on leave or entered an area where weapons were proscribed. He felt there was an incompleteness about him at such times. Flashes of near-panic would spur a chill of terror until he reminded himself that the separation was temporary and nonthreatening; having a weapon at hand was his normal state of being.

A weapon was the soldier's ready partner in defense. It was the tool of his trade. With a good weapon he felt prepared; without one he was naked and exposed to the enemy's malevolence. The well-trained fighting man understood his weapon, its capabilities, limits, and its needs. Confidence that his armament would perform when properly cared for was vital to the mettle needed to confront other men on the battlefield.

A soldier used many weapons, but for most only one was his alone. Hand grenades, Claymore mines, and anti-tank rocket launchers were among the many munitions available in Vietnam. They were as deadly as were personal weapons, yet they were different: They were expendable. They did not require the constant high level of maintenance that a personal weapon demanded. They lacked the same general applicability in combat. It was the machine gun he carried, the pistol, the shotgun, the M79 grenade launcher, and, most of all, the rifle with which the fighting man had a unique relationship.

As important as this association was, the feeling a man had for his weapon was rarely personal. A weapon that failed in combat would be discarded for the first available functional replacement. When the soldier left the combat theater, his discomfort at not having a weapon at hand was born of habit, not affection. His bond with his weapon was inseparably linked to his combat exposure; thus their ultimate permanent parting was accompanied by relief and joy rather than mourning.

Failure of a weapon during combat could destroy the soldier's trust in his weapon and in his confidence in his own ability to perform and survive. Without that confidence, the individual questioned the usefulness of his weapon as a means of self-defense and task accomplishment. It no longer served as a source of comfort and instead became a catalyst for fear; the soldier without faith in his weapon feared that he would be killed or fail his comrades.

Ultimately the soldier knew that his weapon's reliability was primarily his responsibility. Its care therefore took precedence over his own comforts. One veteran in B Company, 2/8 Cavalry recalled a fundamental reality of every combat soldier's daily existence; for him, weapons and their maintenance were "more important than food [and] water. . . .You can live without food or water for a long time, but not if your weapon is not working."[1]

The soldier's relationship with his weapon was a no-nonsense one based on respect. He understood that the weapon would kill him, fellow unit members, or innocent civilians if misused. So there was a cold-heartedness to the closeness: The soldier or marine handled his weapon with notable care only because it had to do his bidding as needed. The weapon had no combat value if it failed him. In that sense the soldier and his weapon were truly one because the individual who failed to maintain his weapon or employ it properly was equally useless in the field.

SOLDIERS' INDIVIDUAL WEAPONS

The individual weapons carried by soldiers and marines in Vietnam included the M1911 .45-caliber pistol, the M79 40-mm grenade launcher, and the M16, amongst others. The .45-caliber pistol had been in the U.S. military forces inventory since before World War I. It was carried primarily for short-range personal defense or use by medics, officers, or others whose jobs at times made carrying a larger weapon difficult.[2] Shotguns were not carried in large numbers but were effective in conditions where dispersion of shot, blast, and intimidating noise was beneficial. Such situations included dense jungle fighting, urban combat, and other situations in which close engagements were expected or the shock of a shotgun's noise would help to overwhelm an adversary.

The M79 grenade launcher and versions of the M16 rifle that included a supplementary grenade launcher fired a variety of 40-mm rounds. The weapon's original purpose was to provide units a means of engaging targets between the distance a man could throw a hand grenade and a mortar's minimum range.[3] The grenade launcher's high-explosive munitions armed only after traveling fifteen meters (to ensure that the ensuing burst did not injure or kill the firer). A necessary design feature, the 15-meter distance made some men hesitant to carry the M79 because of the short ranges at which many Vietnam engagements occurred. Grenadiers and M60 assistant machine gunners were issued a .45-caliber pistol for self-defense at these ranges, but the pistol's lack of accuracy and the time necessary to draw and fire the weapon made it a less than an ideal means of protection. Though the M79 had a shotgun round for close contacts, the grenadier had to have the appropriate round loaded or go through a time-consuming process of breaking his weapon open, extracting the round, and replacing it with another. The process was not conducive to survival in a confrontation with an automatic rifle-carrying enemy at close range. The shotgun round on occasion proved insufficient for protection, further reducing a soldier's confidence in the M79.[4]

Given the shortcomings associated with carrying the grenade launcher, it is not surprising that 1st Cavalry Division soldiers had mixed views regarding the system. One found it preferable to the M16, stating that a soldier should be provided with "a personal weapon . . . that he can *trust*. I got rid of my M16 as soon as I could, finding that I had more faith in my M79 and later my shotgun."[5] Another thought the M79 was "one of the greatest weapons they ever made. When you have a sniper in a tree or something, you can just fire the M79 and it'll just bust him all open."[6]

Thomas G. Rhame, B Company, 1/12 Cavalry commander from November 1967 to March 1968, at times found those who carried the weapon less enthusiastic. He recalled that some lacked confidence in the weapon to the extent that they had to be threatened with a court martial before they would leave a base camp armed only with the grenade launcher and a pistol. Rhame considered the weapon "totally unsatisfactory."[7]

One 1st Cavalry Division veteran recalled an instance of "heavy contact with the 33d NVA Division during which the M79 man wouldn't move up and engage. Instead he passed his M79 forward with three HE rounds for others to use."[8] Another observed that "the men that carried the M79s were the hardest to get to fire."[9] The hesitation may have been related to the problems with firing the grenade launcher in jungle or other close terrain in which a round could strike an object and bounce back into friendly positions. As a company commander noted, "Down in the jungle you just can't fire that HE round because you're going to get more casualties yourself than you're going to inflict."[10]

The M79's lack of an immediate close-in engagement capability meant that grenadiers were at risk in short-range combat. Some units compensated by having other soldiers provide security for those carrying the M79, but this inhibited riflemen's freedom of action and was unfeasible in some terrain. The XM-148 was an initial attempt to redress these problems. It gave the soldier a weapon much like the M16, but beneath the rifle barrel the soldier or marine had a grenade launcher similar to the M79. He thus could fire either 5.56-mm rifle rounds or 40-mm grenades. The XM-148 was rejected by the army, however; the testing agency concluded that the "over and under" combination had technical shortcomings that they felt made it unsatisfactory for combat.[11] The testing agency may also have been influenced by infantry leaders, a majority of whom found that too many grenadiers participated in firefights as riflemen. These leaders considered the resulting decrease in grenade fire unacceptable and expressed a preference to retain the M79 with .45-caliber pistol or similar combination in lieu of adopting the M16 with XM-148 system. Men who had to carry the M79 in combat, however, favored the M16 with XM-148.[12] Their desire for a better means of self-protection was eventually met when a modified combination of M16 rifle and grenade launcher was approved later in the war and issued as the M203.[13]

It was the ubiquitous M16, however, that was the infantryman's primary individual weapon in Vietnam. A loaded M16 was nearly four pounds lighter and over five inches shorter than its predecessor, the M14.[14] While the reduced weight was important from the perspective of wear on the soldier carrying it, the lesser bulk and length also made it a quicker rifle to employ: It took less time to point the barrel and engage a target. That speed could make the difference between survival and death when confronting an enemy at short range.

Beginning in 1967, some 1st Cavalry Division soldiers also received limited numbers of the new CAR-15 submachine gun. Similar to the M16A1 in appearance, operation, and maintenance, the CAR-15's reduced length made it even easier to use in small spaces, such as interiors of helicopters, and facilitated a more rapid response from point men and others in situations in which speed of action was especially critical. Leaders also liked the weapon; it gave them increased firepower (as compared to the .45-caliber pistol) without the bulk of the larger M16. The advantages came with a cost, however; the shorter barrel reduced accuracy, especially at longer ranges.

Adoption of the M16 had come after extensive and often heated debate. Any consideration of replacing the American fighting man's rifle guarantees controversy. Old soldiers and veterans question the need, others the cost. Arguments are ignited by the teething problems accompanying the introduction of almost any new weapon. The revered M1, adopted by the army in 1936 and used throughout World War II, and the M14 rifle, introduced in the late 1950s, both had technical problems that took several years to correct. Unlike the M16, however, neither of those weapons became the standard during wartime, when the cost of shortcomings was measured in soldiers' lives.[15]

The army initially had no intention of replacing the M14 in the 1960s. The costs related to that rifle's introduction and lack of evidence regarding the M16's clear superiority were arguments against displacing the larger, heavier piece. Additionally, the M14 used the 7.62-mm round that had been accepted by North Atlantic Treaty Organization (NATO) nations as that organization's standard; the AR15 (as the M16 was earlier known) used a smaller 5.56-mm projectile.[16] The Powell Board, a group of officers that took its name from its senior member, General Herbert B. Powell, convened in late 1958 to consider replacing the M14. It recommended against the move in part because it concluded that the smaller AR15 round would not meet the demands of combat.[17]

This recommendation did little to stop replacement deliberations, however. A subsequent September 1962 report strongly favoring the AR15 over the M14 spurred Secretary of Defense Robert McNamara to ask that the army reconsider its decision to retain the older rifle.[18] The army conducted its own Rifle Evaluation Study in November and December of 1962; it included an analysis of the AR15, the Soviet/Warsaw Pact AK47, and two modified versions of the M14. The researchers found the AR15 had several advantages, including less recoil than the M14, which had "resulted in bruised shoulders and cut lips" and made some soldiers hesitant to fire.[19] The study, however, concluded that the M14 should be retained, not in small part because the AR15 had a considerably larger number of malfunctions during testing than did the M14. The army conducted an internal investigation after the objectivity of these findings was questioned. Though no significant wrongdoing was proved, the test results had been tarnished by the accusations.[20]

Under pressure from the secretary of defense, notably his announcement of the closing of the M14 production line at the end of 1963, the army ordered 85,000 M16-series rifles in November of that year.[21] Positive reports from American advisors in Vietnam and a 1965 request for purchase of the weapon by the Military Assistance Command, Vietnam, provided further impetus for full adoption.[22] That decision eventually came in 1967 for all U.S. forces other than those in Europe, and in 1968 it was extended to include them as well.[23] Well before that time, however, members of the 1st Cavalry Division had been issued the rifle and had employed it against the enemy in Southeast Asia.

Division training with the new rifle was minimal because the weapons were received only days prior to the men's 1965 departure for Vietnam.[24] The most significant impact of this late issue was that the organization's officers and noncommissioned officers were as inexperienced with the weapon as were their men.[25] Replacements' rifle proficiency also suffered, the new soldiers having been trained on the M14 in the United States only to receive an M16 when assigned to the division.

The new weapon was favorably regarded by many despite these difficulties. J. D. Coleman, who commanded B Company, 2/8 Cavalry, found that his soldiers had a great deal of confidence in the M16 and preferred it to the M14 because of its lesser recoil. Perhaps the best known display of confidence in the M16 came at the conclusion of the 1/7 Cavalry's fight in LZ X-Ray. The units' commander, Lt. Col. Harold G. Moore, stood before a group of reporters and declared that "brave American soldiers and the M16 won a victory here."[26]

Reports of excessive numbers of weapon malfunctions from units that had received the M16 were not long in coming.[27] The 1st Cavalry Division was not immune to the problems. One B Company, 1/5 Cavalry veteran dryly observed that his "M16 ammo would jam. As a point man this wasn't the best news."[28] Another soldier's unit "had the original M16s and in sand they jammed. I saw eight fellow squad members die because of this."[29] The army sent training teams into the combat theater to teach men how to better maintain their rifles, and steps were taken to ensure that soldiers being assigned to Vietnam had been trained in the use and maintenance of the M16.[30] Whether through formal training or via word of mouth, soldiers quickly learned what was needed to better the chances that their weapons would remain in working order. Franklin D. Miller's first of six Vietnam tours was with the 1st Cavalry Division. He described what became his first actions on waking each morning soon after his March 1966 arrival:

> The first thing you did in the morning when you woke up, and I mean the *very* first thing, was to jack a round out of your weapon's chamber and slide a new one in. Overnight, moisture would accumulate in the barrel and chamber, and that tiny bit of water could eventually ruin your whole day.
>
> As soon as every member of the element was awake, we'd take turns cleaning, oiling, and pulling normal maintenance on our weapons. We'd clean our weapons in shifts because obviously we didn't want to have every weapon apart should the enemy visit us. Weapons were top priority.[31]

Problems with the new rifle were not limited to the army. Marines received the M16 later in the war but suffered the same shortcomings. Some went into battle with their cleaning rod assembled and taped to their rifle stock, ready for quick removal and use to force a jammed round out of the chamber.[32] The Marine Corps's official history includes the telling understatement that "marines had discovered through bitter experience that the M16, if not cleaned regularly, was prone to jamming."[33]

The humidity, dust, and rains of Vietnam posed serious problems for those trying to keep their weapons in working order. So-called "mad minutes," during which all soldiers fired their rifles and machine guns at a predesignated time, offered the quite practical benefit of keeping the enemy off guard. It was also an opportunity to dispose of questionable ammunition. Confirming Miller's observations regarding the effects of weather on rifle rounds, a division veteran explained that his unit "shot up old ammo quite regularly. Many of us kept our M16 loaded with a cartridge in the chamber. Most of the ammo would oxidize and jam in the weapon—even in the clips [it] would 'turn green.'"[34] Other soldiers developed their own solutions to M16 problems. One "found that WD-40 kept my weapon [M16] firing even in very sandy and wet conditions. Relatives sent the WD-40 lubricant from home."[35] Others found that the answer was an alternative personal weapon.

For many, lack of confidence in the M16 translated into a belief in the superiority of the enemy's rifle. These soldiers believed "AK47s were worth their weight in gold. They were so accurate and trouble free, everybody wanted one."[36] A second veteran wrote that "the M16 would misfire when it was wet or dirty. The AK47 would never misfire. We had one and tested it. It was a better weapon."[37] A third found that "M16s were not very effective in combat conditions in SVN [South Vietnam]. Continuous jam-ups and breakages. We would have done considerably better had we been issued AK47s. My weapon (M16) would only fire 3 to 4 rounds on semi-auto[matic] before jam-up."[38]

Steve Siegel of C Company, 2/7 Cavalry, was trained on an M14 in the States and went through two M16s and an AK47 before picking up an M60 during the November 1965 fighting on LZ Albany. His first M16 jammed on firing the third round, the second after four magazines. He picked up an AK47 but quickly discarded it; "everybody was shooting at sounds" because the vegetation made it impossible to see more than a few meters. Siegel found to his consternation that firing the enemy automatic rifle immediately drew heavy fire from his fellow soldiers, who mistakenly thought him an NVA adversary.[39]

As mentioned, the AK47 was in fact tested during an army rifle evaluation study and found wanting. The enemy's weapon was considered to "in no way" meet an infantryman's demands, in part because the bolt could not be locked in the open position. This was a flaw from a safety standpoint and because the rifle could not indicate that the last round of ammunition had been expended.[40]

Writing about the British and French at Waterloo a century and a half before, Paddy Griffith observed: "[T]he truth of the matter is that both sides believed their enemy had superior muskets, just as in Vietnam both sides believed the enemy had the better assault rifle. It is only natural, after all, that one should imagine a weapon is more dangerous if it is carried by an enemy rather than by a friend."[41] Such beliefs, however, hardly encouraged soldiers' trust in their weapons.

FIRST CAVALRY SOLDIERS' CREW-SERVED WEAPONS

The primary squad crew-served weapon in Vietnam was the M60 machine gun. This system, in a modified form, was also the door gunners' armament on UH-1 model helicopters, popularly known as "Hueys." Early in the war the 1st Cavalry Division's rifle platoons had an authorized strength of forty-four men. This included three ten-man rifle squads, a heavy-weapons squad of eleven men (squad leader plus two machine gun teams, each with a machine gunner, assistant gunner, and ammunition bearer; and two 90-mm recoilless rifle teams with a gunner and assistant gunner in each), a platoon leader, platoon sergeant, and radio-telephone operator. Some leaders modified their platoons to provide their units with more firepower; they acquired a third machine gun and formed three teams. The third team also allowed allocation of one machine gun team to each rifle squad. The platoon leader could alternatively keep a machine-gun crew under his control or assign additional crews to a particular squad as missions and terrain dictated. The gunner was the primary operator and generally carried the weapon with some ammunition; his assistant gunner carried additional belts of 7.62-mm rounds that he fed into the weapon during engagements. Few units retained the cumbersome 90-mm recoilless rifle, if they ever included it in the first place.[42]

Machine-gun crews were often critical to a unit's success. In describing M16 malfunctions, an artillery forward observer with C Battery, 1/77 Artillery Battalion, who accompanied A Company, 2/12 Cavalry, on missions, recalled that "some men fired and got a jam after a few rounds from carbon build-up. Some men got a jam from overheating their rifle. THANK GOD THE MACHINE GUNS DIDN'T."[43] Coleman thought the M60 "was a magnificent weapon. . . . The machine gunners felt invincible. . . . It was better than anything the NVA could field."[44] Coleman regularly put one of his M60 gunners second or third in the column when his force was moving in a file, a short "starter belt" of ammunition in his weapon so that the gunner could immediately provide the unit with a large amount of firepower on contact.[45]

Soldiers vied for the privilege of carrying or acting as assistant gunner for an infantry platoon's M60 machine guns. The competitor who gained the coveted status put himself in jeopardy. The VC and NVA both understood the power inherent in the gun and its influence in a firefight; its operators were therefore primary targets. Nevertheless, many soldiers who wanted to make a difference in battle saw the M60 as the means to do so and willingly accepted the risks.

CONCLUSION

Regardless of its type, a weapon was only of value if it was employed against the enemy. It was the instrument that allowed a soldier or marine to protect himself and comrades, or to keep an adversary's head down while the unit maneuvered into better positions. Every man was expected to use his weapon in support of the whole. Those who did not use them when they should and could have were less than worthless; they failed to meet their minimum responsibilities and attacked the fundamental trust upon which unit cohesion depended. Nevertheless, at times the fulfillment of these minimum responsibilities demanded extraordinary courage.

3

Engaging the Enemy
Allow me to introduce . . .

On the first hour of my first day
In the front trench I fell.
(Children in boxes at a play
Stand up to watch it well.)

Rudyard Kipling, "The Beginner"

In combat situations, your desire to live overrides your brain.

1st Cavalry Division respondent 81

One study of combat behavior observes that "of all species, homo sapiens has the most feelings."[1] The nature and intensity of emotions differ from man to man, and even within an individual over time. To look for a single explanation for soldiers' combat behavior, or to expect all soldiers to possess common motivations, is to understand neither the nature of humankind nor that of the soldier in war. It is true that men experiencing conflict share some motives, respond to similar stimuli, and work toward the achievement of common goals. Much can be understood by studying these commonalties, but only if each warrior's individuality is constantly kept in mind.

One element in comprehending the fighting man is understanding his willingness to destroy the adversary. It was long assumed that soldiers, while often seeking ways to avoid battle if given an alternative, had little compunction about killing the enemy once they confronted him on the battlefield. This supposition has more recently undergone closer scrutiny. Students of soldiers' willingness to engage the enemy have identified (and become attached to) two general categories: soldiers who completely failed to fire their weapons and soldiers who discharged their weapons but deliberately missed their human targets. In the former case, analysts thought that breaking the barrier of participation was the major step in creating an effective soldier. With the latter problem, a high volume of fire in no way implied effectiveness; finding a solution would be more complex. The cases raised separate but not necessarily unrelated questions: 1) Why would a soldier not fire at an enemy? and 2) Would he deliberately miss when firing?

THE "NO-FIRE" SCHOOL

Killing is one of war's most fundamental acts, inevitably associated with strong emotions that, especially early in a soldier's combat experience, may include powerful inhibitions. Yet only occasionally has a military leader broached the subject of soldiers' unwillingness to fire their weapons. World War II general Lucian K. Truscott did so in his memoirs, *Command Missions,* writing that he

> was surprised to find what a relatively small proportion of individual weapons available in any unit were ever employed in action. One would think that every unit engaged in combat would employ every possible weapon, for battles are won by destroying or threatening to destroy the enemy. But this had not been so in the actions in which our infantry and armored battalions had been engaged. Our investigation revealed that . . . each of them had been won by a fraction of the unit with the assistance of supporting arms—artillery, naval gunfire, machine guns, bombers, tanks.[2]

Truscott concluded that leadership and training were the factors that determined the quality of a unit's performance.

It was the work of S. L. A. Marshall that brought the issue of the American fighting man's willingness to fire to the forefront. The controversy that resulted from his findings has already been discussed. The words that spurred the debate were as follows:

> On an average not more than 15 percent of the men had actually fired at the enemy positions or personnel with rifles, carbines, grenades, bazookas, BARs, or machine guns during the course of an entire engagement. Even allowing for the dead and wounded, and assuming that in their numbers there would be the same proportion of active firers as among the living, the figure did not rise above 20 to 25 per cent of the total for any action. . . . If he had so much as fired a rifle once or twice, though not aiming it at anything in particular, or lobbed a grenade roughly in the direction of the enemy, he was scored on the positive side.[3]

Marshall was specific in stating that his average figure of 15 per cent was for the entirety of an engagement. If an action lasted over a period of several days, only fifteen out of every one hundred men would ever attempt to engage the enemy; the other eighty-five would fail to do so. Further, "terrain, the tactical situation, and even the nature of the enemy and the accuracy of his fire appeared to have almost no bearing on the ratio of active firers to non-firers." A soldier's level of experience also had little effect.[4]

Marshall was in what could be called the "no-fire school," those who believed that some soldiers would not fire under any circumstances. For him "the failure of the average soldier to fire is not in the main due to conscious recognition of the fact that the act of firing may entail increased exposure. It is a result of a paralysis which comes of varying fears."[5] The primary of these, in Marshall's view, was a soldier's fear of his own aggression, a fear born of society's prohibition against taking another human being's life.[6]

The already-mentioned general officer refutations of S. L. A. Marshall's findings were joined by researchers' well-supported rebuttals. Based on more rigorous analysis than Marshall's, Samuel Stouffer's study of American soldiers reported that World War II veterans considered "shooting before they are able to see their target" the third most common error made by new replacements in 1944 northwestern Europe.[7] World War II historian Martin Blumenson also concluded that Marshall's estimates were more likely based on personal judgment than on values founded in rigorous analysis.[8] Francis C. Steckel found that "diaries captured from Japanese soldiers revealed a myth among the enemy that Americans, supposedly motivated only by money, were paid by the number of times they fired their weapons. These Japanese observers could find no other explanation for the high volume of American small-arms fire."[9] John G. Westover, who worked closely with Marshall during World War II and had been present for many of the interview sessions, described him as "intensely practical" and a man who "considered statistics 'an adornment' of belief."[10]

Whether fact or fabrication, there is no doubt that S. L. A. Marshall's writings stimulated considerable research on the subject of soldier performance under fire. Several writers attempted to explain the shortcoming. James R. Ebert considered the impact of fear on performance in his *A Life in a Year: The American Infantryman in Vietnam, 1965–1972*. A soldier was "either a shooter or a shaker," one new man was told soon after his arrival to the 1st Cavalry Division's 2nd Battalion, 7th Cavalry. That soldier found "that being a shooter was something that did not come automatically with the uniform. A man had to 'build into it,' and until the first several enemy contacts, it was impossible to tell whether a replacement would shoot or shake."[11] Another member of that battalion substantiated this concern. Randy Hoelzen of C Company, 2/7 Cavalry, remembered "being absolutely scared shitless" and being of little value during his initial contact, though most soldiers "handled things well and eventually blended in."[12]

Writing after World War II, the U. S. Army Medical Corps's Stephen Ranson found that "freezing" was one of many normal reactions to fear. Vietnam veterans' freezing under fire, therefore, could have been a physical reaction to "combat stress and the fear resulting from it."[13] Yet while this might explain the occasional failure, it did not provide an explanation for failures on the scale of those proposed by Marshall. Ranson found freezing was "abnormal if more than transitory, if inappropriately induced, or if it prevents the soldier from accomplishing movements necessary to his own safety or that of others."[14]

Observations by men with extensive combat experience and others whose research was far more rigorous than that conducted by S. L. A. Marshall nevertheless concluded that American fighting men did, at times, fail to engage the enemy. No veteran would be surprised by such a finding. Combat can be an overwhelming experience, especially for those with only limited prior exposure. Sheer terror, instinctive self-preservation, or not knowing how to react to a situation all could inhibit a soldier's willingness or ability to use his weapon, yet these forces were generally temporary in effect and influenced only a small number of fighters at any given time. There was little, if any, legitimate evidence that eighty-five of every one hundred men failed to fire.

THE "DELIBERATE MISS" SCHOOL

A second group of authors addressing soldier unwillingness to engage the enemy comprises those who believed in the "deliberate miss": Soldiers fired their weapons, but did so with no intention of hitting or killing their adversary. This phenomenon, rather than concerns regarding a complete failure to fire, was the more frequently addressed before World War II. One author supported such a conclusion by citing a late-eighteenth century Prussian experiment in which the soldiers of an infantry battalion hit a one-hundred-foot by six-foot fabric target 60 percent of the time at a range of seventy-five yards—a far higher success rate than that evidenced by casualties in actual engagements.[15] Given a two hundred-man enemy regiment, the 60 percent hit rate led him to conclude that up to 120 of the enemy should have fallen to the first volley in combat.[16] That two battalions struck only thirty-two of the enemy during an actual engagement in 1717 was taken as evidence that the soldiers were deliberately missing their human targets.[17] The analysis reflected either poor logic or a limited understanding of combat, however, because:

(1) Regiments of the day did not form in single ranks; men would have been positioned behind others, protected from fire by the bodies of their comrades to their front;

(2) Dispersion between men to the right and left was necessary to allow soldiers to raise their weapons to fire, reload, and pass forward or to the rear, so the enemy did not present the unbroken surface of a sheet of cloth;

(3) Soldiers of the day were generally not six feet tall, so hits on the upper part of the sheet would have been misses in combat (Frederick the Great, writing shortly after the cited example, implied that soldiers of his day were between five feet five and five feet six inches tall);[18]

(4) A soldier in ranks did not present a uniformly rectangular target. Further, he would turn his left shoulder toward the enemy when engaging, thereby further reducing the surface area exposed to his adversary.

Taking these considerations into account while still granting 60 percent accuracy results in a rough estimate of 40, rather than 120, enemy being struck by a volley. This does not take into account soldier exhaustion; blinding smoke; noise; dust; the screaming of wounded, officers, and noncommissioned officers; incoming fire; and the many other factors characteristic of the battlefield that made concentration and hitting a target difficult. Considering these many elements, striking only thirty-two of the enemy lends little evidence to the notion of men deliberately missing an enemy advancing upon them with intent to kill.

Those writing of poor marksmanship were more likely to attribute factors other than an unwillingness to destroy fellow human beings, however. Ardant Du Picq blamed his soldiers' poor marksmanship on two factors: (1) the jostling they received as they stood in ranks during battle and (2) their anxiousness to fire before the enemy could fire at them. In the latter case, Du Picq believed a soldier "is instinctively in haste to fire his shot, which may stop the departure of the bullet destined for him. . . . Perhaps it is better said that who fires least expects to be hit most."[19]

Therefore, Du Picq wrote of soldiers who, far from hesitating to fire, were anxious to fire. While Marshall concluded that fear prevented soldiers' engagement of the enemy, Du Picq found fear to be an almost irresistible source of firing. Rice C. Bull of the Union Army's 123rd New York Volunteer Infantry Regiment likewise found his compatriots only too willing to fire at their enemy. Writing of his personal combat experiences, he recalled that "we were warned not to fire before ordered to do so, but as soon as the Johnnies opened on us some of the men commenced. Most of us, however, held our fire until we saw the line of smoke that showed that they were on the ridge; then every gun was fired. It was then load and fire at will as fast as we could."[20]

Steckel noted that some interviewees told of too great a willingness to fire among World War II soldiers: "Sentries became 'trigger-happy,' or over anxious to shoot first, often with tragic results. Men who forgot a password or failed to hear a challenge were killed or wounded by their own guards. Such incidents were all too common, especially at night."[21]

This also proved to be the case in Vietnam. Robert Mason of the 1st Cavalry Division's B Company, 229th Helicopter Battalion, recalled, "Every night there's a bunch of firefights on our perimeter. A lot of it's our own troops shooting at our patrols coming back to the line. . . . Up there last night . . . five guys in a patrol were killed trying to get back in."[22] Marine D. E. Bonsper was nearly killed in a similar incident. He went outside his unit's perimeter to check on his men when a listening post (LP) failed to respond to a radio check. Approaching the position in the pitch blackness of a Vietnam night, he called out the name of the marine who was to have been on the radio. Bonsper recalled the result:

> Almost as soon as my words were out of my mouth, the entire area a few yards to our front erupted in muzzle flashes. I heard a loud burst of automatic fire and listened to the cracks as the rounds passed by my head. My guide was hit and went down.... [His] eye was lost but he lived. The LP? The marine who was supposed to be on watch was asleep. My calling his name had startled the two other marines who were legitimately asleep. They had instinctively picked up their M16s and opened fire.[23]

Veterans of Vietnam and earlier wars have cited many other similar instances. This anxiousness to fire, born of fear, training, or caution, demonstrates a willingness to shoot to kill.

Perry Jamieson provided another reason for poor marksmanship in his discussion of soldier performance during the Spanish-American War. Spanish troops in defensive positions were confronted with American soldiers who, as their commander Frederick Funston described, "fairly combed the top of that dike with bullets. We were advancing at a walk and it was point-blank range, and our fire so disconcerted the enemy that though they plied their rifles with great vigor, they were not exposing themselves enough to get any sort of good aim."[24]

Gen. George Patton recognized the disruptive effects of incoming rifle fire. He advised soldiers to use "marching fire," during which "one round should be fired every two or three paces. The whistle of the bullets, the scream of the ricochet, and the dust, twigs, and branches which are knocked from the ground and the trees have such an effect on the enemy that his small-arms fire becomes negligible."[25]

A man on the receiving end of such intense fire would likely be pleased were he able to kill those so threatening him. However, instinct, the sense of self-preservation, causes men to press themselves to the ground as they wait for the danger to pass rather than rising up to return fire. Hardly unwilling to engage their foe, they find it difficult to put that action ahead of instinctively protecting themselves, even when such inaction is illogical and hastens their demise.

WHY MEN SHOT TO KILL

Despite its significance and the attention it received, the issue of whether men hesitated to fire, or if they fired whether they did so with the intent to kill, remained unresolved through war after war. So too did the underlying question of why men would try to avoid killing other men. It is helpful to approach these concerns from the opposing perspective: Rather than asking why soldiers hesitated to kill, ask instead why men *did* kill in battle.

Psychiatrist Franklin Jones noted that a small minority of soldiers had few reservations about their duty to kill and killed with no questions or remorse. Others agreed. Based on his World War II experiences, John Glenn Gray suspected that the willingness to destroy an adversary was something inherent in most combatants:

> Anyone who has watched men on the battlefield at work with artillery, or looked into the eyes of veteran killers fresh from slaughter . . . finds hard to escape the conclusion that there is a delight in destruction. . . . The satisfaction in destroying seems to me peculiarly human, or, more exactly put, devilish in a way animals can never be.[26]

There were other men, those who killed but took no pleasure in the act. Ernie Pyle, one of World War II's preeminent war correspondents, described a soldier whose willingness to engage the enemy was based not on delight in destruction but rather a resigned acceptance of its inevitability: "Buck Eversole had no hatred for Germans, although he had killed many of them," Pyle wrote. "He killed because he was trying to keep alive himself. The years rolled over him and the war became his only world, and battle his only profession. . . . 'I'm mighty sick of it all,' he said quietly, 'but there ain't no use to complain. I just figure it this way, that I've been given a job to do and I've got to do it.'"[27]

Some men's minds helped them deal with the killing and other combat stresses by achieving a state of detachment. Gray wrote of World War II soldiers' training and fatigue combining to allow them to enter "a dazed condition in which all sharpness of consciousness is lost," a state in which "they can be caught up into the fire of communal ecstasy and forget about death by losing their individuality, doing what is expected of them because it has become automatic."[28] John Ellis similarly noted that "automatons" was "a very appropriate word in this context. For few men remember feeling much fear in actual combat or, indeed, much about any of their feelings and actions."[29] Steckel believed this detachment was a way for the fighting man to escape the trauma of combat:

> Combat evoked a dreamlike state of mind that distanced soldiers from the horrors of the battlefield. The vision of burning equipment and mangled bodies, the indistinguishable sounds of enemy and friendly fire, the screams of the wounded, and the smell of the dead were too much to comprehend all at once. Soldiers found themselves uncontrollably focusing on something else, unable to realize and appreciate fully what was happening around them until it was all over.[30]

Bradford Perkins wrote of the same phenomenon as he looked back on his World War II experience. He attributed both heroic and foolish acts to what

he called the "glaze of war" as men performed acts while believing themselves somehow distant from the dangers of combat.[31]

The shared physical and mental anguish that was inseparable from combat
bonded men in a manner possibly unmatched in other aspects of life. The
mutual dependence on which survival depended helped build this closeness.
Mortar fragments tore at the psyches of those physically unscathed as thoroughly as they shredded the flesh of those they left dead or maimed. The reaction was at times hatred and a desire for revenge. John Dollard found that
79 percent of his Spanish Civil War veterans thought the killing of a close
friend made others better soldiers.[32] Gray similarly found that "when the
soldier has lost a comrade to this enemy . . . [h]is reason for living is to seek
revenge; not an eye for an eye or a tooth for a tooth, but a tenfold retalia-
tion."[33] Marine E. B. Sledge noted much the same emotional change after
twenty-two marines were killed during a patrol in the World War II Guadal-
canal campaign. He wrote of the resulting hatred between American
marines and their Japanese adversaries, a resentment felt

> deeply, bitterly, and as certainly as danger itself. To deny this hatred or
> make light of it would be as much a lie as to deny or make light of the
> esprit de corps or the intense patriotism felt by the Marines with
> whom I served in the Pacific. . . . This collective attitude, Marine and
> Japanese, resulted in savage, ferocious fighting with no holds barred.
> This was not the dispassionate killing seen on other fronts or in other
> wars. This was a brutish, primitive hatred.[34]

Japanese cruelty drove Filipino Benjamin de Leon to become a guerrilla and
motivated his killing of Japanese occupiers. Four Japanese soldiers raped a telephone operator in his village; de Leon once completed the obligatory bow to
a sentry only to be slapped nonetheless. The invaders stole the food and be-
longings of the townspeople. "We had a good life before they came," de Leon
recalled, "and they did bad things."[35] For de Leon, killing was retribution.

Jones identified six emotional responses to casualties among comrades: (1)
anger, (2) grief, (3) horror, (4) guilt, (5) bonding, and (6) dependency on the
mission.[36] Farley Mowat wrote of a highly regarded regimental commander's death in World War II Italy after which the deceased leader's men
showed several of these reactions:

> On the Assoro scarp the crew of an 88-mm gun laid their weapon over
> open sights. And when the cloud of yellow dust rose clear of the fox-
> hole, Sutcliffe was dead, and the I.O. [Intelligence Officer] lay dying.
>   Prior to this moment all of the soldiers of the Regiment who had
> been killed had died in the confusion and tumult of action. Their loss
> had not been deeply perceived as yet, and hatred had not grown from
> their graves. This new stroke of death was something else again.

The tragedy had a remarkable effect. It irrevocably and utterly destroyed the pale remainder of the illusion that war was only an exciting extension of the battle games of 1941 and 1942. The killing of the C.O. before the battle seemed to be an almost obscene act, and when the news came to the men it roused in them an ugly resentment. The emotions stirred by the first skirmishes with war were only awaiting crystallization, and now they hardened and took form. Hatred of the enemy was born.

One more element had been added to the moods of battle and with its acquisition the Regiment reached a new level of efficiency as an instrument of war.[37]

A soldier in Vietnam saw his hatred of the enemy as having a very practical element. His fear and anger were born of being on the receiving end of incoming fire; his response was to eliminate those threatening him:

We know we can overcome our fear only by facing it. So we begin to focus on the men who are the source of the danger and of our fear. It concentrates inside us and through some chemistry is transformed into a fierce resolve to fight until the danger ceases to exist. But this resolve, which is sometimes called courage, cannot be separated from the fear that has aroused it. It is, in fact, a powerful urge not to be afraid anymore, to rid himself of fear by eliminating the source of it. And the only way of eliminating it is through the use of fire-power.[38]

Du Picq too saw a connection between willingness to fire and men's emotional state. He believed that firing, whether with the purpose of killing or not, served as a necessary physical and emotional release in addition to its being a defensive reaction. The stress of standing motionless in ranks was unbearable; firing was an alternative to uncontrolled retreat. "The coolness of men cannot be counted on," Du Picq wrote; "It is necessary above all to keep up their morale; one ought to try above all to occupy and soothe them. This can best be done by frequent discharges."[39] He cited the Roman Civil War battle of Pharsalus as a prefirearms example, noting, "Pompey had given his men orders to await the charge without stirring, and to let Caesar's army break its ranks upon them. . . . Pompey's immobility was an error because there is in every one an animation, a natural ardor that is instilled by the onset to the combat. Generals ought not to check but to encourage this ardor."[40] Writing some one hundred years before Du Picq, Maurice de Saxe noted that "the same troops, who if attacking would have been victorious, may be invariably defeated in entrenchments."[41] One of Dollard's respondents, when asked for reasons a soldier was fearful during action, wrote that it "depends on how active you were. If inactive, more fear."[42] Marshall agreed, believing that "any constructive use of [a soldier's] muscle power, and especially putting him at a job which he can share with other men, may become the first step toward getting him to make appropriate use of his weapons under combat conditions. Action is the great steadying force."[43]

For some soldiers, killing was simply common sense. Ebert wrote of one soldier who believed that all that mattered was "to survive and stay alive for a year. That was just the most important thing that there was. If something would have got in the way of me staying alive, I'd of had to kill it. That's what made me fight."[44]

Observers of soldiers' behavior in combat report widely differing responses. Some found the riflemen of World War II and before only too anxious to fire. Others concluded that men had not fired at all or fired with no intention of killing. Of course, no two riflemen's motives or responses to situations were completely identical. Indeed, an individual soldier might himself respond differently to similar situations over time. Some engaged the foe but were less aggressive than others; a few were unfazed by danger. These same variations characterized America's soldiers and marines in Southeast Asia during the Vietnam War.

VIETNAM AND THE AMERICAN SOLDIER'S WILLINGNESS TO ENGAGE HIS ENEMY

As a general rule, 99 percent of the time if they get shot at, they're going to shoot back unless they're hit.

Company Commander, 1st Cavalry Division

Questions posed to 1st Cavalry Division and Fort Leavenworth veterans regarding willingness to engage were focused on whether men fired their weapons rather than how effective that fire was. In other words, they addressed the "no-fire" issue rather than directly investigating the "deliberate miss" proposition (though respondents' comments provided insights regarding both). Veterans made it clear that the American soldier in Vietnam was rarely reluctant to discharge his weapon in combat. At the same time, however, there were many cases of soldiers not firing when the situation apparently dictated that engagement was appropriate. To explain this apparent anomaly, it is necessary to look both at why men in Vietnam at times did not fire in combat and why they chose to kill the enemy when they did choose to engage.

Only nine of the 258 1st Cavalry Division respondents reported that they had never fired at the enemy during their service in Vietnam.[45] Thus, 97 percent of that 258 recorded that they had engaged an adversary on at least one occasion. First Cavalry Division veterans also responded that they engaged the enemy in 99 percent of the instances in which they believed that they were themselves threatened. From the first-person perspective, therefore, there appears to have been little reluctance to draw a trigger against the foe.

The number of times a soldier used his weapon during a tour was a function of his duties, his location, and the specific period he served in Vietnam. Almost three of every ten veterans felt they were in life-threatening situations less than ten times during their time in Vietnam; over eight in ten felt that they had experienced such situations fifty times or less. Only 6 percent of the 1st Cavalry Division veterans confronted such danger one hundred times or more. A disproportionate number of those responding that they had been in life-threatening situations one hundred times or more were helicopter crewmen. Though pilots, crew chiefs, or those assigned as helicopter door gunners made up only 8 percent of division respondents, they together represented 38 percent of those who thought themselves in life-threatening situations one hundred or more times.

The apparently low values for the number of times some soldiers considered their lives endangered reflected the nature of the conflict during much of the war. Soldiers could spend extensive time on operations with few sightings of confirmed enemy. A member of B Company, 1/8 Cavalry, serving in Vietnam in 1966, for example, believed that his unit made contact only once in every one hundred attempts to ambush the enemy.[46] The greater exposure of helicopter crews, on the other hand, was likely due to their frequently flying into or out of "hot" landing zones, those from which the enemy fired at their aircraft as they approached or departed the area. Given this generally infrequent contact with the enemy, it is unsurprising that a quarter of the respondents had engaged the enemy less than ten times and eight in ten had done so on less than fifty occasions. Only 7 percent fired at the enemy in over a hundred engagements.[47]

When men did engage, those armed with rifles used automatic mode (during which pressing the trigger resulted in continuous firing) 44 percent of the time on average.[48] The value varied depending on the unit, however. Many 1st Cavalry Division leaders interviewed in 1966 had limited the number of soldiers in a squad who were allowed to fire on automatic. The number ranged from one (normally the point man, the individual at the head of a column during patrols) to three. Other units had no restrictions. Often soldiers were directed to fire on automatic only in specific instances. For example, many would use this mode during the opening moments of an engagement when a large volume of fire was needed to seize the initiative from an enemy who had initiated the action. After this first outpouring, soldiers switched to the more easily controlled and less ammunition-consuming semiautomatic fire mode (in which one round was discharged for every pull of the trigger).

First Cavalry Division leaders soon noticed their men's greater willingness to use their weapons than S. L. A. Marshall had reported was the case in World War II and Korea. Officers and noncommissioned officers were particularly impressed by the "uniform rate of fire" they heard during engagements. Those listening to the outgoing fire from the other side of LZ

X-Ray during that autumn 1965 battle in Pleiku Province heard a constant, heavy volume of fire rather than the sporadic, ragged fire characteristic of only a few men using their weapons. Aware of Marshall's findings from earlier wars, they later conducted an informal study to determine why their men were so willing to employ their weapons. They concluded that the following were critical factors:

- excellent 1st Cavalry Division training
- division esprit de corps
- high individual soldier motivation
- the M16's lesser "kick" when fired
- soldier confidence in the M16 (concerns regarding malfunctions were not yet widespread)
- superb noncommissioned officer leadership that ensured that soldiers fired and fired properly.[49]

Veterans of the 1st Cavalry Division not only responded that they themselves were willing to engage the enemy; they also found little hesitation to do so in their fellow soldiers. Though roughly half of the veterans had witnessed at least one incident in which a soldier failed to use his weapon when he apparently should have, their estimate of the percentage of those armed with individual weapons who fired when it was appropriate was 82.8 percent. For men with crew-served weapons, the estimate was 86.9 percent participation. The equivalent values based on responses from Fort Leavenworth veterans were 83.8 and 90.7 percent, respectively.

Though values of over 80 percent seem encouraging compared with previous analyses, they still raise the question of why between one and two soldiers in ten did not fire during engagements with the enemy. Those addressing the issue with regard to their own failures to fire frequently cited other responsibilities. Leaders at all levels noted that positioning fellow soldiers, calling for artillery or helicopter support, resupplying their men with ammunition, and similar responsibilities took precedence over personally firing at the enemy. This behavior was in keeping with their training and the expectations of both those they led and their own leaders. It is the duty of leaders to first guide the actions of others and establish the conditions for success rather than personally engaging the enemy in situations other than those in which their direct participation is essential to unit survival.[50] Lt. Col. Hal Moore "was tempted to join" his 1/7 Cavalry soldiers as they poured fire into the enemy trying to overrun LZ X-Ray in November 1965, "but resisted the temptation. I had no business getting involved with the actions of only one company; I might get pinned down and become simply another rifleman. My duty was to lead riflemen."[51]

As has been noted, a man's duty position significantly influenced the likelihood he would have the opportunity to engage the adversary. Medics, radiomen, forward observers with the responsibility to call for fire support, and machine gun assistant gunners had jobs with responsibilities that made firing individual weapons a secondary concern. Medics were allowed to carry weapons only for self-defense and use in defending their patients. U.S. Army regulations and the Geneva Convention both directed that chaplains were not to carry weapons, as they were considered "noncombatants." However, a post-war study based on eight hundred responses from combat chaplains reflected that 8 percent used their weapons in Vietnam, most for protection of themselves or their soldiers.[52] Chaplain Curtis Bowers was photographed carrying a .45-caliber pistol and two hand grenades while he served with the 1st Battalion, 327th Airborne Regiment, in December 1965. For Bowers the weapons were "more a defensive thing to have just in case." He stopped carrying the pistol after being "chewed out" by a senior officer, but kept a hand grenade in his ammunition pouch. The enlisted soldier who assisted a chaplain was to also provide his defense, but at times there was insufficient room on a helicopter for both the chaplain and his assistant to fly into combat.

Bowers never used his weapons in combat, though he "was very tempted to fire once. . . . I resisted that urge and just threw [another soldier] hand grenades instead." The individual to whom Bowers threw the grenades was Lt. Jim Gardner. Gardner lost his life in the action; he posthumously received the Medal of Honor for his heroism.

Of the four chaplains serving in the brigade during Bowers's tour, only one did not carry a weapon. This officer, a Catholic priest, died in action on 4 May 1966, the first of thirteen chaplains killed during the war.[53]

First Cavalry Division men with the greatest likelihood of engaging the adversary were warrant officer aviators, enlisted soldiers assigned to helicopters (primarily door gunners), and officer aviators, respectively. Infantry machine gunners, squad leaders/platoon sergeants, other enlisted soldiers in combat positions, officers, and enlisted men not serving in combat positions followed in order. That squad leaders and platoon sergeants tended to have more engagements than their subordinate squad members may appear surprising, as these are leadership positions. However, unlike platoon leaders and other officers, these men more often found it necessary to lead by example during firefights, their behavior encouraging men to follow suit. While an officer would tend to be occupied with sending reports, calling for fire, coordinating logistical resupply, and arranging for medical evacuations, corporals and sergeants maneuvered fighting men and directed fires, frequently by firing themselves. Some leaders increased the ratio of tracer rounds (rounds that had a glowing trail when fired) to ball (non-tracer) munitions to better allow their unit members to see where they wanted them to fire.

A finding by those conducting a study during the Korean War would also help to explain this tendency for enlisted leaders to engage more often than their subordinates. Aggressiveness ratings for noncommissioned officers at squad and platoon level increased with rank, perhaps because those who demonstrated such behavior were more likely to be promoted to leader positions. Thus men in these jobs had demonstrated greater aggressiveness than the norm, and this behavior had been reinforced through promotion.

Aviators apparently fired more because they had more opportunities to engage the enemy. Other men had jobs that put them in situations during which firing weapons was to be avoided if possible. Long-range reconnaissance patrols, for example, were to focus on acquiring intelligence rather than finding and engaging the enemy. Men on such missions therefore sought to avoid detection and refrained from firing in any but essential circumstances.

Though many recalled cases in which their duties kept them from firing, veterans rarely cited others' duties as causes of comrades not engaging. There are several possible explanations for this apparent contradiction. Many respondents were often not located close to those whose duties demanded restraint in weapons use and thus could seldom have observed them during combat. Some soldiers may not have cited other duties because of the way they perceived the survey question, which asked whether they had seen a soldier not fire when he should have. Respondents may not have included those soldiers with duties that precluded their firing in the group of those that should have engaged.

"Fear (the soldier 'froze')" was cited most frequently as the reason that another soldier did not engage the enemy when the situation seemed to demand it. Nearly half of the 1st Cavalry Division veterans had seen a soldier fail to fire his weapon on at least one occasion; 80 percent of those respondents cited fear as a cause.[54] This fear had many forms. Some veterans recalled obvious cases of cowardice. One recalled a group of soldiers who cowered in a bunker while others fought off a heavy ground assault against their fire base.[55] A second wrote of a fellow noncommissioned officer who "was sent to the rear base camp for court martial" after freezing under fire for the fourth time.[56] Another saw a soldier who "turned and ran from [the] enemy,"[57] and a fourth man believed "some people simply put an M-16 on the ground, buried their heads, [and] fired at nothing."[58]

J. D. Coleman had served in Korea before his tour in Vietnam. He blamed poor training and weak leadership for soldier failures during that earlier conflict. He "saw a reluctance to close with the enemy" in units other than his own, as well as a hesitation to "'put their heads up' when under fire. They froze in their foxholes and wouldn't put their heads up. . . . They were not well trained, not well motivated."[59] Two researchers studying U.S. marine performance in Vietnam wrote that signs of combat exhaustion included crying, hyperventilation, and "acute incapacitating anxiety (more commonly known as 'clutching' or 'freezing')."[60] These analysts' conclusions parallel Ranson's World War II findings: Cases of freezing under fire could have been caused by men being overwhelmed by the pressures of combat. As was the case with Ranson's observations, the effects were rarely found to be more than a temporary phenomenon.

Leadership was critical in getting men to act under fire regardless of whether or not the desired action was returning fire. Sgt. Julius C. Durham was one of only two who survived when his platoon was ambushed. He found it extraordinarily difficult to get recent arrivals to react correctly during the action. "The new men were down on the ground; they were firing, but it was hard to get them to move," he related. Durham was acting platoon sergeant and had been assigned to the rear of the platoon to keep the unit together; "I had to make each man move individually. Some of them I had to lift up."[61] In another instance, a 1st Cavalry Division unit was receiving sporadic incoming fire during a helicopter medical evacuation. The battalion commander, Lieutenant Colonel Stevenson, "flew into Delta Company's LZ shortly before dark and assisted [company] leaders in the evacuation of the wounded. [The] chief difficulty was getting people to move while still under occasional small arms fire. The presence of their battalion commander proved the inspiration necessary to see all the wounded evacuated rapidly."[62]

Cases cited as "fear" in veteran responses may have been perceived differently by the men under fire. One soldier said his "platoon LT [lieutenant, the platoon leader] chickened out and let a large NVA force through our ambush without engaging them." The veteran's view of his leader's judgment in allowing "a large NVA force" to pass unmolested might be somewhat harsh if the lieutenant had judged the risk of engaging such a large force too great. Such was the case when Tom Renard and two fellow marines in the Third Reconnaissance Battalion were on a mission south of Da Nang. Renard describes a case in which good judgment seems to have dictated forgoing engaging an enemy force of initially unknown strength. He recalled that "we were poorly set up—lying against the embankment with the VC [Vietcong] walking down a trail on the other side, and we couldn't tell how many were coming. I knew all they had to do was to pop grenades over that small hump of earth and we would be dead. In that area there just weren't any good places to remain unseen and undetected. Anyway, we just lay there and let those VC go by."[63]

A third veteran was undecided as to the motivations underlying a comrade's failure to fire, concluding that it was "possibly fear. [He] did not want to give his position away. [He] heard the enemy shooting but couldn't see him," in a case where the man not engaging may have had no target or not squeezed the trigger for legitimate reasons.[64] Another cited "fear of exposure to hostile fire—laid low" in a case that could have been either truly fear-induced "freezing" or good judgment during a period of intense incoming fire.[65] What appeared to be fear to some may have been something quite different in reality. Even when the cause of a man's actions was fear, that fear could have many faces. Rarely was it the visage of cowardice.

One infantry platoon leader recognized that such cases were often based on an accurate assessment of the situation: "Many soldiers don't return fire because they are behind a tree or log under heavy suppressive fire. Once artillery or other units create a distraction of fire with the enemy, these same soldiers will return fire with relish."[66] Another veteran recalled that many factors influenced a soldier's behavior in combat, any of which could explain why a man fired or failed to do so: "I did see soldiers not firing their weapons when we were being fired at. I will not and cannot evaluate whether they should have fired or not. . . . My guess is that they were staying low for the moment and they may have been low on ammo. It was also difficult to know exactly where the rest of the company was."[67]

Experience level and shock were among the factors that influenced how greatly fear influenced a marine or soldier. Shock struck when hours of stationary duty in a defensive position or the lethargy of a sweat-soaked trek were violently disrupted by the sudden pandemonium of a firefight. Tolerating such a psychological blow was more difficult if it had never before been experienced. A 1st Cavalry Division veteran recalled that when soldiers failed to return enemy fire it "was usually during their first fire fight experience and was mainly due to fear or the unsure feeling of how to respond."[68] Another admitted that he did not fire during one of his earliest encounters due to "fear. . . . I am ashamed to admit this."[69] Reasons given for other soldiers not firing included an individual's being "new in country and an FNG who may have panicked when we came under fire." [70] "He did not have the confidence he could hit anything,"[71] or, simply, "This happened to new people."[72] Another division veteran described the unfortunate product of one new soldier's terror:

> We had one person killed with D/1/8 [D Company, 1st Battalion, 8th Cavalry] who was a new replacement because he was apparently looking for a foxhole with a concrete lining. As he was dying he was talking about "I couldn't find a hole." He was hit about 10–15 seconds after we received the first shots and was standing up looking confused. He didn't respond to the "get down" yells by the other troops even though we were either against rice paddy dikes or in the water.[73]

Though an inexperienced soldier was understandably more susceptible to confusion under fire, men with previous combat experience were by no means exempt. No two combat situations were alike, and many factors made each event difficult to fathom. The response to most enemy-initiated contacts was to immediately return fire, drop to the ground, and seek protection, after which part of the American unit engaged the adversary with covering fire while other elements maneuvered to destroy the opposing force. As they did so, men often lost track of fellow unit members and found it hard to determine the locations from which enemy fire was coming. Individuals fired despite this disadvantage; soldiers were trained to engage places that seemed likely to conceal the enemy. As George Patton noted from his World War I and World War II experiences, outgoing rounds tended to intimidate opposing soldiers and reduce the effectiveness of their fire even if the rounds did not strike a target. The prescribed counter to a close ambush took advantage of this suppressive effect. In these cases the enemy suddenly opened fire at short range, generally from positions chosen because they offered the receiving unit little protection. The standard response was to turn into the enemy fire, direct a high volume of fire toward the adversary, and march through his positions. These actions were designed to seize the initiative from the ambushers, force them to keep their heads down, and allow the American unit to walk into the ambush site to destroy the enemy from behind.

What sometimes kept men from firing was a combination of not knowing where the enemy was and being unsure of the location of one's own men. Other causes were attributable to the confusion that more often than not characterized a firefight. Men failed to fire because of "a combination of confusion, fear, and misorientation," a "combination of 'fear' and just [being] overwhelmed by what was happening in [the] initial stages of [a] fire fight," and "fear for some times but others . . . just confused and didn't know what to do."[74]

Terrain and security concerns seldom allowed units to use formations in which all men were located on line with targets directly to their front. As a result, men at times could not fire because other members of their unit were between the enemy and themselves. This was frequently the case when North Vietnamese or enemy guerrilla forces attacked only one portion of a firebase. Men on one side of the perimeter could not fire in support of those being attacked for fear of hitting their comrades in the back. Similarly, terrain or vegetation sometimes restricted movement to a single file during patrols; marines or soldiers could not engage an enemy because other Americans to their front or rear blocked their line of fire.

Veterans cited several other equally legitimate reasons for not using their weapons. Training and unit policies dictated that targets be engaged with weapons other than rifles or machine guns in many instances, especially at night. The enemy would probe perimeters in an attempt to draw fire so that the flash from defenders' weapons would reveal their positions. NVA and Vietcong sappers considered machine gunners primary targets; the killing power of such weapons marked them for early destruction in any attack. Security dictated that means other than rifles or machine guns be used to engage the enemy in these cases. Grenades, artillery or mortar fire, claymore mines (which could be command-detonated: a soldier could fire them at will rather than the mine being triggered by enemy disturbance), helicopters, or similar "indirect" means helped to deny the enemy detection of American positions.

At times an individual would refrain from firing because weapons other than his armament might be more effective for the task at hand. Foliage, rolling terrain, and other conditions could make engagement with direct-fire weapons (which required "line of sight," an unbroken line between the firer and target along which a bullet could travel) impractical. Such cases required weapons capable of putting rounds through or behind obstacles. Enemy mortar or artillery attacks similarly provided no targets against which those on the receiving end could directly retaliate. They instead had to reply in kind with calls for aircraft fire support or, if close enough to the South China Sea, naval gunfire.

Less frequently noted reasons for not engaging included weapons malfunctions, actual or feared ammunition shortages, so brief a contact that it was impossible to respond, wounding of a man in the opening moments of an attack, and operating in a no-fire zone where engagement was proscribed. Several soldiers also blamed other men's improper training or inexperience. A veteran of B Company, 2nd Battalion, 8th Cavalry, twice "saw a new point man, seeing his first NVA or North Vietnamese, turn around and ask if he should fire."[75] A second veteran noted that the "point man spotted enemy soldiers across open area. He stopped to alert command instead of engaging. He should have engaged."[76] Another 1st Cavalry Division soldier found his weapon inadequate to the task as he stood "naked on top of a shower stall putting water in. I threw the water can at enemy, but the round fell way short!"[77]

Revenge motivated men in Vietnam just as it had in previous conflicts. Sergeant Willie Williams saw many of his fellow soldiers killed by the enemy during the first half of his 1966 tour. Williams found "after that, killing didn't bother me. . . . After I saw the way our people were dying, the trigger pulled easier."[78] A marine reacted similarly after he saw the enemy shoot and kill a wounded comrade. Subsequently his "whole attitude started to change. [He] went from being scared to death to being madder than hell."[79] Veterans noted that a soldier could ill afford to wait for such an excuse, however: "Most of all the individual cannot wait to get mad or scared after some buddy is blown away to decide he's going to shoot. The few people that I saw not shoot had to be convinced that the enemy meant business. It was sad but they became some of the best or deadest soldiers."[80] A second former 1st Cavalryman found that some new arrivals believed killing required a mutual antipathy; he "heard a guy say at base camp: 'If I don't f— with them Cong they won't f— with me'—how wrong."[81]

Eli Ginzberg's study of World War II veterans identified some men who "had been so strongly indoctrinated with the commandment that killing is a sin that, even though they were not conscientious objectors, they were still unable to function in combat."[82] Vietnam veterans also recalled a limited number of instances in which moral conviction acted as a brake on firing. Twenty 1st Cavalry Division veterans and one Fort Leavenworth soldier believed that this had kept some other soldier from engaging, at least once.

A 2nd Battalion, 7th Cavalry veteran wrote that two soldiers who had refused to fire claimed that moral beliefs underlay their failures, but his "personal opinion is that it was fear."[83] Other respondents found a refusal to fire a legitimate response; often the nonfirers supported their fellow soldiers in other ways. D Company, 1/12 Cavalry's Walt Kudlacik "had a medic who was a conscientious objector in the platoon. He chose not to carry a weapon during his tour. When asked if he would fire a weapon if our platoon was being overrun and some of his buddies might die if he did not, his answer was he would not fire a weapon. He was still respected for his deep conviction against weapons."[84] A third veteran recalled two unit members who would not fire because of religious convictions but who carried ammunition for others.[85] Those describing these refusals based on moral grounds generally did so with no bitterness, noting that the men otherwise demonstrated their loyalty to unit members while standing by their beliefs.

Personal and group pressures influenced some men's willingness to kill. One personal factor was survival: Du Picq's observed desire, in a soldier, to kill the enemy before he was himself killed. Another was the soldier's need to demonstrate his ability to perform, what some called a "gut check." A soldier knew his job was to confront and kill other men; completing the act was confirmation of his status as a warrior. Sgt. Steve Hansen recalled "feeling that I had been tested and found to be a man" after the 1965 fighting in LZ X-Ray.[86] Responsibilities to a soldier's primary group have been cited by many authors as underpinning various combat behaviors. After bravery so extraordinary he was awarded the Medal of Honor, the 1st Cavalry Division's second lieutenant, Joe Marm, simply asked: "What would the fellows have thought of me if I had been afraid to do it?"[87] "Letting comrades down" was listed by far more Israeli combat veterans (40.4 percent) as "the most frightening aspect of battle" than any other, including "loss of limb, injury" (26.6 percent) and "death" (20.7 percent).[88] Despite the rapid turnover in personnel due to the twelve-month rotation, transfers, and combat casualties during Vietnam, soldiers developed a bond with their fellows that drove them to fight.

CREW-SERVED WEAPONS

S. L. A. Marshall's claim that only 15 to 25 percent of American soldiers fired during World War II engagements overshadowed his conclusion, readily accepted, that "men working in groups or in teams do not have the same tendency to default of fire as do single riflemen."[89] He found that willingness to fire was greater among crewmen serving their weapons than was the case with individual riflemen. Both division and Fort Leavenworth responses supported a similar conclusion.

As noted in the previous chapter, the average for crew-served weapons participation exceeded that for individual weapons users in both surveys. Those manning crew-served weapons also averaged more engagements during their tours in Vietnam and were more likely to fire when in a life-threatening situation. Veteran responses provide some insight into the reasons for this greater participation. Men assigned machine guns were chosen for differing reasons in various units, but the designations were deliberate. The selection was left to platoon sergeants or platoon leaders in J. D. Coleman's company. Assignments were based on a combination of a soldier's training on the M60, his "affinity for it," and the expertise he demonstrated in the machine gun's use, but all those selected had volunteered for the job.

Despite the discomfort of carrying the heavier machine gun during patrols, experienced men seldom saddled new personnel with the task. Ebert's conclusions supported those of Coleman and emphasized the importance of the weapon to a unit: "Humping the M60 was hazardous and fatiguing duty. It was hazardous because the gun drew a lot of enemy attention in a firefight. . . . But, heavy and cumbersome as it was, giving the machine gun to a new man was not advisable if the unit anticipated having to use it."[90] A former platoon leader in Vietnam wrote that "crew members of crew-served weapons (primarily M60s) were selected partially because they could and would fire—thus they always fired."[91] David Hart, who during his service with C Company, 1/5 Cavalry, served as rifleman, squad leader, platoon sergeant, and platoon leader while an enlisted man, wrote that "the only crew-served weapon we used in the field was the M60 machine gun, and I do not recall seeing these gunners holding back. I would guess that they were selected for their aggressive tendencies, and were thus more inclined to quickly open fire and continue suppressive fire."[92]

A former lieutenant in the division stated he "had the same machine gunners for eleven months and they carry it just like it's a little baby."[93] Another found that "in a peacetime company the most disliked job is the machine gun," due to its bulk and weight, "but over here these people fight for them. You tell a kid, 'You're going to be a rifleman,' and he says 'Oh, no, sergeant; I want to be on a machine gun team. Give me that ammo,' and he straps on 400 rounds of machine gun ammo and carries it all day long because he knows that M60 is going to really get somebody up there."[94]

James Johnston's squad of marine machine gunners found written evidence of their enemy's belief that these larger weapons posed an especially dangerous threat in World War II. He recalled that marines on Peleliu "found some printed matter written in Japanese. . . . It said that the Americans' most effective weapon was their light machine gun and that in order to defeat the marines, the light machine guns must first be destroyed." Johnston recalled the result: "From the way they came at us, . . . I guess they must have believed it."[95]

Soldiers and marines in Vietnam knew the responsibilities and the risks associated with being a machine gunner. One believed that "90% of an infantry company's firepower in Vietnam was the M60 machine gun rather than the M16."[96] Those volunteering to carry the M60 recognized that their fellow squad members depended on this firepower; they also realized that they were a priority enemy target in any fight. A 1st Cavalry Division company commander recalled his men's dedication and bravery when an enemy .50-caliber machine gun opened up on his unit and hit four men. The officer recalled that "the machine gun team was right up there behind the four that got killed and the man on the machine gun started moving out down the trail where he could set up that machine gun and start shooting back at that .50. Of course, that .50 just greased him and killed him instantly. The assistant gunner just kicked him out of the way and got behind the machine gun and he was killed too. Then the other man in the machine gun team kicked him out of the way and got up there and he was wounded."[97]

Like their Union and Confederate forefathers who rushed forward to hoist fallen colors only to fall under the resultant hail of enemy fire, Americans in Vietnam understood the risks but nevertheless volunteered to serve on M60 crews.[98] Such men realized that the machine gun's firepower was crucial to both their own and their comrades' survival and success. They also realized that the machine gun had a motivational effect similar to that of the colors Civil War soldiers had been so desperate to save. Those earlier soldiers knew well that others would surge forward in the defense of their colors, that morale would suffer an often crippling blow were they to see their flags fall. Similarly, those manning machine guns in Vietnam knew that the pulse of an M60's supporting fire comforted and motivated riflemen moving against an enemy trying desperately to stop them.

There are additional factors that may have influenced the perception or reality that machine gunners fired more frequently. Marshall noted that heavier weapons were moved less during engagements and therefore firing pauses would be fewer. Additionally, soldiers and marines with many differing duty positions carried rifles or another individual weapon. Though few of their comrades cited other responsibilities as a reason fellow soldiers did not fire, it is nonetheless likely that at least some observing squad leaders, platoon sergeants, platoon leaders, company commanders, radiomen, field artillery forward observers, or medics would have seen them not firing due to the demands of their jobs and considered this when estimating the percentage of individual weapons carriers using their weapons.[99] Machine gunners had but one job: to inflict as much damage as possible on their enemy.

CONCLUSION

The responses of Vietnam veterans reflected that many, perhaps the majority, of soldiers did not engage the enemy on at least one occasion. Few men believed that in most cases this failure to engage was anything other than a temporary or occasional phenomenon. Both 1st Cavalry Division and Fort Leavenworth veterans concluded that over 80 percent of a unit could be expected to fire during any particular engagement. At times all members of a unit would have employed their weapons; on other occasions terrain, the shock of an adversary's attack, or another factor reduced a unit's fire to far less. Typically, however, with leaders focusing on leadership tasks, medics helping wounded, some men maneuvering to better positions, others lying wounded, assistant gunners feeding machine guns, and several in positions where vegetation, fellow soldiers, or terrain blocked their line of fire, an average of between one and two in every ten men did not fire. A small number of these were truly overwhelmed by the situation and their own fears. A smaller number refused to fire because of moral convictions, though they generally assisted their fellow fighters in other ways. The evidence suggests that very few were habitual cowards or found their trigger fingers stayed on more than the rare occasion. There is also little evidence that those who employed their weapons lacked the desire to hit their human targets.

Yet while 80 percent seems acceptable, especially so if one believes that Marshall's statistics from World War II and Korea are valid, there were still men who failed to fire when they should have done so. Better preparation for combat would have conceivably readied men for the shock of war and thereby helped them fight through the crush of noise and pandemonium to engage in situations where too many were simply overwhelmed. That units composed of better-prepared men would have been more effective is obvious. That their casualties would have been fewer likewise seems a given. Not only would those firing have been less likely to die themselves, but their fire would have killed or suppressed enemy otherwise able to inflict casualties on fellow unit members. Getting it right in training, properly readying marines and soldiers for war, would therefore have meant that more sons and fathers would have returned home alive.

4

Training
Learning the Steps

Ignorance is not only *always* wrong, but it is *the* evil of the world. It is not by ignorance that we stimulate the endurance of our men, for it is by knowledge and understanding of the realities of war that we do so.

J. F. C. Fuller, The Foundations of the Science of War

No modern soldier enters the army fully prepared to go to war. He must adjust to a strange environment under the tutelage of those more experienced than he is, much as a newborn adjusts to life with the guidance of its parents. For those bound for Vietnam, only a matter of weeks lay between their first day of military training and deployment to combat in Southeast Asia. In those too few days they had to learn the bulk of what they would need to survive; there would at best be time only for fine-tuning after they joined a unit. What a man learned during his training frequently determined whether or not he returned home alive.

The U.S. Army confronted a conundrum during the Vietnam era. The ultimate objective of its training was preparation for fighting and winning in combat. During the 1960s and until it left Southeast Asia, however, the army always had at least two major overseas responsibilities challenging its readiness: Vietnam and the defense of Western Europe. The Vietnam War included irregular Vietcong and regular NVA threats; both forces were far more likely to confront American units as foot soldiers than mounted in vehicles. A ground war in Western Europe was envisioned as primarily a clash between mounted regular armies; NATO armor and mechanized forces would fight Warsaw Pact units on the plains and in the cities of Europe to defend vital U.S. interests. The primacy of those interests influenced the service's training, doctrine, and procurement policies.

An example of the sometimes competing priorities was the previously discussed debate regarding the infantryman's basic weapon. Not only was the M14's 7.62-mm round the standard agreed upon by NATO members; the weapon's greater weight was less of an issue in Europe, where soldiers tended to rely on vehicles for battlefield mobility rather than foot movement. Similarly, the Marine Corps had to prepare its men for contingencies worldwide in addition to meeting the demands of combat in Southeast Asia. It, like its fellow service, faced competing training demands as it prepared men for service in the corps.

Fortunately, some aspects of individual and unit training were applicable regardless of the type of conflict envisioned. Recruits had to learn the fundamentals of handling their weapons, the basics of first aid and field hygiene, and fundamental military discipline. Other training requirements were unique to specific conflicts—for example, elements particular to given terrain, the extent to which soldiers had to deal with booby traps, and the tactics used by the enemy. Furthermore, different organizations had different capabilities and thus different training requirements even within a given theater. Infantrymen in some units in Vietnam rode trucks into an area of operations; in others they were transported by armored personnel carriers, and in yet others men walked into combat. Those in the 1st Cavalry Division flew.

Training centers in the United States found they could not prepare recruits to serve effectively in West Germany while simultaneously providing adequate preparedness for Vietnam. Forces in Europe were not actively engaged in combat as were those in Vietnam, but the ever-present threat from Warsaw Pact forces required that arriving soldiers be ready to perform their duties. Nonetheless, American units in Europe had the time to train and integrate new arrivals into their organizations without the threat of a man's first mistake being fatal. Organizations in Vietnam had no such leisure. The new man reporting to a combat unit in Southeast Asia had two immediate adjustments to make: one to his new unit and the second to his first combat. The replacement gap, that abyss between the new man's expertise and what he needed to be combat ready, kept the new arrival from full and immediate integration into a fighting team.

Clausewitz wrote that "it is immensely important that no soldier, whatever his rank, should wait for war to expose him to those aspects of active service that amaze and confuse him when he first comes across them. If he has met them even once before, they will begin to be familiar to him."[1] Training was the means to expose the uninitiated and narrow this gap that would ideally be closed before the soldier and his unit first experienced combat together.

Whether in the United States or in Vietnam, training was continually adapted as lessons learned in the conflict were combined with new doctrine and weapons to prepare men for the war's constantly changing character. Adaptation inspired new tactics; new tactics demanded revised training; the enemy adjusted, thus precipitating further American changes in a continual competition for advantage. Some changes in tactics influenced the way war was waged at its higher levels, such as developing a concept of fighting based primarily on the helicopter. Other changes were more subtle but, for the man at the cutting edge, no less significant. The enemy's introduction of a new booby trap or mine had little impact on the oversight of the war from Saigon, but it was of great interest to the soldier on patrol. Lessons of the past complemented more recent revelations to bring about the introduction of new methods for facing battlefield challenges.[2]

TRAINING IN THE UNITED STATES

The mental preparation and lessons taught in eight weeks of Basic Combat Training (BCT) were the first steps in a soldier's training process; they established the foundation for Advanced Individual Training (AIT) during which further skills essential to a soldier's particular specialty were taught. These skills were, in turn, the basis for more training after a soldier joined his unit.

The expansion of the army brought on by the Vietnam War caused a related increase in U.S. training capabilities. The army went from ten major training centers in 1964 to sixteen three years later. The number of basic training companies increased from 310 to 630 and AIT companies from 60 to 140 during the same period. Even with these additions, the army could not train incoming soldiers fast enough to meet the demands of the war; skill levels in some specialties declined as the conflict in Southeast Asia continued.[3]

The marines also struggled with the sudden influx of recruits. The duration of both their basic and advanced training programs was reduced in an effort to fill the combat theater's hunger for replacements. This lost preparation time was in some ways compensated for by increased efficiencies in training, but at least one very significant loss could not be overcome. Before late 1965, every new marine spent a minimum of three months with his unit before deploying overseas. Each man therefore had the opportunity to establish ties with comrades on whom he would rely in combat; those men, in turn, had the time to make the new marine a reliable member of their organization. Thereafter, however, most recruits went directly from centralized marine training to Vietnam and their first unit.[4]

BASIC COMBAT TRAINING (BCT)

Basic Combat Training took a civilian and made him a soldier or marine. The course of instruction sought to improve a trainee's physical fitness, give him fundamental combat skills, and otherwise prepare the man for military life. His training included introduction to the concept of discipline—a concept of far greater scope than most recruits imagined.

First there was self-discipline. An individual had to perform without constant supervision; he was responsible for his own actions—actions that could save or sacrifice a comrade during combat. If he fell asleep on watch it could mean the death of his entire squad. The man who carried unnecessary weight in his pack could become a heat casualty, necessitating helicopter evacuation and compromising his unit's location. Self-discipline included an understanding of teamwork and the benefits of subordinating self-interest to the welfare of the squad or platoon. The most skilled marine or soldier could at times not do what two less-qualified men could accomplish. The individual was less important than the whole. No man was essential to a well-trained unit, for the business of war was too important to allow one man to be so crucial.

Second, there was fire discipline. Undisciplined use of weapons could cause ammunition shortages or result in the death of comrades. The man who fired a rifle at night instead of opting for a hand grenade or claymore mine revealed his position and potentially opened his unit's defenses to penetration. The recruit learned that fire discipline included ammunition conservation and selective use of an M16's automatic capability. As one 1st Cavalry Division veteran summarized, "Discipline! Discipline! Discipline! A well-placed shot by a disciplined, well-trained rifleman is far more effective than a random hit caused by filling the area with automatic fire."[5]

Du Picq wrote, "No one can stand against an Achilles, but no Achilles can withstand ten enemies who, uniting their efforts, act in concert."[6] Du Picq understood the value of unit discipline: every man had his role and performed it for the welfare of the whole. The soldier on point focused his attention forward as he looked for booby traps or enemy to the front; he relied on the slack man (the second soldier in a column) to protect him should an enemy be in the trees overhead. Both men looked to the flank guards to warn of dangers from the right or left.[7] Unit discipline made the whole more than the sum of its parts only if each part was equal to its task.

There was no end to the refinements of discipline. The combat soldier had to practice light discipline. Lighting a cigarette at night could give away his position because the flame could be seen for kilometers in open terrain. Similarly, the slightest of sounds could compromise an ambush that had been occupied for hours if one man violated noise discipline.

Discipline made responsiveness possible. Basic training taught the recruit to obey orders first and ask questions later. Speed of response in combat could mean the soldier lived through a situation rather than dying.

BCT was where a trainee learned how to apply discipline in the execution of his elemental soldier skills: breathing properly as he squeezed the trigger on his weapon, maintaining his rifle and overcoming a malfunction if it jammed, throwing a grenade without exposing himself more than was essential. Discipline included controlling his food consumption so as to have sufficient sustenance before the next resupply and drinking so as to not prematurely exhaust the water in his canteen. Discipline was key to the combat unit's success and its men's survival. The foundation of discipline included dedication, confidence, expertise, experience, and savvy. The new man was by nature a weak link.

Discipline alone was insufficient. Basic and Advanced Individual Training also built the recruit's physical condition to a minimally acceptable level. The emphasis on physical conditioning during stateside training, the recent arrival in Vietnam discovered, had an aim beyond simple harassment. The continuous exertion of humping a pack on long marches, bearing up under the ubiquitous heat of Southeast Asia, and being able to fight after completing dash after dash against an enemy position as strength-sapping rounds cracked around his head demonstrated to the replacement that being fit was key to surviving and not failing others in his unit.

Leaders repeatedly spoke of the need to acclimatize new soldiers upon their arrival in Vietnam. The climate made this necessary regardless of the physical conditioning newcomers had undergone in basic and AIT, and that climate showed no mercy to any newcomer. Marine Corps captain Dave Ramsey spoke of reinforcements that his 3rd Battalion, 3rd Regiment received during the summer of 1965. These men, who Ramsey thought "had not been acclimated at all," immediately suffered heat casualties despite entering combat in the relatively cooler hours after sundown.[8] Problems such as these were exacerbated by the reduced emphasis accorded physical fitness during stateside preparation.

Stouffer found that World War II soldiers' evaluations of their own physical fitness was directly related to how well they believed they were prepared for combat.[9] Michael Doubler similarly noted that most Second World War "soldiers felt that field exercises with tough, realistic battle conditions, regular and rigorous physical fitness training, running obstacle courses, and long field marches of twenty-five miles with full field equipment best prepared them for battle. These activities reflected the broad consensus that the single best way to prepare a soldier for combat was to improve his stamina and physical strength."[10]

Although physical fitness was no less important in preparing men for the rigors of operations in Vietnam, observers from sergeant major to general agreed that physical training was not as strenuous as it had been for World War II and Korean War veterans. Command Sergeant Major Stanley R. Marcille served in the combat zone in both those wars and had two tours of duty in Vietnam. He contended that physical toughness had been too greatly deemphasized in early training; the trainees themselves told Marcille they needed more conditioning.[11] Shortfalls in this area were compounded by the use of trucks to move soldiers to and from training sites. Whereas their counterparts in earlier wars marched to and from rifle ranges, the trainees of the Vietnam era rode, saving time but providing less toning of soldiers' bodies for the combat that was but weeks away.[12]

Finally, basic training shared with all army preparation the ultimate goal of building every soldier's confidence in his own abilities as a fighting man and his army's capability to defeat the enemy. In theory, training was to produce a soldier who was capable and confident and who would be a valued member of his unit.

ADVANCED INDIVIDUAL TRAINING (AIT)

After Basic Combat Training, soldiers moved on to Advanced Individual Training for further education in their particular specialties. Infantry AIT included both individual and small-unit training. Men learned how to position weapons and move under the covering fire of machine guns and artillery. All received training on the weapons essential to infantry combat. Depending on their infantry specialty, they also received instruction about how to serve as a member of a rifle squad, mortar crew, or antitank weapons team.[13]

First Cavalry Division veteran respondents training represented the typical myriad of experiences found in any army division in the combat theater. They underwent BCT in eighteen different locations. They were scattered over twenty-three locations for AIT, but more than a quarter of them completed AIT at "Tigerland" in Fort Polk, Louisiana.[14] Over the course of the war, Fort Polk prepared more American soldiers for service in Vietnam than any other training center in the United States.[15]

Fort Polk and Fort Gordon, Georgia, began conducting a modified version of the standard AIT early in the war—a nine-week course designed specifically for infantrymen going to Vietnam.[16] The first six weeks were dedicated to sharpening and expanding the trainee's knowledge of fundamental infantry skills, such as weapons training and use of a map and compass. The focus of training in the final weeks of the course was patrolling and other field skills directly applicable to soldiers' pending Vietnam assignment. Instruction covered the establishment of defensive positions, village searches, booby traps, and actions against snipers.[17] The ninth and final week of Fort Polk infantry AIT was conducted in an area that included a detailed replica of a Vietnamese village.

Fort Polk had a reputation for toughness most men found warranted. Those 1st Cavalry Division veterans who commented on their Tigerland experiences generally found it difficult, memorable, and necessary. One veteran summed up his nine weeks of advanced infantry training at Fort Polk, Louisiana as "extremely difficult. . . . I was *glad* to get to Nam to get a break from Fort Polk." However, when he "got to Vietnam and completed my training at Camp Evans, it all became clear why we were trained like that. I credit my survival of Vietnam solely upon my excellent training and the great unit I was with. I was wounded in action in January 1968 in an enemy ambush. If I had not been trained the way I was I would have died for sure. It seems so hard when you go through it, but it's only for *your* own good."[18]

REPLACEMENT TRAINING IN VIETNAM

It was impossible to prepare America's soldiers for all aspects of Southeast Asian combat, regardless of the quality of training at Fort Polk and other centers. No training could totally prepare a man for the death of a comrade. No rehearsal could induce the level of fear experienced when the enemy fired rifle, artillery, mortar, and rocket rounds with the intention of killing. The 1st Cavalry Division's innovative use of helicopters and the many demands on the army training system ensured that replacements coming to the division needed further preparation before they were assigned to units.

Leaders quickly found it necessary to create a school for newcomers, much as divisions had done during both of the world wars. The British had discovered a similar requirement for special schooling during World War I. Medical officer Capt. J. C. Dunn wrote that training for replacements arriving in France for service with the Second Battalion, His Majesty's Twenty-Third Foot, The Royal Welch Fusiliers, in July 1916 "hardly amounted to a 'lick and a promise'; it did not fit the men to take part in any operation. They had fired only five rounds of ball cartridge; many of them did not know how to load and unload a rifle, to fix and unfix a bayonet."[19] The situation was little different for some Americans in that war. James Cooke wrote that "in 1917, most of the eager soldiers would train with wooden mock-ups of rifles, machine guns, and mortars, and some would go to France without even the most rudimentary instruction in rifle assembly, care and cleaning, or marksmanship."[20] David M. Kennedy similarly observed that, during World War I, "the average doughboy at the Meuse-Argonne had seen perhaps four months of training in camps. Many had seen but a few weeks. Some had been cycled so swiftly from induction center to war zone that they had never handled a rifle and had to be given a quick ten-day course of instruction upon arrival in France."[21]

Leaping forward to a conflict a generation later, one author concluded that individual training during World War II "had three main purposes" in the armies of all belligerent nations: "to rid the conscript of civilian preconceptions about his 'rights' and personal freedom; to familiarize him with the weapons that he was likely to have to operate, mainly the rifle, mortar and machine gun; and to give him some experience of the noise and confusion of actual combat. Armies succeeded best at the first of these tasks."[22]

Units' establishment of schools to bring replacements' skills to acceptable levels and provide new men time to acclimatize had been considered one of the American army's most important adjustments to its World War II personnel replacement system.[23] In Terry de la Mesa Allen's 104th Division, "replacements went through ninety hours of intensive training over a twelve-day period after arriving with their new outfit. Weapons firing consumed a great portion of time."[24] Twenty-four percent of officer veterans from World War II Pacific and Italy cited "inadequate training of our troops for combat" as an important shortcoming.[25] Ellis wrote of issues similar to those the 1st Cavalry Division would confront twenty years later when using helicopters: in North Africa, "armour and infantry rarely underwent joint training and thus had little understanding of each other's abilities or problems."[26]

Thus leaders in Vietnam found that their replacements exhibited the same training deficiencies as had men two decades before. Newcomers to Southeast Asia required additional weapons training, further inoculation against the shock of initial combat, and the help of veterans to learn many of the lessons key to survival. John A. Fesmire judged early replacements "weak in weapons training and weapons employment techniques" when they reported during his November 1965–April 1966 tenure as commander of C Company, 2/7 Cavalry.[27] A second division veteran noted the benefits the 1st Cavalry Division replacement school offered him, fresh from soldier stateside training: "When I first got to Vietnam, I was put out into the field with no pretraining about the area. Later in 1966, the Cav started a two-week training camp for new incoming troops. This sure did help cut down on the stupid mistakes that they made and cut down the injuries. This also gave them time to settle down their nerves and learn about what to watch out for, like booby traps."[28]

The need for supplementing replacements' stateside training did not lessen as the war progressed. Some veterans believed that stateside training produced a less qualified soldier in the conflict's later years. A 1st Cavalry Division veteran who went through basic training twice because of a break in service thought his instruction better when he went through it in August 1967 than when he repeated the experience in November 1972: "The training in '72 was like scout camp while our motto in '67 was 'the more sweat in training the less blood in combat.' After basic training in '72, I found myself unsure of the people I had [gone] through training with."[29] Another found that during his "second tour of duty in Vietnam, the quality of the new troops arriving after completing their stateside training was so poor that it was almost murder to send them into the field."[30]

Despite efforts by trainers in the United States and Vietnam, the army and marines found it difficult to maintain combat proficiency because combat losses and other kinds of attrition reduced their reserve of regulars while short service obligations and the twelve-month rotation rushed one-term soldiers through their ranks.

Another factor that very likely influenced the diminished skill levels found in some men was the mandate from the secretary of defense that all services take a set number of recruits from groups scoring below the previously allowable minimum score on entry tests.[31] For example, this program (designated "Project 100,000") required that between a fifth and a quarter of new marines be from Armed Forces Qualification Test Mental Group IV. No one scoring lower than those in this group was allowed to serve in the military. Many of these men were fine additions to their services, but some had difficulty picking up skills during training or meeting the demands of their assigned duties.

First Cavalry Division leaders conducted their in-country training with several objectives in mind.[32] They sought to redress shortfalls in BCT and AIT and help their men to adapt to local fighting conditions. Specific elements of the division replacement course were altered over time to address new missions, fresh terrain, or unusual enemy tactics, but it necessarily included instruction on the M16 and procedures pertinent to helicopter operations. Division leaders found that men needed further familiarization with their personal weapons; each weapon also had to be zeroed before a soldier went into combat. The preliminary training also gave men the opportunity to adjust to the differences between firing at live targets and practicing on a rifle range. In the former case the target was more often than not invisible; when visible it was often moving. Jack W. Pellington, a reconnaissance sergeant with the 2/12 Cavalry, was one of many veterans who noted such discrepancies. He recalled that "in Vietnam, nine out of ten times you were fighting a well-concealed ghost. You fired in the direction of the enemy sound, or if lucky, at a muzzle flash. A visible target was a rarity."[33]

Most new soldiers had also never been trained in helicopter assault techniques. They needed instruction on how to position themselves on the ground prior to an aircraft's arrival so that they would move to the correct position on the helicopter during loading and how to handle their weapons and other equipment so as to avoid accidental misfires or entanglements as they exited. They needed to learn the proper procedures for jumping from an aircraft, both when it had landed and when it was hovering over stumps or other obstacles. They had to be taught how to move to the appropriate location on the landing zone and help establish a perimeter defense, what to do if the helicopter crashed before passengers could exit, and how to move around the aircraft to avoid being struck by the tail or main rotors. These and many other considerations were essential in training personnel because of the 1st Cavalry Division's reliance on aircraft.

Refreshing combat skills was a second end served by in-country training. This included reviewing BCT and AIT lessons that had atrophied during the leave many soldiers took between AIT and their reporting to Vietnam. Veteran soldiers who had not yet experienced combat, and even those with previous Vietnam tours, also needed to hone combat skills. Refresher training was also a component of programs designed to ready men with time in Vietnam who were assuming leadership responsibilities. The division ran a course for those so designated in addition to the replacement program. A 1st Cavalry Division veteran who served on its cadre described this course in some detail:

> In my last three months in Vietnam I served as OIC [officer-in-charge] of the division's combat leader course. One man from each line company in the division attended a 2-week school in the division rear (Bien Hoa) where myself and 6 NCOs . . . taught/reviewed all of the basics for squad leaders—with an eye on how things were 'really done' as opposed to 'by the field manual.' We covered small unit tactics, leadership, weapons, map reading & land navigation, first aid, demolitions, artillery adjustment rapid procedure and intelligence. I think this type of course might have been beneficial on a company level—taking a company for one week and exposing them to a 'lessons learned' approach where each person might get an idea of the jobs & responsibilities of others as well as refreshing the subjects many might not have had since basic or AIT. Heavy emphasis would be placed on weapons—including those often carried but sometimes seldom used (claymores, LAW M-72, etc.). We did this in the CLC (everyone fired a LAW and we had claymore demonstrations) with rotations and replacements. A company could go through a review like this every 6 months (which might also be linked to a stand-down). I recall our students scoffing at the idea that we might be able to actually teach them anything when they arrived but almost all left with the feeling that the school had been beneficial and that they really had learned something.[34]

The division's third in-country training objective, after teaching newcomers about weapons and equipment and refreshing their combat skills, was to inform them about the procedures, customs, and expectations that were the norm in their new unit. The trainers passed on the lessons learned from combat operations that had yet to be incorporated into stateside preparation. They also attempted to instill an initial sense of pride by drawing on their organization's exploits in Vietnam and earlier wars. The division school was an opportunity to begin building the esprit de corps that was a first step toward each man's performing as a team member under fire. Finally, these initial training sessions were periods of acclimatization, a chance for new men's bodies to adapt to the Vietnamese climate under conditions where others' lives would not be endangered if a man collapsed under the Asian sun or lagged behind while his body adjusted to changes in diet.

When the division first opened its replacement training center in the autumn of 1966, there were sufficient veterans with combat experience to ensure that those newly arriving received the benefit of instruction from the wise. Men with the division when it initially deployed the year before had not been so fortunate. Though there were some senior leaders in the officer and noncommissioned-officer ranks who had seen combat in World War II, Korea, or both, few had been exposed to the mix of regular and irregular warfare that confronted a soldier in Vietnam. None had fought as airmobile soldiers. Terry Musser found that his training had not "been that bad except that we weren't ready for air assaulting into hot LZs [landing zones under enemy fire]. You can read about them in a book and they can tell you about it, but until you actually have been to a hot LZ there is no conception of what it is. Nobody was ready for it."[35]

Veterans looked back on their early training in Vietnam as an essential part of preparing for the coming test of fire. A young officer who was eventually assigned to B Company, 1/8 Cavalry, described the division's course as it was conducted in its first weeks. The instructors were a captain and three senior noncommissioned officers, all of whom had been in Vietnam for nearly a year. Training included instruction on

> operations of the division, how it was broken down, what type of units they had and a little bit of air mobility tactics. I went through with the privates and the noncoms. Then all the junior officers in the group went over to where they had a rappelling tower and they taught us helicopter rappelling techniques and how to seat ourselves in the helicopter. . . . We were given an orientation on Vietcong tactics, uniforms, and shown a wide variety of captured weapons. We were given a class on mines, booby traps, punji stakes, and for a final phase of the course, we had a small patrol out here on Hon Kon Mountain. The jungle there is quite thick, quite steep, and very realistic. We went out in squad size—well, more of a reinforced squad, with one of these cadre members with us to advise us—but we ran it ourselves. Got the experience and got a little bit of the feel of the jungle. . . . I gained quite a bit from it.[36]

When Thomas Rhame arrived in the combat theater in later 1967

> every man who came into the 1st Cavalry Division, me included, underwent two weeks of training back at An Khe, at the base camp. They had a two-week, in-country acclimatization and conducted training in airmobile operations. I would say it was pretty beneficial because the soldiers got very rapidly acquainted with the helicopter. . . . They ran a pretty effective booby trap training program. They set booby traps up where patrols would go and, as the soldiers would go in, smoke would go off and the soldier would rapidly see that if it had been the real thing he would have killed himself and three or four other people.[37]

John E. Robbins commanded A Battery, 2/19 Field Artillery from November 1967 to mid-April of the following year. He found the 1st Cavalry

Division school instructors taught "the airmobile kinds of things that you did because we didn't have anything back in the States teaching people how to be airmobile soldiers in-country. This gave the kids a lot of confidence. It also gave them an opportunity to adjust to the climate and the humidity."[38] Another 1st Cavalry Division veteran was a great believer in the division school's efforts to help him make it home alive:

> I was probably one of the best stateside trained infantrymen the U.S. Army ever sent to Vietnam. Yet not all of the stateside training in the world could have helped me survive Vietnam. You also had to have someone up above watching over you to make it back home. However, the "First Team" did try to increase the odds for survival by sending all newly arrived "Sky Troopers" through its jungle school (which was first rate) before assigning them to a combat unit. Such a policy of re-familiarization with weapons and tactics, and adjustment to terrain before assignment to a frontline unit, should be continued if the rigors of war allow it.[39]

Some commanders found it necessary to provide further training even after a new man went through the two-week division program. Joe Driscoll did so as commander of Headquarters and Headquarters Troop, 1/9 Cavalry (Aerial Reconnaissance), passing on Vietnam-specific tactics that his unit had developed and found effective.[40]

Active operations often precluded dedication of time to formal training after a replacement left the division school; John Fesmire used patrols around his base camps to break in recent arrivals when the enemy was not active locally.[41] James E. Tindall's aerial field artillery battery (equipped with Cobra attack helicopters carrying both guns and rockets) ran a two-week orientation course for replacements that included firing fifty to one hundred rockets from their aircraft on training ranges. New pilots initially flew in the front seat of Cobra gunships rather than serving as the backseat aircraft pilot-in-command.[42] Establishing replacement schools or conducting supplemental training frequently overburdened the organizations. The Department of the Army's 1970 "Study of the Twelve-month Vietnam Tour" found that newcomer inexperience "required units to conduct training sessions beyond those normally expected of a unit. Many units, already short of personnel, struggled with personnel turnover without corresponding decreases in mission workload."[43]

In addition to training replacements, units honed and refreshed the skills of all their members to maintain fighting trim. As a 1st Cavalry Division veteran put it, "There were occasions when even combat troops needed refresher training on makeshift rifle ranges set up around fire bases during lulls in the fighting."[44] Weapons had to be repeatedly zeroed. Though every soldier was trained to remember his zero, the value could change after a weapon suffered the shocks endemic to combat operations or was exchanged for a replacement rifle. Refresher training frequently also included instruction on weapons maintenance, use of weapons (both friendly and enemy) other than those normally carried by the soldier, and the ubiquitous unit drills. These training periods were further used to pass along lessons learned by other units and to redress deficiencies noted by unit leaders during recent operations. One officer recalled an instance during which "a VC [Vietcong] soldier bolted from hiding in the midst of my platoon. At least 16 guns were aimed at him as he dashed across an open paddy to the jungle beyond. He made it. Not one shot of the dozens of rounds fired hit him. I pulled my platoon off line for two days of weapons training. After that they were better."[45]

Another leader conducted daily training to reinforce fire discipline and other fundamentals during periods in firebases, stressing the use of aimed fire rather than excessive reliance on area fire with the M16 in automatic mode.[46] Thomas Rhame remembered that "every time we hit a firebase, we went into a weapons qualification and a weapons familiarization firing exercise and conducted a patrol training class. . . . I found that new people needed to shoot a lot."[47]

John D. Fuller commanded C Company, 1/7 Cavalry, in the latter half of 1970 and found that certain skills had to be taught at company level. Potential point men and slack men required extensive additional training before they were allowed to assume these critical roles.[48] Marine units likewise often conducted additional training. The commander of Battalion Landing Team 2/4 (2nd Battalion, 4th Marine Regiment) in 1968, Lt. Cdr. William Weise, established a program in which all marines rotated through marksmanship, camouflage, patrolling, security, and other training one company at a time. Night training received special emphasis. One of Weise's subordinates understood his commander's motivation, observing that Weise "believed that his most important responsibility was to make sure not a single life would be lost because the men weren't properly trained."[49]

Drills dominated much of this infantry unit training. Leaders had their fighting men repeatedly practice actions that had to be instinctive during engagements. These included actions to take if ambushed at close range, responses to sniper fire, and how to maneuver against a position while other unit members provided a base of fire to cover the movement. Trainers worked to make selected actions automatic so that a man would not hesitate the extra fraction of a second that might cost him his life. If the enemy ambushed a patrol at close range, for example, soldiers learned to turn immediately *into* the incoming fire and return a heavy volume of outgoing fire. The seemingly logical alternatives—either immediately hitting the ground or seeking the nearest cover away from the ambush—left the uneducated exposed in the middle of the beaten zone of his adversaries' weapons or impaled on punji stakes, if not blown apart by well-positioned booby traps or mines located along likely escape routes. Having a soldier accept that the best way to deal with a close-range ambush was to turn into the fire of the enemy was a challenge. At least one 1st Cavalry Division soldier refused to accept that solution. In describing an enemy ambush he revealed both his understanding of the problem and his lack of confidence in the technique:

> Over here when a Cong sets up an ambush, they sense that you will be moving this way so they are going to set up what is known as a killing zone on the trail. You are supposed to come through here and he is set up where you have to come up the hill to get to him. It's going to be rocky and thick. It isn't going to be easy getting up to him and out here you are going to be right out in the open. So they tell you when you get hit to charge the thing. Sure, run up that hill, run up there and spit right down the barrel of that .50 so they can blow your head off real good. It just wouldn't work; it's true, you've got to do something and in an ambush you don't have time to think. . . . But this thing of trying to assault them is no good. But you have to do something, that's true.[50]

An Australian officer writing about the Korean War recalled problems he encountered when training soldiers how to react to a close ambush. He found that the solution was to fully explain the logic behind the drill:

> A definite "immediate action" drill was laid down and included in the syllabus of training for reinforcements at the Divisional Battle School in Japan. It was here that great difficulty was encountered in putting over this particular technique. These troops, without any experience of war, were not impressed with a technique which called for them to "walk into" a well-concealed force of, say, fifteen Chinese, all firing fully automatic weapons from a position of great tactical advantage. . . .
>
> Instructors responsible for training in patrolling techniques were encouraged by the school staff to adopt a new approach: the battle situation was to be described realistically and in detail. Then the fact of there being a natural, undisciplined reaction to run away was to be acknowledged. Usually this caused intensified interest in the squad. . . . It was demonstrated geometrically that the quickest way out of trouble was to pass directly through the enemy to a position immediately behind rather than attempt to follow the natural inclination to run away or by-pass the ambush.
>
> From this point on the change in attitude was marked. Necessary refinements to this aggressive but at first glance apparently foolhardy action were eagerly adopted. Assimilation was hastened and the required standard was achieved quicker and with less need for close supervision by forceful instructors.[51]

William L. Hauser articulated the logic behind all such drills:

> There is no substitute for repetition in training. . . .
>
> Threat of death or maiming is surely the ultimate distraction; unless the soldier has been drilled . . . he cannot be expected to keep fighting . . . under stresses of shot and shell, confusion, uncertainty, and the infectious fear of his comrades.[52]

Routinization led to instinctive reaction. Ebert recalled how "reaction could be so automatic that a man under fire might feel detached from his actions, separated from the control of his own response. As Layne Anderson put it, 'You don't really think; you just act on instinct.' "[53] Another soldier described this almost unconscious drill behavior as making "no value judgments, no conscious decision. You just flow with the experience."[54] When Franklin D. Miller's first fatal engagement of the enemy came, "the kill was very fast, very quick. There was no thought process involved. It was basically a 'scare' kill: you see somebody and you shoot immediately. . . . I saw them run and before I was even aware of it I was raising my M16 to my shoulder and it was going off."[55] Another 1st Cavalry Division veteran recalled that "the greatest danger was in the opening seconds of a firefight. It was crucial that the point element or other section of the unit first engaged with the enemy immediately expend as much firepower as possible against the NVA to keep their heads down. This required instant firing of M16s in the automatic mode to neutralize the enemy. Extreme care had to be taken to ensure that everyone did not have to reload at the same time and thus allow the NVA to destroy us with overwhelming firepower during the pause."[56] Years after Vietnam the army still saw the value in these observations and cited them in its "Winning in the Jungle for Squad through Battalion Operations" pamphlet: "Quick fire techniques must be second nature to every soldier. Engagement distances are usually so short that known distance firing techniques are not effective. In short, he who shoots first 'wins.' "[57]

Some units complemented formal training sessions with a buddy system that took advantage of more experienced soldiers' expertise, a scheme that had also been used by organizations during the Second World War and in Korea.[58] Ebert wrote that "arranging for veterans to look over the shoulders of the new men helped prevent accidents. Most soldiers recalled these mentors with genuine fondness as friends who in great measure preserved their lives."[59] George F. Smith's unit used a buddy system during his October 1969 to May 1970 command of A Company, 1/5 Cavalry, a period during which the unit spent a large amount of time patrolling near the Cambodian border.[60] There was very limited time to prepare new men for combat, he recalled, aside from "a little remedial training in base camps."[61] This procedure of matching a new man with a veteran was made standard procedure in many 1st Cavalry Division units. A soldier in A Company of the 1/8

Cavalry related that his unit "never put a new man out there by himself. We put him with an old man to show him the ropes and talk to him and tell him what to expect. That way the guy doesn't get shook up, and if something new happens, he'll know exactly what to do."[62]

SHORTFALLS IN TRAINING THE VIETNAM SOLDIER

The discrepancies between stateside training and actual fighting conditions that eventually caused the creation of the division replacement school became apparent soon after the 1st Cavalry Division's 1965 arrival in Vietnam. Steve Ebert wrote that "many ordinary riflemen began to sense that something was wrong after a month or two in Vietnam. Gerry Barker . . . was a new NCO with the 1st Battalion, 8th Cavalry, during the battles in the Ia Drang Valley in November 1965. It seemed to Barker that when his unit first went over there, 'we really made every mistake in the book. We were not trained for it. We were trained to fight World War II, and we were bad.' "[63] Division schools helped to redress serious shortcomings in training and experience over the duration of the war, but there were at least four areas (in addition to aircraft operations–related skills) that constantly required attention when new men arrived. These were weapons training, battle inoculation, mental preparation for combat, and better replication of the environmental conditions in which the soldiers would fight.

Weapons Training

Survey respondents most frequently cited weapons skills as needing improvement. There is little doubt that the early use of M14s for training in the United States and the issue of M16s to the division's soldiers after they arrived in Vietnam was the root of early shortcomings. The 1/5 Cavalry's Bob Franklin joined his unit in December 1966; "The only weapon I saw or handled was the M14 rifle. On arrival in Vietnam I was issued an M16 rifle and was told that it was easy to field strip and that I would catch on. No instruction or zeroing was done."[64] Another division veteran "trained in basic with a M14 and had only three days with a M16. After basic I never used a M14 again, and while in [AIT at Fort Sill, Oklahoma, as an artillery forward observer], never used an M16 at all."[65]

A third veteran recalled with some bitterness that his M14 instruction and other facets of his basic and advanced training did little to prepare him for Southeast Asia. He trained at "Fort Dix in winter and Fort Lewis in winter then seven days leave—then the Nam. Does that sound smart? I'm very lucky I'm alive."[66] A fourth, with service in B Company, 2/5 Cavalry, received stateside training "on the M14, [and was] then sent to Vietnam and handed a M16. I didn't know the first thing about the weapon, wasn't told how to fire or clean it. I wasn't even issued ammo until I complained. I asked for directions and was told to see my sergeant. Hell . . . being a PFC [Private First Class] I wasn't going to bother a 1st Sergeant. Our company went out in the field three days later and that was that."[67] The problem was not limited to M16 training, however. Though it was frequently the sidearm they carried in Vietnam, one young medic never received .45-caliber pistol training during his predeployment training. While on his last leave before going overseas, his "dad, a marine WWII combat vet, was quite surprised that I had not even handled a .45. He produced one and trained me on it before I went to Nam."[68]

A veteran of B Company, 1/8 Cavalry, summed up what was perhaps felt by all of these individuals when he concluded that poor weapons training "killed more than Charlie ever did."[69]

Fortunately this problem occurred less frequently in later years as M16s were made available to stateside training centers. Nevertheless, marksmanship continued to be an issue. An infantry veteran who served three tours and eventually rose to the rank of command sergeant major concluded that soldiers were rushed during their weapons training; they therefore failed to learn how to fire accurately at long range and how to wisely use automatic fire. This poor preparation was particularly ill-advised in his view, as "good marksmanship training and hard discipline are the two ingredients which make an infantry platoon successful in battle."[70] Sherman Flanders had two tours with the army and another pair as a civilian in Vietnam. He found that "in 1945 to 1960 rifle company personnel spent more time on firing ranges . . . and each man had to fire [the] M1 [rifle], carbine, BAR [Browning Automatic Rifle], .45 [pistol], machine guns, and 2.35/3.5 [bazooka antitank weapons] each year. [Around] 1960 rifle company personnel only fired their own assigned weapon for qualification each year. [The] old system was best; [soldiers were] better qualified, more familiar."[71]

Despite Flanders's confidence in earlier training procedures, Donovan reported that the American Korean War soldier was "keenly aware of his lack of training. Everyone interviewed recommended that all infantrymen going through basic training be given sufficient experience and instruction in the use of all infantry weapons (with the possible exception of mortars) so that they could fire and disassemble any one of them. This would seem a sound recommendation in view of the fact that in the group of 483 men questioned on the number of weapons they had been assigned for use in combat, one-third had used at least two kinds."[72]

Like Donovan's Korean War veterans, those who had served in Vietnam believed that soldiers should have also been given more extensive training with multiple American and enemy weapons. Weapons malfunctioned or were damaged in firefights; if a man could not immediately correct the problem, the soldier sought the nearest available replacement. Often this was not the same type of armament he normally carried. An infantry platoon had men carrying M16s, M79s or another form of grenade launcher, .45-caliber pistols, and at times M14 sniper rifles or shotguns in addition to machine guns. There was also a reasonable likelihood that the nearest available weapon had belonged to the enemy. As one veteran described the situation. "A soldier knows his M16. In a firefight, it malfunctions or breaks or whatever. Next to him [there is] a fallen comrade with an M79 grenade launcher or an officer lying there with a .45 auto[automatic pistol]. Does the soldier know how to use either one?"[73] A combat photographer felt "all soldiers need to be cross-trained on a variety of weapons. Even though my personal weapon was the .45, I had several occasions that required me to fire [the] M60 and M16 (both were weapons I was not familiar with)."[74]

Specialist Fourth Class Bill Beck was an assistant M60 machine gunner when he landed in LZ X-Ray and found himself going through a series of weapons to both defend himself and help save his unit as the NVA closed in on the 1/7 Cavalry position. He was with fellow soldiers Theron Ladner and Russell Adams during an enemy assault on their A Company sector. Moore and Galloway wrote of how Beck went to the aid of a soldier with a chest wound. Beck wrapped the man's "first-aid pack and a plastic wrapper over both holes, screamed for a medic, got his M16, and tried to fire it at the NVA shooting at us. It was all shot to hell."[75] He then moved to and bandaged an officer who had also been hit by enemy fire:

> I got his M16 and tried to fire it and it was inoperable. I took his .45 pistol and fired into the jungle toward the enemy. Somewhere along the line I picked up an M79 grenade launcher from a dead guy and tried to fire it, and it was no good. . . .
>
> Just then I heard Ladner screaming "Beck, Beck, *help!* Adams is hit." I ran back. Russ was on his back staring at me, the M60 lying on its side. The side of his head was a mess. . . . The enemy knew they had shot him and were closing in on us from the front and right front thirty yards out. I righted the M60 fast and started firing at them. . . .
>
> Suddenly the M60 jammed. We were being assaulted and I could see the enemy twenty-five yards out. It's surprising how fast you think and act in a situation like that. Lying prone I opened the feed cover, flipped the gun over and hit it on the ground. It jarred the shells loose. Debris from the ground had caught in the ammo belt when Adams was hit. I flipped it right side up, slapped the ammo belt back in, slammed the feed cover closed and began firing again. It seemed like a lifetime, but wasn't more than five or ten seconds.[76]

In addition to concerns about weapons familiarity, men expressed concern that weapons training was not sufficiently realistic. One of S. L. A. Marshall's recommendations for improving the number of firers was to make rifle training more like actual combat. He later attributed increases in the number of riflemen firing during Korea and Vietnam to adoption of his suggestions.[77] Philip Sheridan of American Civil War fame had made a similar suggestion long before Marshall. In 1885 he directed the use of "more realistic targets, profiles of soldiers representing an enemy skirmish line."[78]

Many other 1st Cavalry Division veterans supported calls for greater emphasis on weapons skills needed in combat. Foremost among these was the ability to rapidly engage the adversary. As one observed, "more training is needed in firing their weapons in simulated combat situations. It's one thing to learn the use of a weapon on a firing range, and quite another when someone is shooting back at you."[79]

A second who had been point man for five and a half months, and later took the "slack man" position of second in column while a squad leader, wrote that "first contact with [the] enemy is usually fast and picking the weapon up to aim can cost you your life."[80] Squad leaders in D Company, 1/8 Cavalry, worked "with the troops on marksmanship (short range) when we were on artillery fire bases. The targets were fuse cans and grenade packing cardboard cans that we engaged rapidly at different angles," he recalled. "Squad leaders would set up the cans while the soldier was looking the other way. Then when he was back by the soldier, he would tell him 'gray cans now.' The soldier would have to turn around and identify the gray cans and shoot them but not the black or green cans. It was an impromptu drill in shooting and target identification. We shot up about 150–200 rounds per month on that type of drill per person."[81]

Another veteran emphasized that "quick fire tactics and training are very helpful [when] detecting a concealed enemy or an enemy who may be on patrol as you are. In most situations encountered while on patrol, especially near the 'point,' quickness in reaction is important."[82] Units taught these "quick kill" techniques to allow soldiers to more rapidly engage the enemy during chance encounters. Some also issued shotguns to point men to increase the area covered with an initial pull of the trigger.[83] Quickness often came at a cost, however. Many veterans recalled soldiers who missed targets at very short range due to a combination of using quick fire techniques and automatic fire.

Veterans additionally saw a need to conduct unit as well as individual weapons training. One veteran was a radioman who opted to carry a rifle. He recalled that he often had little idea of where much of his company was located and thus did not fire at times for fear of hitting his fellow soldiers.[84] To overcome such problems and to maximize the effectiveness of unit fire, one officer found it critical to "train them to fire weapons as a part of team development. Teach them weapons training as a squad, not individuals. Show them from BCT what integrated fire is and how they rely on each other."[85] The marines' Lieutenant Jerry Siler similarly understood the need to provide weapons training for his unit. In a procedure that was the reverse of that employed by many units, he had his "guys trained to fire the first round on semiautomatic and then switch to automatic fire. If possible, they were also to aim in on the VC that corresponded to their number in the patrol. The number-one man would sight on the first man in the enemy team, and so forth. This would keep all of us from aiming in on the same one or two."[86]

Although at first largely attributable to a lack of M16s for stateside preparation, shortcomings in soldiers' and marines' ability to employ their weapons did not entirely cease when initial training programs eventually received sufficient rifles for recruits. New arrivals required supplementary training and an opportunity to zero their assigned rifle; veterans needed occasional refresher instruction. Well-conceived unit weapons training complemented these individual sessions to meld the many into a unified whole. As a man's weapon was his basic implement of war, it is unsurprising that skills related to its use were most cited by veterans as needing greater attention.

Battle Inoculation

Battle inoculation—training conducted with the objective of immunizing a soldier against the shock of unexpected events in combat—was hardly a new concept when introduced during Vietnam. In its broadest sense, the approach has included everything from striving for realism during training to positioning soldiers in bunkers as artillery impacted in the immediate vicinity. When designed properly, it put soldiers in situations similar to those likely to overwhelm a man when he first confronted them in combat.

Ninety-seven percent of the Spanish Civil War veterans participating in Dollard's study believed that "giving a man a real picture of the dangers of battle will tend to make him a better soldier."[87] F. M. Richardson recognized battle inoculation's value for newcomers: "All men should have detailed knowledge of the weapons which may be used against them and of the nature of the enemy who will be using them."[88] Richard Holmes quoted a British parachutist who during the Second World War "could see the other blokes in the section, and when one of them got hit he was thrown back so hard by the bullet I was sure he'd had it, but he was OK. . . . It was unbelievably confusing, far, far worse than even the most confusing exercise."[89] In their post–World War II study of combat neuroses, Roy L. Swank and Walter E. Marchand found that men initially underwent considerable mental and emotional anxiety accompanied by a number of physical abnormalities resulting from fears associated with the shock of early combat experiences. However, "gradually the men became adapted to the existing conditions of battle. They became familiar with the sounds of their own, as contrasted with the enemy's, artillery and automatic small arms weapons. From the sound they could determine the caliber of artillery fire and how close the projectiles would fall, thereby knowing when to 'hit the dirt.' Without being conscious of it, they chose paths of approach which afforded concealment and cover, and they constantly watched for snipers in trees and hedges. Smoke and fire disciplines at night became automatic, and the soldier was always well oriented to his own and the enemy's strength and position."[90]

Physical reactions to combat could be delayed, however. The pressures of constant exposure to danger, extended periods of sleep deprivation, and being responsible for the marines in his squad eventually caused James Johnston to collapse "with a series of convulsions. It was beyond my power to control them . . . I finally gave up and let the convulsions run their course." Johnston concealed the event from his men and quickly recovered from it, but he long remembered the harsh demands of combat, which he found "unbelievably depleting both physically and mentally."[91]

Soldiers eventually learned the skills that helped them to survive. The knowledge often came after considerable stress and the loss of comrades whose initial ignorance and reaction to the shocks of their first combat did not provide them the opportunity to become battle wise. Effective battle inoculation in many cases clearly could have reduced stress and the casualty rate among new men.[92] Elmar Dinter concluded that "training can help considerably in reducing the fear of the unknown and unexpected. Thus, for example, tanks should no longer appear as frightening monsters to the infantryman. He must get used to tanks by becoming familiar with them. . . . The first time an enemy machine gun opens fire from behind anxiety is increased considerably, even in an exercise. The more this is repeated the more the soldier learns to trust in his group, in the efficacy of his cover, and in his own weapon."[93] Herbert Gardiner Lord had earlier written of the danger of inexperience and the value of proper preparation during the World War I. "In battle," he noted, the unexpected appearance of the enemy or the sudden explosion of a large shell nearby

> may throw a battalion of soldiers into terror before they know what has happened.
>
> In general, then, we may say the element in a situation most likely to set off fear is surprise. It will always do it. . . . But the surprise in situations disappears to a great extent when one has become familiar with those situations in which surprise occurs. So training involves becoming, as we say, used to such situations. First make-believe situations of surprise have to be met. In mock-battle startling appearances of mock enemies, sudden loud explosions at unforeseen times and in unexpected places, breed familiarity. The soldier gains to some degree the attitude of expecting that almost anything may happen anywhere at any time.[94]

Writing after World War II, Hans Kissel similarly concluded that "the more unexpectedly [shock in combat] occurs, the less significant does it need to be" to cause soldier panic.[95]

The Canadian army may have been the first to employ a form of battle inoculation to prepare for twentieth-century conflict. Instructors at a World War I training center threw grenades with very small charges over trainees' heads. The French later adopted similar practices during the war.[96] Though the British apparently did not use such techniques, two of their prominent medical officers wrote of the need for precombat conditioning.[97] Lord Moran, having served with the First Battalion of the Royal Fusiliers from the autumn of 1914 into the spring of 1917, railed against those who thought realistic training would traumatize a soldier and thus sought "to hide from him what war is really like until he finds it out for himself. It would be as reasonable to keep the medical student away from disease because some may become a little too introspective and get it into their heads that they themselves are suffering from the same malady."[98] J. C. Dunn, Moran's aforementioned counterpart with the Second Battalion His Majesty's Twenty-Third Foot, The Royal Welch Fusiliers, "was convinced . . . that more emphasis should be placed on training before a recruit reached his unit, and that this should include what a later generation referred to as 'battle inoculation'—exposure to shell and rifle fire."[99] Interestingly, Dunn saw a benefit for organizations whose men had received innovative training. He "believed that experienced soldiers soon became uneasy if they were joined by drafts who had no training and were unable even to fire their weapons." Dunn, in his post–World War I response to a War Office Committee Enquiry into "shell shock," believed that unfamiliarity with the noise of combat scared new arrivals. He suggested having them accompany resupply teams for two weeks before sending them into their frontline units so as to lessen the shock of that introduction.[100]

Battle inoculation was readily accepted as a valuable part of World War II training. Both the British and Americans used procedures such as firing live rounds over soldiers' heads and having "enemy" dummies spring from buildings. The British tried (but later abandoned) trips to slaughterhouses as part of the process.[101] By 1943, American basic training put virtually all soldiers "through an infiltration course which required crawling over rough ground for about eighty yards under live machine gun fire. From time to time infantry troops were exposed to the sounds of nearby artillery fire and took part in maneuvers which introduced realistic battle stimuli" with the objective of reducing "the disruptive effects of fear in battle."[102] American combat veterans from the North Africa and Sicily campaigns, when asked what kind of precombat training was needed to better prepare soldiers for their first combat, most frequently responded that soldiers should be put under live fire and in other realistic battle conditions.[103] In a survey of veterans from the Italian campaign, 81 percent (again, more than any other response) cited "going through tough, realistic battle conditions on maneuvers" as an important element of a soldier's training before his deployment overseas.[104]

The British formed "battle schools" in early 1942, and it was from these institutions that the term "battle inoculation" came.[105] One of their aims was "to condition men to the noise and turmoil of war by using the maximal amount of live ammunition and high explosives throughout the course."[106] Trainers were cautious in the use of such conditioning, not wanting to overwhelm recruits with excessive use of live fire and noise in early sessions. Previous experience had demonstrated that inoculation could instill a fear of combat in inexperienced men if the training was not properly calibrated.[107]

A more sophisticated form of battle inoculation featured firing various friendly and enemy weapons to familiarize soldiers with their characteristics. One combat veteran found this technique valuable even for veteran soldiers, as it taught troops "who have been in quite a number of battles . . . to distinguish between Bren and Spandau fire, between the whistle of our own shells and those of the enemy. They go to ground as soon as there is any noise of firing, although it is not directed at them. This often disorganizes an entire battle, especially at night."[108] The value of battle inoculation was validated when a number of British officers who had undergone the process claimed that it had prepared them well for their first experience under fire during the Battle of Alamein.[109] Pacific marine E. B. Sledge told a similar tale. During prebattle training, one of his veteran instructors "blew the whistle and we got down. He announced each type of Japanese weapon and fired several rounds from it over our hole into the bank. . . . This was one of the most valuable training exercises we underwent. There were instances later on Peleliu and Okinawa which it prepared me to come through unscathed."[110]

Lucian Truscott described an episode that demonstrated this need to familiarize soldiers with the conditions of friendly fire on the battlefield. During his first days of battle command, some of his men panicked upon hearing the sounds of friendly artillery fire landing over a half mile away. Truscott wrote that "it had never occurred to me that naval gunfire passing over the heads of an infantry battalion could cause such panic that the battalion would take to its heels and disperse so that it required most of two days to collect the stragglers."[111] He blamed faulty training, finding that the

> battalion was not familiar with the characteristic sound of naval gunfire passing overhead. Having just landed on a strange and hostile shore, advancing in darkness on a dangerous mission, and entering battle for the first time, the battalion was keyed to a high pitch of nervous tension. It broke completely under a new and terrifying sound. Our training had been at fault for we had failed to accustom men to all of the unfamiliar sounds of battle.[112]

Leaders recognized that certain enemy weapons held a special terror for soldiers. Though the reactions of soldiers in various armies differed, the German's Stuka dive bombers, 88-mm antiaircraft guns (when used against ground forces), and mortars all held top position as "most-feared weapon" for Allied forces at some point during the World War II. A 1944 British VIII Corps report noted that "it is obvious that the most frightening weapon has been the mortar. In quiet periods it would be advantageous to use captured German mortars as a method of battle inoculation."[113] Stouffer similarly saw value in such training, though he found that over time soldiers' fears became less based on a weapon's imagined capability to do harm than on demonstrated fact. He suggested that precombat familiarization with enemy weapons and their characteristics would help men to discriminate between real and assumed capabilities.[114]

Earlier, Dollard found that his Spanish Civil War veterans had feared a certain weapon "either because it is especially common and dangerous, perhaps the case with artillery shells, or because something about it arouses irrational fear, perhaps the case with air-bombing. The machine gun should probably be high on the list because it is actually dangerous, but the men may feel that, though dangerous, it is in the realm of the familiar and that they know how to cope with it."[115] The threats that inspired a special fear in Spanish Civil War veterans were bomb shrapnel (listed by 36 percent), trench mortars (22 percent), artillery shells (18 percent), bayonet and knife (16 percent), and expanding bullets (16 percent). During the Korean War, American soldiers overwhelmingly cited the enemy's 120-mm mortar as the most feared weapon, with burp guns and artillery coming in a distant second and third, respectively.[116]

The penalty for an army's failure to properly prepare soldiers for their initial combat was borne by the men themselves. The cost could be death, as was the case with the replacement who ran about seeking a "foxhole with a concrete lining" in his first and last firefight. The luckier escaped to experience other engagements, hopefully the wiser for having learned from early mistakes.[117] Injuries could also be mental. Ahrenfeldt quotes two World War II medical officers as stating that "a large proportion of patients admitted to a neuropathic military hospital revealed that their neurotic breakdown was either determined or in part precipitated by the unaccustomed stress of noises, such as gun-fire, shell-bursts, exploding bombs, sirens, planes, and dive-bombing," and concluding that "fear, which is simply a normal protective instinct, can be countered by enlightenment, and aerial bombardment is unlikely to achieve its demoralizing object if the experience is not a complete surprise. . . . Repetition of bombardment noises would appear to assist in raising the power of endurance and in enabling the individual to stand up to this new form of attack."[118]

Like these men from earlier wars, many who arrived in Vietnam had never undergone familiarization with indirect fire. They faced similar unknowns and potentially disorienting effects. Ebert wrote that "no matter how good their training was, soldiers and marines were rarely prepared for the confusion and noise, the chaos and disorder, or the death and suffering encountered in battle."[119] Veterans agreed. Like their World War II counter-parts, they felt that more realistic battle inoculation training was called for. One recommended that army training should "have soldiers witness incoming fire. . . . Small arms fire from companion soldiers even directed away is very scary or unnerving."[120] Another likewise felt "training should be more realistic. My Basic and AIT training did not prepare me for real combat [with] artillery. Nothing like the real mortar and rocket attacks and ground attacks that took place in Vietnam. We trained down-range at Fort Sill [Oklahoma] only a few times."[121] William J. Jones recalled no battle inoculation training at all during his 1967 basic and advanced training at Forts Lewis and Polk, respectively. Only when he was selected to attend the Noncommissioned Officers Course at Fort Benning, Georgia, did he have to crawl under wire while receiving small-arms fire overhead or experience artillery rounds going over his position.

John Purdy recalled similar training during his 1967 infantry AIT at Fort McClellan, Alabama in which he and his fellow trainees crawled "under barbed wire where we had live fire over our heads and quarter pound blocks of TNT [going off around us]. The day time was scary, but at night you could see where the tracers were going and it was way over our heads."[122] That Purdy had the confidence to look up and recognize the lack of danger itself demonstrated the value of the exercise. Such training instilled confidence while familiarizing the trainee with the shaking of the earth and chaos of noise that heavy fires precipitated.[123] A veteran who had served both as a platoon leader and company commander during Vietnam supported the call for greater use of battle inoculation in preparing men for the noise confronted in combat, for "soldiers are not so much afraid as they are overcome by the sounds of battle."[124]

Like soldiers twenty years earlier, those in Vietnam felt more training was needed to prevent the newcomer from succumbing to the confusion that was characteristic of virtually any combat engagement. No training could fully prepare the inexperienced soldier for war's challenges, but it could help reduce the impact of combat's original shock to a manageable level, and that reduction could be the discriminator between death and survival. Breen's Australian Vietnam veterans believed that nothing "they endured during training prepared them for the shock of their first contact with an enemy firing at them. By the same token, if the subject came up, I do not know of any of them who felt that their battle inoculation was a waste of time or resources."[125] A 1st Cavalry Division veteran understood the potential costs of battle inoculation, but concluded they were worthwhile, given the benefit accrued: "I know soldiers will get hurt and killed in this kind of training, but they will be more ready to get into the fight. It took a little while for new soldiers over there to get the feel for combat. Sometimes they didn't live that long."[126] He recognized, as many soldiers and marines did, that the occasional unfortunate loss in training is repaid many times over in combat.

Mental Preparation

Instilling confidence in his weapon and readying a soldier for the shock of combat were both critical elements in mentally preparing him for the ultimate test of war. The soldier had to believe himself able to fight and win. Dollard's veterans found that "having planned in advance how to meet possible dangers in battle makes a man a better soldier" (agreed with by 98 percent of those responding) and that a soldier "who expects to be afraid in battle and tries to get ready for it makes a good fighter" (58 percent).[127] In Soviet soldier training programs "emphasis [was] placed on upon the need for confidence in themselves, their equipment, and their leaders."[128]

The form such mental preparation took was critical in determining its eventual success or failure. While serving as Army Commander, South-Eastern Command, in 1942, Gen. Bernard Montgomery wrote of the need for the building in soldiers of "a true offensive spirit combined with the will-power which would not recognize defeat," not the hatred for the enemy that had dominated much of British training and which Montgomery believed futile.[129] On the other hand, Dollard found hatred of Fascism acted as a significant motivating force for members of the Abraham Lincoln Brigade, though it must be remembered that his group consisted entirely of volunteers perhaps more idealistic than the norm in most armies.

Both Moran and Baynes witnessed a phenomenal mental transformation in the recruits who came into the British army just before World War I. Each saw value in the mental preparation that resulted in exceptional dedication to a man's regiment and helped to build the cohesion so crucial to units in battle. Moran did "not doubt that many unpromising specimens were transformed by training; in particular by that part of training which consists in inculcating *esprit de corps*. I remember men recruited at the street corner by starvation who came to act on the principle that if the Regiment lived it did not matter if they died, though they did not put it that way. This was their source of strength, their abiding faith; it was the first of all the creeds that in historical times have steeled men against death."[130] This "fierce loyalty to the Regiment," Baynes believed, "was the strongest single influence on the lives of everyone in the battalion. . . . The biggest thing of all was that the battalion should do well; this bound all ranks together as nothing else could. For a member of the Scottish Rifles there was one overriding fear, and that was that he should let the battalion and his company down when the great moment came."[131]

American units do not use the regimental system in the manner of their British counterparts, but a similar pride can nonetheless be inspired by good leadership and fellow soldiers' esprit de corps. E. B. Sledge repeatedly cited the importance of the camaraderie and sense of family he felt as a member of K Company, 3rd Battalion, 5th Marine Regiment, during World War II. It was home to men whose sense of reality was otherwise shattered by the stresses of combat; not failing his unit mates was a powerful motivation to carry on even in the most gruesome of circumstances.[132]

Men's anticipation of their first combat experience also affected their initial effectiveness. John Ellis quoted a British noncommissioned officer in World War I who, recalling his experiences during the Battle of the Somme, remembered that "I hadn't gone ten yards before I felt a load fall from me.... I had been worried by the thought: 'Suppose one should lose one's head and get other men cut up! Suppose one's legs should take fright and refuse to move!' Now I knew it was all right. I shouldn't be frightened and I shouldn't lose my head. Just imagine the joy of that discovery! I felt quite happy and self-possessed." Ellis went on to comment that "most accounts of men's experiences in assaults agree that the feeling of fear vanished as soon as they went over the top."[133] An officer across No Man's Land from Ellis's NCO, Ernst Jünger, similarly recalled a surprised German soldier's reaction to his first combat in the trenches:

> Behind me is the recruit who was so handy with his machine-gun when we had our glimpse of the English this morning. His face is as white as a child's who has not slept. It is his first "show" and I ask him: "This isn't how you fancied it would be at the depot?" "Oh Lord, sir, I thought it would have been far worse!"[134]

During his studies of Americans in World War II, Ginzberg found "some men collapsed even before they got into combat. Many soldiers admitted that, horrible as combat was, it frequently was less bad than what they had imagined it would be. A considerable number became so anxious about combat they were unable to complete their training; others became upset when their unit was alerted for overseas shipment; and still others when they were about to enter the line. When the general environment contains a threat to life or limb, some people become ineffective long before they actually enter the danger zone. Their reserves have been eaten away by their fears."[135] The marines' E. B. Sledge vividly described the horror as he awaited movement toward the shore of Peleliu and his first combat. Sledge, who would perform his duties well and survive both that campaign and Okinawa, found that

> the suspense was almost more than I could bear. Waiting is a major part of war, but I never experienced any more supremely agonizing suspense than the excruciating torture of those moments before we received the signal to begin the assault on Peleliu. I broke out in a cold sweat as the tension mounted with the intensity of the bombardment.

My stomach was tied in knots. I had a lump in my throat and swallowed only with great difficulty. My knees nearly buckled, so I clung weakly to the side of the tractor. I felt nauseated and feared that my bladder would surely empty itself and reveal me to be the coward I was.[136]

Ulysses S. Grant's courage under fire apparently also required less mettle than did remaining cool before the bullets began to fly. Writing his wife Julia, Grant confided that "there is no great sport in having bullets flying about one in every direction, but I find they have less horror when among them than when in anticipation."[137] Grant was not alone in his precombat nervousness; many American Civil War leaders put their men through drill or manual of arms as they awaited battle so as to calm them.[138]

Members of the 1st Cavalry Division in Vietnam recognized similar fears in replacements coming to their units from the United States. Veterans thought that stateside training was failing to adequately mentally prepare recruits—that in fact it unnecessarily intimidated new men by making them overly fearful of combat. A member of B Company, 1/8 Cavalry found "these people come over here scared. . . . Someone back there is scaring them to death. They're telling them they're fighting daily or something over here. . . . They just try to scare them too much."[139] Desire to make training tougher than war, but to do so without intimidating a new man, was the objective. The preparation need not have been complex. Simply providing time for inexperienced soldiers and marines to participate in frank discussions with mature combat veterans was found to be beneficial.

Vietnam veterans understood that the need for conditioning of the mind was as fundamental to a soldier's training for war as was his physical preparation. "We need a course for new soldiers on the psychology of combat," one veteran wrote, "taught by *qualified* combat veterans, on what to expect and what to do to maintain fire discipline until the appropriate time."[140] Another preferred informal opportunities to frankly discuss "the odds in various circumstances of being killed while engaging enemy in combat, e.g., if surprise is on our side, should you duck or shoot first? If surprise is on the enemy's side? If you're outnumbered? Also, drill soldiers on survival skills, like not going to the aid of a wounded buddy until you know what and where enemy forces are. And equip soldiers with some realistic sense of what conditions may be like, e.g., faulty leadership, time required for ammo resupply, [and] confusion of enemy forces with civilian neutrals."[141] A third believed "cool heads prevail and *live*. . . . When I was in infantry training we never learned about the 'big picture' in combat support, e.g., air, artillery, helicopters. Combat trainees should realize: a) know your terrain, b) understand your enemy and the cause that he is prepared to kill you for," and finally "c) unity is strength."[142] After similarly stressing the need for more realism in training, a fourth veteran concluded that he did not "think training should stop at weapons. . . . You can't imagine what it's like until you've been there."[143] Another was more blunt: "Try to get the average GI guy to know he has to kill or be killed."[144]

Mental preparation had value in addition to that as a prophylactic against shock. Drill and reactive thinking alone were insufficient for dealing with combat. Training had to instill individual initiative. J. C. Dunn related the cost of failing to do so in his description of a World War I attack during which the "wire was so poor that a man had only to put his foot and his weight on it to make a way through." Yet soldiers lined up to pass through a hole; the time lost as men waited "to file through the few gaps made by the resolute let Jerry man his parapet and get up his machine-guns. It was fairly plain that there had been no lack of leadership, but the irresolute mass had not been trained out of the habit of the turnstile."[145] Men must understand that control of their fate in combat is very much in their own hands despite fortune's holding of the ultimate card.

Perhaps the best mental preparation for combat was simply high-quality training. Done well, training built a soldier's belief in himself and his readiness to succeed in battle. Kellett noted that effective training "provides a soldier with a degree of self-confidence in his military skills and in his physical stamina that is valuable in combating fear. The sense of professional pride that exists among well-trained troops has consistently been shown to be a powerful motivation in itself."[146] Stouffer found a direct correlation between the confidence a soldier felt in his own abilities and his symptoms of fear: "Men who reported the largest number of physiological symptoms of fear tended to show less confidence in their ability to perform successfully in combat. . . . Fear reactions in combat may be due, in part, to an attitudinal factor—the feeling that one has not had sufficient training for one's combat job."[147] A study of British deserters concluded "that technical mastery of a weapon was only half of training, and was worth little unless accompanied by confidence in the ability to use it under battle conditions. . . . If [a soldier] felt that his training had been skimped or hurried, or that he was being given a job for which he had not been trained, he would lack confidence; his morale would be low."[148]

This inculcation of self-confidence proved crucial in Vietnam. A postwar study concluded that "training is an important component of the soldier's reaction to a stressful situation. Whether or not the soldier is well trained is often less important as far as mental health is concerned than his perception that he is. A soldier who thinks he is well trained has more confidence in his ability to survive a war."[149] Others concurred, understanding that in addition to the knowledge of how to accomplish critical tasks, what the soldier "needs is to experience the actual physical carrying out of the performance in response to kinds of cues which would occur in combat. Not only must the trainee know what behaviors are appropriate under various conditions and how to perform them, but *he must know that he knows* if he is to face combat conditions with confidence."[150] A man's confidence in his combat abilities and in his capability to deal with the unexpected calms preoperation fears. It is a confidence born of a belief in his ability to defeat his enemy and survive the event.

Replicating the Combat Environment

Mimicking the physical environments in which combat would take place was a fourth element essential to readying the marine or soldier for war in Vietnam. Men had to understand the nature of the environmental challenges they would confront. Dense vegetation, for example, was the catalyst for many soldiers' fears. The darkness below the jungle canopy and the difficulty of detecting camouflaged enemy bunkers wore on even experienced soldiers. Better preparation for specific combat environments gave soldiers the skills and confidence fundamental to confront the terrors of these and other unknowns.

Lt. Col. A. A. White, Command Psychiatrist for Eastern Command, India, during World War II, credited better training as one element in improved British performance during western Burma's second Arakan campaign.[151] Further, training allowed warriors to develop tactics suited to various terrain types. Discovering, during combat, that established techniques were unsuitable meant suffering a surprise potentially costly in lives and confidence. It was far better to learn the lessons in rigorous precombat exercises. Similarly, Americans at the U.S. Army's jungle training center during the Vietnam era found that a "conventional attack of an objective will normally not work in jungle terrain. It proved virtually impossible to deploy a platoon on line and overrun an objective while moving up hill in the thickly tangled jungle."[152] Creighton Abrams believed that every infantry soldier going to Vietnam ideally would have gone through this four-week course in Panama, but manpower demands did not permit the additional training time.[153]

Combat veterans also urged that other environmental realities be emphasized. The aforementioned invisibility of the enemy was as much a characteristic of fighting in Vietnam as it had been in previous wars. L. D. Holder, a Vietnam cavalry troop commander, wrote that

> the enemy is only seen clearly in ambushes or meeting engagements. After initial contact, he finds cover/concealment. Training should reflect that. It should emphasize unit fire into *areas* of *concealed* targets. Aimed fire should be mixed into such exercises by the initial, then occasional, presentation of clearly visible targets, but unit fire with all the problems of direction, distribution and control should be *the norm*. We have this wrong. [We] mustn't stop with individual marksmanship or with clutter free squad courses if we want to improve volume, effect, [and] control of fires.[154]

As in previous wars, night worked to magnify both real and perceived difficulties presented by terrain and a thinking adversary. American soldiers in

Vietnam too often supposed their enemy possessed a superiority in night fighting much as they believed him better able to fight in the jungle. A 1st Cavalry Division veteran considered his night training "inadequate—always has been. Night training builds confidence. GIs [were] afraid to shoot at night [as they might] give [their] position away."[155] An A Company, 1/7 Cavalry, platoon leader recommended that soldiers should have been run "through a series of day patrols and night ambushes to exhaustion to familiarize [them with] problems of shifts and team sleep, snoring, disorientation, and resulting attitude shifts."[156]

Good training instilled both ability and confidence. Essential to that confidence was a soldier's or marine's belief that he was prepared for whatever contingency the battlefield held in store for him. Replicating the shocks, surprises, ruses, abuse, accidents, and other tribulations of combat instilled in men a faith in their ability to deal with the unknown and unpredictable. No preparation could expose the warrior to all scenarios, but well-designed instruction honed his skills and helped him to believe himself ready.

ADDITIONAL ASPECTS OF COMBAT TRAINING

There were other areas in which Vietnam veterans felt their combat preparation had fallen short. Several cited a failure to more frequently use veterans to train the inexperienced soldier. Clausewitz realized that the experienced soldier saw combat in a way no newcomer could. The veteran was therefore an invaluable resource in the preparation of the inexperienced for war. "In war," he observed, "the experienced soldier reacts rather in the same way as the human eye does in the dark: the pupil expands to admit what little light there is, discerning objects by degrees, and finally seeing them distinctly. By contrast, the novice is plunged into the deepest night."[157] The value of using veterans to train new men was overwhelmingly supported by the responses of Dollard's Spanish Civil War veterans, 99 percent of whom believed that "having a veteran soldier explain to the men on the basis of his personal experience the life-saving importance of the things they are learning . . . tends to make them better soldiers."[158] Commanders would have needed to rotate instructor veterans often, however. Years before, Ardant Du Picq reminded commanders that the value of prior exposure to combat diminished quickly with time: "Nothing, especially in the trade of war, is sooner forgotten than experience."[159]

When Stouffer asked veterans returning to the United States how combat-experienced men could be best used by the army, 40 percent responded that they should "be used as instructors or cadre men to pass along their practical knowledge to soldiers who had not been overseas yet."[160] Stouffer hesitated to recommend such a policy, however, for "the returnee instructor's frequent point of view is summed up in this not untypical comment of an ex-combat man who was instructing in an Infantry Replacement Training Center: 'I do not agree with this kind of training. There has been pitifully small or no progress toward jungle training. All overseas men know we can't fight by the book!!! Much training in U.S. is very useless—no practical jungle training whatever—wrong psychology in dealing with recruits.'"[161]

Training centers in the United States nonetheless drew very heavily on veterans returning from Vietnam. In 1966, then Vice Chief of Staff of the Army Abrams wrote that "training centers are manned with returning veterans from Vietnam wherever possible."[162] The situation was somewhat different from Col. Hal Moore's perspective. After commanding the 1/7 Cavalry during the November 1965 fighting at LZ X-Ray and later leading the 1st Cavalry Division's 3rd Brigade, he rotated back to the United States the following June. Moore had hoped that "my next assignment would be to the Infantry School at Fort Benning, where I could pass along what I had learned in Vietnam to the young officers who were headed for combat. It was not to be. In fact, only one of the hundreds of officers who had gone through airmobile training and a year in the field with the 1st Cavalry Division was assigned to the Infantry School."[163] Despite Moore's disappointment early in the war, by late 1968 over 90 percent of the instructors in Fort Jackson's 3rd AIT Infantry Brigade were Vietnam combat veterans, and other veterans were being used to prepare West Point and ROTC cadets as well as young officers on orders to go to Vietnam.[164] A 1st Cavalry Division veteran wrote that "the best training a young soldier could get would be just to really sit down and talk to and learn from another who has seen, felt and lived through the real thing. . . . We had many little tricks that have been lost and to re-learn them in another fight will cost many good men's lives."[165] Otto Lehrack described an episode in which a marine veteran aided a newcomer but demonstrated his perception of the relative importance of training versus self-preservation:

> One day during the day we were sitting in our position and I was talking to a fellow that had over a year in country. . . . He was taking me under his wing and telling me what I should and shouldn't do. As I was talking to him, some sort of noise sounded far off on one of the adjoining mountains. This guy's eyes seemed to dilate, his chin tightened, and the next thing I knew he was making a move toward the hole. And finally he turned around and said, "Get into the hole." I did what he told me to do and I said, "What's going on?" And he said, "That report, that sound that you heard, was a recoilless rifle." And he went on to explain what a recoilless rifle could do. But I noticed that first he took the opportunity to use his knowledge to obtain cover and safety.[166]

Some practical knowledge was given less emphasis than veterans thought appropriate. They believed that training in map reading fell short of combat demands. Several 1st Cavalry Division veterans believed that they should have been better trained in this skill because their units were at risk in situations in which leaders failed to read a map correctly or could not, if disabled, rely on subordinates to accurately read a map.[167] A veteran infantryman in A Company, 1/7 Cavalry, felt "that all soldiers should be trained to read maps better. Often my unit was lost in Vietnam. At one time it cost the lives of several servicemen."[168] A fellow veteran from A Company, 2/8 Cavalry, believed not only that "jungle training in [the] U.S. wasn't enough to [adapt] to the jungles of Vietnam," but that soldiers required "more training in map reading. I was in a situation where I had to call artillery. Due [to the] little experience or knowledge in map reading [it] was very difficult. But my fellow comrades' lives [were] in danger. Every soldier should have a good knowledge of map reading."[169] A veteran whose Vietnam service was with A Company, 2/12 Cavalry, from July 1967 to July 1968 considered it essential that every soldier be able to read a map and use a compass so as to be able to assume control if his leader falls in combat:

> While officers and NCOs are giving the orders in battle, too many times they are killed or wounded. The outcome of a firefight may rest on a corporal or private's shoulders [and] their ability to carry out orders, report back, and adjust firepower. . . . I could tell you a dozen stories or more where an RTO [radio-telephone operator] or corporal has done his job after officer or sergeant was killed or wounded. . . . To destroy the enemy you must call in firepower and that firepower depends on your map and compass work.[170]

CONCLUSION

Though the training a soldier received prior to departure for Vietnam might have been imperfect, valiant efforts were made to prepare him as well as possible. The multiple demands on the armed services to meet national security needs combined with its inexperience in fighting the type of war confronted in Vietnam to make determination of training requirements very difficult. The first marines and soldiers deployed to Vietnam underwent the schooling of combat, the most expensive education in the world. Their sacrifices were the cost of knowledge applied in the preparation of others.

When veterans of the 1st Cavalry Division recalled what they considered shortfalls in their preparation for Vietnam, many of their concerns echoed lessons cited in earlier wars—lessons overlooked because they were either obscure, ignored, or thought not to pertain to a conflict so presumably unlike World War II or Korea. Combat experience gained in those two previous conflicts was valuable, but fighting in Vietnam included both conditions similar to those of earlier wars and new challenges. Veterans recognized the need for skill with their weapons and confidence in the weapons themselves, as well as the necessity of exposing the trainee to combat-like conditions before he was compelled to experience them when his life was on the line. They saw a need for mental preparation as an accompaniment to physical training and skill development. All quality training was recognized as a step toward the building of the confidence so crucial to individual and unit performance. Soldiers recommended the use of veterans as trainers both to take advantage of these men's combat expertise and to help trainees believe that they were learning what was crucial to success in combat.

Small unit operations characterized the fighting in Southeast Asia. Leaders turned over quickly as a result of combat losses and six-month command tour rotations. Too often newcomers were deprived of a veteran's lessons by his sudden departure at the end of a twelve or thirteen-month tour. Many veterans therefore recommended that all soldiers be trained in skills that in previous wars were thought necessary only for commissioned or noncommissioned officers. The soldier or marine with but a few months of combat experience not infrequently found that responsibility for his unit's survival fell to him. Trained properly and given a chance to live through his initial combat experiences, the veteran American fighting man in Vietnam often found himself responsible for training and leading others during the ultimate test of combat.

5

The Twelve-Month Tour
Home by Midnight

When young men who are still growing are forced to enter military service and thus lose all hope of returning safe and sound to their beloved homeland, they become sad, taciturn, listless, solitary, musing, full of sighs and moans. Finally, they cease to pay attention and become indifferent to everything which the maintenance of life requires of them. . . . Some years ago this disease was rather common but now occurs very rarely since the wise arrangement was instituted of limiting the period of military service to a definite number of years.

Leopold Auenbrugger, Inventum Novum of 1761, *quoted in* War Psychiatry, *Franklin D. Jones et al., eds.*

I feel the biggest mistake made in Vietnam was the replacement system. I feel units should be trained together before they go in combat. I am a tennis pro; I can't play with a different partner every day. That was what was happening in Vietnam with the replacement system.

First Cavalry Division respondent 64

Ardant Du Picq wrote that "a wise organization insures that the personnel of combat groups changes as little as possible, so that comrades in peace time maneuvers shall be comrades in war."[1] One hundred years after he penned those lines, Americans fought the Vietnam War with its soldiers serving tours of one year's duration, each man being assigned individually to a unit that only in exceptional circumstances had he seen before his wartime arrival. Unlike soldiers in any of his nation's previous wars, virtually every soldier knew that he had twelve months to serve as he first stepped onto Vietnamese soil.[2] No aspect of the American fighting man's combat experience more dominated his perspective than this one-year tour (thirteen months for marines arriving in Vietnam before late 1969).

The authors of the United States Marine Corps Vietnam history unequivocally labeled the fixed tour "the most important policy influencing morale. . . . The most important thing to almost every Marine was his rotation date."[3] Letters home regularly cited the number of days until a man's return. Units had a dual hierarchy, one of rank and another of days left "in-country," in which fewer days equated to a superior status. When a man rotated back to the "World," everyone's place in the chronological rankings increased by one. Experience was respected; "short-timer" status was envied. Many a soldier's waking thought, whether he was on a squad perimeter deep within jungle foliage or in the relative safety of one of the U. S. Army's large base complexes, was "X and a butt days."[4] Jerome Dowling, who had served as division psychiatrist for the 1st Cavalry Division, found that the number of days remaining in one's tour could also act as the basis for social relations: "A common bond between two people can be set up on the basis of a similar DEROS [Date of Estimated Return Overseas, the date a man was to leave Vietnam] . . . say plus or minus one month, whereas it is rather difficult for a 'short timer' to find much in common with someone who has 364 days to go."[5]

The rotation system offered no advantages based on location of assignment within Vietnam, none due to the type of duty the soldier performed. The infantryman forward and in frequent contact with the enemy had the same 365 days to serve as did his rear echelon counterpart who rarely if ever handled a weapon. Though it was argued that setting a firm date for rotation benefited the individual soldier by giving him a fixed goal on which to focus, it required frequent introduction of replacements into combat. New arrivals' inexperience made them more likely to die, be wounded, or suffer neuropsychiatric problems than were veterans with more time in the field. The benefits provided to the individual soldier were therefore questionable.

The twelve-month individual tour was rooted in recommendations made after World War II, twenty years before. Thereafter, even in the relatively peaceful years of the pre-Vietnam Cold War, fixed tour lengths and a policy of individual rather than unit rotation disrupted unit cohesion and undermined training programs designed to maximize combat readiness. These shortcomings were recognized but could be tolerated in the interest of equitably distributing the strains of being assigned for long periods overseas and the burdens of family separations due to unaccompanied tours. It was the welfare of the individual, rather than organizational efficiency, that provided the basis for the army's rotation policies.

This emphasis on the individual was not common to all of the world's armies. The British had historically rotated units rather than individuals. Nineteenth-century British regiments were what historian Correlli Barnett called "a completely insulated world in which a soldier spent his entire career." Officers were at times assigned to positions outside their own units, but an earlier policy of similarly moving noncommissioned officers or "other ranks" had been discontinued.[6] This primacy of the unit was maintained through and beyond the First and Second World Wars. Baynes wrote that at the initiation of the former

> one of the most important points to remember about the army was that it was a long-service army. At Neuve Chapelle there was not a man in the ranks of the 2nd Scottish Rifles with less than five years' service. . . . Not only did soldiers serve for a long time, but they usually remained for most of their service in the same company, or at least the same battalion. . . . When the attack was launched at Neuve Chapelle many men in each company had been in it for up to seven years or more. The result of this was that there were ties between many soldiers which were stronger than one can easily imagine.[7]

Though groups of individual replacements came into British units, the men were frequently from the same region and had gone through training together, thus somewhat mitigating the sense of entering a completely new environment alone. The same procedure characterized the British Army's replacement policy during World War II. Men knew the unit to which they would ultimately be assigned soon after entering the "depot battalions" in which they completed their initial combat preparations. If a man was sent to another organization during an emergency, he was reassigned to his originally designated unit as soon as was feasible.[8]

WORLD WAR II

Great Britain and other Commonwealth nations retained this focus on unit rather than individual primacy throughout World War II. It was not without its drawbacks. Soldiers stayed with their units and units stayed in combat theaters. Men fortunate enough to survive thus spent years in and out of fighting. An officer with the British Army's 7th Hussars in North Africa in World War II summed up the seeming hopelessness of the soldier's situation: "The actual business of fighting is easy enough. You go in, you come out, you go in again and you keep on doing it until they break you or you are dead."[9] Denis Forman expressed the same fatalism in speaking of his experiences with a Canadian regiment in Italy: "I was lucky: an infantry officer had only two options in World War II—death or being wounded. Virtually none survived intact in the front line through the North African campaign and Italy. I was lucky to be wounded."[10]

It became apparent early in the war that the resultant stress on those who survived without serious physical wounds was such that many eventually reached their mental limit. In writing of Canadian soldiers in *Combat Exhaustion,* Copp and McAndrew noted that "the battles of the spring and summer of 1942 and especially the withdrawal to the El Alamein line forced acknowledgment of large numbers of cases that seemed to be associated with fatigue and nervous exhaustion."[11] Brig. G. W. B. James, a psychiatrist with the British Eighth Army, concluded "men can probably do two years after which there is an increasing risk of nervous breakdown."[12] Cpl. Ralph Pearse of Britain's 2nd West Yorkshire Regiment was by 1943 "quite convinced that he could not survive the war. 'Both Sid Wright and I were sure by this time that we couldn't go on coming through battle after battle alive. Like Sid, I'd become a fighting man and nothing else; no hope of anything else but more fighting, until in the end we knew we must be killed. We didn't care much. We knew it was inevitable.'"[13] This fatalism developed despite the British policy of periodically rotating units out of the front lines to rest their soldiers.

Like their Commonwealth allies, American soldiers also remained with their units until death, wounds, collapse, or the war's end relieved them, but the GI had no prior affiliation with the unit to which he was assigned before reporting. There was no guarantee he would return to his original outfit if he were wounded. The American policy of individual rotation had become the standard in 1912, when the previous practice of rotating units back to the United States after short stints overseas was abandoned. Prior to 1912, units deploying for foreign service transferred soldiers with commitments shorter than a specified number of months to other organizations. The objective of this policy was to minimize the number who would have to be replaced before the unit returned to home station. Though this change was originally implemented in peacetime, it likely influenced adoption of a similar system for wartime personnel management.[14]

Americans therefore suffered the same trepidation regarding their eventual fate as did their allies. However, U.S. units were not periodically rotated out of the line to provide rest periods. Only a break in the action or the good fortune to be selected for a respite allowed the surviving veteran a break from the combat, barring his being wounded. A Department of the Army study recognized the strains such a system imposed on the soldier: "The stark realities of combat disclosed that under such a system combat soldiers could look forward to an ultimate destiny which could be nothing other than wounds, mental or physical breakdown, or death itself. This grim prospect brought the realization that continuous combat for divisions required a rotation program."[15]

Many did not survive the odds of continued exposure unscathed; fewer still survived in infantry units that bore the greatest weight of enemy steel and lead. Within infantry organizations it was the rifleman whose chances of becoming a combat casualty far exceeded those of other American soldiers. Infantrymen included riflemen, infantry platoon leaders and company commanders, mortar men, and a number of other skills and positions. Riflemen made up only 11 percent of a World War II infantry division's strength, but on average suffered 38 percent of its combat casualties. One study of the U.S. Army's 3rd, 34th, 36th, and 45th Infantry divisions in Italy found that infantrymen of all types suffered 92 percent of those units' battle casualties.[16] Eighty-two percent of all American army battle losses over the duration of the war were infantrymen.[17] An Army Ground Force headquarters report written soon after World War II noted that in fifty-seven infantry divisions in which infantry soldiers made up 68.5 percent of the authorized strength, those men suffered 94.7 percent of the division's battle casualties.[18]

In U.S. Fifth Army rifle battalions fighting in Italy, almost half of the men initially on unit rolls were gone after fifty days in combat. Only 18 percent of the initial group were with their units after 150 days, and with the passage of three hundred days only three of every one hundred original men remained. Two-thirds of these losses were due to deaths, wounds, or missing soldiers. The remaining one-third were lost to disease, psychiatric evacuation, administrative causes, or nonbattle injuries.[19] The impact at unit level was that divisions lost over 100 percent of their authorized strength during the course of the war. Eighteen of the sixty-five American infantry divisions committed in combat during the Second World War had cumulative losses greater than the number of soldiers they were to have on their rolls.

The infantry units within these organizations were undergoing turnover at rates far greater than those in other divisional organizations. Infantry regiments in some divisions lost the equivalent of two and one-half times their authorized strength over the course of the war.[20] The situation was much the same in the Marine Corps. James Johnston recalled that his machine-gun squad suffered 300 percent casualties during World War II fighting in the Pacific.[21]

Losses due to physical wounds were accompanied by psychological injuries as the stresses of combat and constant exposure to danger wore the few surviving men down. The authors of a 1949 study by the U. S. Army's Surgeon General's Office believed that these neuropsychological losses were directly attributable to prolonged exposure to the possibility of being killed or badly wounded. They concluded that "psychiatric casualties are as inevitable as wounds due to gunshot and high explosives."[22]

In addition to concluding that an individual rotation policy was necessary to reduce the number of psychiatric casualties, General Devers, commander of the U.S. 6th Army Group in World War II, believed that divisions should spend no longer than thirty to forty consecutive days on the line in active areas.

The army experimented with several rotation policies during that war. A June 1943 directive allowed theater commanders to return soldiers "whose morale or health had deteriorated and whose effectiveness could not be restored by intratheater rotation."[23] Commanders differed in their application of this guidance, however. Those in the Caribbean Defense Command and North Africa established rotation policies, but General MacArthur at first cited lack of sufficient shipping and manpower as an obstacle to initiating any such policy in the Southwest Pacific theater.[24] Throughout the remainder of the war, policies between theaters continued to differ and were changed even within commands. When MacArthur later put a system in effect, the standards for rotation were modified and the number of days for rotation increased on several occasions. Such increases were inevitably accompanied by a subsequent surge in neuropsychiatric casualty admissions.[25] Despite these losses and recognition that a well-considered rotation system was needed, no uniform policy existed by the cessation of hostilities.[26] Too often the programs that did exist were used to rid a unit of undesirable personnel rather than returning the deserving to the United States.[27]

Several postwar studies considered the rotation issue. A September 1946 Army Ground Force analysis determined that a policy was needed. It recommended relief of soldiers from frontline service after one year and concluded that an individual rotation policy was preferable to a unit-based system. A second study recommended that rotation in future conflicts be based on a point system in which a soldier was credited for length of service, number of wounds, citations for bravery, overall performance, and family necessity.[28] The World War II experience and postwar analyses influenced the decision to establish a rotation policy soon after the beginning of the Korean War.

KOREA

A rotation system for American soldiers in Korea was instituted in April 1951, approximately nine months after North Korean forces began the conflict with their late June 1950 invasion.[29] Headquarters, 1st Cavalry Division, summarized the Eighth United States Army, Korea (EUSAK) policy as one in which those soldiers serving with divisions would rotate on a "first in, first out" basis, with men in forward combat units receiving top priority; for others, service periods were based on the type of organization to which they belonged and the risks they were likely to experience in that unit type.[30] Eighth Army further refined the criteria by identifying factors to be considered favorably in determining priorities among soldiers eligible for rotation: "time spent in close proximity to the enemy; time in extremely hazardous service; continuous overseas service; physical condition with consideration given to wounds; and honorable service without a record of courts martial."[31] However, no officer or enlisted man was to be "rotated until an acceptable replacement is available and capable of carrying on the work of the rotatee."[32]

Problems arose immediately. Requirements to return soldiers whose enlistment had already been extended a year due to the war's outbreak, whether they had seen combat or not, precluded sending men home who met the standard for return based on their time with a fighting unit.[33] Further, reservists who had been involuntarily recalled to active duty were to be released by the end of 1951. The result was that only 60 percent of the soldiers initially returning to the United States rotated because they met the combat criteria for service in Korea. Planners were also concerned that the number of men leaving Korea could not be replaced fast enough to avoid endangering combat readiness.[34] Even were sufficient numbers available, most replacements were men straight out of basic training; there were insufficient experienced leaders to take the place of senior noncommissioned officers if the army met its rotation goals. Similarly, some skill specialties lacked the requisite numbers of soldiers elsewhere in the army to meet the demands of the combat theater. The skills in great demand in combat were sometimes in less demand elsewhere in the army.

Combat theaters were often short of persons with appropriate training even before the introduction of rotation. The solution in many cases was to deny such men and women timely rotation and to rapidly return them for additional combat tours once they got back to the United States.[35] Units compensated by requiring specialists to train replacements before the former were allowed to leave. In sum, such policies had adverse effects on the long-term retention of affected soldiers.

An army-wide officer shortage also delayed the rotation of many commissioned officers. Their commanders sometimes removed them from positions at the front, despite the shortages their departure created, to alleviate the strain of combat leadership. General Van Fleet, Eighth Army commander, felt in June 1951 that "the combat effectiveness of Eighth Army is seriously jeopardized through my inability to replace field and company grade officers who have served in a superior manner, in many cases for as long as eleven months in continuous and severe combat.... Some of the officers rotated prior to arrival of replacements were released by their commanders because they felt these officers had reached a breaking point resulting from a long period of continuous combat and were thereby rendered ineffective, non-aggressive, and detrimental to the combat effectiveness of their units if retained."[36]

These and other problems caused revisions of the rotation plan.[37] Van Fleet told subordinate commanders that it was to be made "'unmistakably clear' that eligibility criteria 'serve only to establish the zone of consideration' for rotation each month" and that the actual selection of personnel for return to the United States remained the responsibility of their commanders. Van Fleet left no doubt that winning the war, not ensuring that eligible personnel rotated home on time, was the primary consideration.[38] In July 1951 a revision of an earlier policy changed the criteria for rotation and extended the time soldiers would remain in the theater, the latter despite the problems with similar extensions in the Pacific theater during World War II. Further modifications of the system were made on several occasions later in the war.[39]

A study completed near the end of the war looked into the possible use of unit rotation in Korea, concluding that "unit rotation is not a feasible substitute for individual rotation during wartime. . . . While unit replacement on a small scale such as the four-man team concept is believed to be practicable, replacement by company, battalion and regiment may result in an entirely untrained unit being prematurely committed beyond the capability of unseasoned troops."[40] Replacement using four-man teams was thought to have payoffs in the form of both higher morale and increased combat effectiveness.[41] The study recommended transfers within the combat theater so that soldiers would spend no more than six months forward of battalion headquarters before being moved to units further to the rear. Those soldiers who had served in "front-line combat" would return to the United States after an average of twenty-four months in the overseas theater; those in the combat support zone would have an average time in the theater of thirty-three months.[42]

The Korean War rotation experience provided the U.S. Army with several lessons. The first was a recognition that wartime theaters had a far greater demand for some specialties than did units elsewhere. Second, it was felt that the army should recognize the greater risks undergone by those at the sharp end, where the threat of death was greater. Third, rotation posed difficulties in maintaining required strengths of combat-experienced leaders. Fourth, the negative influence of establishing a rotation policy and later increasing the time required for rotation was reestablished after its having been a problem during World War II. Unfortunately, many of the same lessons would be revalidated in Vietnam.

VIETNAM

The twelve-month tour has become inextricably associated with the Vietnam War, but both the duration and its uniform application to all soldiers were decisions made only as U.S. strength began to build in the mid-1960s. In 1958 the Office of the Secretary of Defense had established a twenty-four-month tour for those with families in Vietnam, fourteen months for those stationed in Saigon without families, and twelve months for "all others outside of Saigon."[43] The policy was changed in October 1961 to require thirty months for those with families in-country and eighteen months for all others—a change made because of "the urgency for achieving maximum effectiveness . . . in this critical operation."[44] Six months later the Joint Chiefs of Staff recommended a modification to the 1961 guidance, citing the hardships undergone by American advisors assigned to support South Vietnamese battalions. The identified hardships included primitive living conditions, dietary and health problems, isolation, and adverse climatic conditions.[45] By July 1962 the policy had changed yet once more to make a twelve-month tour the standard for all those unaccompanied by families. Military families were evacuated from Vietnam in 1965 and the twelve-month tour was therefore applied to all soldiers stationed in Vietnam aside from general officers and selected colonels whose tours would be between nineteen and twenty-four months.[46] A proposal later that year to extend the tour length to fifteen months was rejected.[47]

Westmoreland recommended no change as the commitment of U.S. combat forces grew. He later wrote that "the adviser was on duty twenty-four hours a day, seven days a week, often under severe field conditions. . . . Almost all advisers operating with troops had recurrent bouts of amoebic dysentery. The harsh conditions provided one of the strongest arguments for a one-year tour of duty, a policy that was in effect when I arrived, and I saw no reason to change it."[48] However, Westmoreland urged that all services use twelve months as the basis for their rotation systems (the marines adopted the twelve-month tour on November 1, 1969). In October 1966, the Secretary of Defense announced that his office had no intention of modifying the twelve-month tour then in effect.[49] It remained the policy for the duration of the Vietnam War.

Perhaps the most notable effect of this rotation policy and those from earlier wars was the existence of a fixed, ever-brighter light at the end of every soldier's and marine's tunnel. Charles Moskos highlighted the significance of this established goal: "For the individual soldier, the paramount factor affecting combat motivation is the operation of the rotation system. . . . Military personnel serve a twelve-month tour of duty in Vietnam. Barring his being killed or severely wounded, then, every soldier knows his exact departure date from Vietnam. The combat soldier's whole being centers on reaching his personal DEROS."[50] Westmoreland wrote that "the one-year tour gave a man a goal. That was good for morale."[51]

Several authors have noted what they found to be a cyclic character of men's Vietnam experiences resulting from the fixed-duration tour. Dowling described three successive phases of apprehensive enthusiasm, resignation, and anxious apprehension.[52] Moskos also believed that a soldier's attitude changed over the course of his twelve-month tour, progressing through initial excitement, a sobering generally brought on by his first serious contact with the enemy, a period of moderate commitment, a peak in commitment as he began to consider himself an experienced veteran, and finally a decrease in effectiveness brought on by short-timer's syndrome.[53]

The twelve-month Vietnam tour was unlike any previously employed by the U.S. military. It applied to virtually all service personnel in Vietnam (albeit later in the war for marines), was never increased in duration, and made no discrimination based on duty position. Its adoption led to controversy during the war. The passage of years has done little to resolve the debate.

ARGUMENTS IN SUPPORT OF THE ONE-YEAR TOUR

Support for the twelve-month tour focused primarily on its benefits for the individual American soldier as evidenced by a dramatically reduced number of combat exhaustion casualties. The authors of the army's *Neuropsychiatry in*

World War II: Overseas Theaters wrote that "the best known lesson of preventive psychiatry in World War II revolved about the establishment of a prescribed, or stated length of, overseas assignment for both combat and noncombat personnel. A growing and insistent demand for rotation was the result of increasing awareness by psychiatrists and others that continued deprivation, hardship, and danger could and did produce mental breakdown or other manifestation of noneffective behavior in most military personnel." They noted that "in Vietnam, the apparent marked reduction of psychiatric casualties over that of World War II and the Korean War has been ascribed in large part to this rotation policy. However, other differences from . . . previous wars have also been credited for the small frequency of psychiatric casualties, including the episodic nature and the lesser intensity of combat in Vietnam."[54]

The same authors also looked to the Southwest Pacific for insights into soldier reactions to combat, finding that admission rates for neuropsychiatric disorders were higher in that theater despite a lesser intensity of combat during the period of their study. They concluded that while extended exposure to combat and morale problems were the primary elements affecting such problems, factors such as climate, lack of a rotation policy, having to operate in jungles, and absence of a man's normal social and cultural environment were also significant.[55]

Others similarly concluded that a rotation policy was desirable but found the single factor of exposure to danger the overriding cause of soldier inability to withstand long-term combat. Edwin Weinstein's and Calvin Drayer's experiences as World War II combat theater medical personnel led them to conclude that psychiatric casualty rates varied more consistently with the intensity of fighting than with any other factor.[56] Two other medical officers, Gilbert W. Beebe and John W. Appel, came to a similar conclusion after reviewing the records of soldiers in World War II Europe, finding that the number of neuropsychiatric problems paralleled casualty rates far more consistently than any other set of factors.[57]

As was the case with physical wounds, it was infantrymen who suffered the greatest number of neuropsychiatric injuries. A study of "old sergeants' syndrome" (described as a condition in which "the anxious, depressed soldier broke down after having lived through months of seeing friends killed"[58]) analyzed the World War II veterans of one division whose frontline soldiers had been in combat continuously for up to seventy-nine days. Ninety percent of the organization's men who suffered from the malady were in the infantry.[59] Dr. Franklin D. Jones also determined that the men who survived failed to form emotional ties with newcomers. Without the support of known and trusted comrades, their confidence waned and left them without defenses against the stresses inherent in a combat environment.[60] A study of American neuropsychiatric casualties concluded that "the breaking point of the median man in World War II was 80 to 90 company combat days (280–315 calendar days in the European Theater of Operations; 640–720 calendar days in the Mediterranean Theater of Operations)."[61]

Copp and McAndrew saw the same trend in the Canadian army during World War II; even the best soldiers eventually reached a point of breakdown after extended exposure to combat. The question was not whether a man would break or not, but rather how long an individual could continue before his collapse.[62]

Farley Mowat recognized that the mental pressures a fighting man had to withstand were not limited to his wartime surroundings. Combat-induced stress was complemented by other burdens with roots back home. Writing of a Canadian regiment in World War II, Mowat observed that

> there were men with children four and five years old whom they had never seen. There were men who had lost their wives and their homes to the long years of separation, but who had clung to a faint and desperate hope that their personal return might restore that which had been shattered. There were men who had served through five years of active service and a year and a half of continuous battle and whose nerves were now only empty sheaths—men who had given of their reserves to the last dregs and who were afraid that one more battle would see them smashed into palpitating inner dust.[63]

Surprisingly perhaps, casualties could have organizational benefits. Personnel losses could be part of a process that allowed a unit to retain its vibrancy and effectiveness. Writing of the First World War, Baynes was almost apologetic as he forwarded a proposition that casualty replacements were invaluable to a unit's ongoing proficiency:

> To give loss of life as a cause of high morale may seem odd, and perhaps a little callous. However, a soldier gets less and less eager to fight the longer he stays in the battle area. A few men thrive on war, but most get progressively more unwilling to face danger as time goes on. . . . Keen, eager young men kept pouring out to replace the killed and wounded, and in this way morale was constantly renewed.[64]

World War II studies similarly found that "the individual replacement system made it possible to keep divisions in intermittent combat indefinitely."[65] New men quickly felt themselves a part of their new units, almost half believing themselves integrated after only a few days.[66] Before long many found them of greater value to their units than men who had been with the organization longer. Stouffer's research revealed that replacements were thought to have reached the average level of efficiency after three months of combat experience. Beyond that point, "not only was the replacement a full-fledged combat man, but our data indicate that for the next several months he was even more likely to be valued as a combat soldier than were his more battle-scarred comrades."[67] Like Baynes and Stouffer, Ellis concluded that fresh men rejuvenated British units during World War II, finding that in North Africa "the only reason units as a whole did not fall apart was that there was a constant flow of replacements." For Ellis this turnover meant that few warriors reached the critical point after which they became neuropsychiatric casualties.[68] Holmes believed that organizations could reach a point beyond which their experience level made them less reliable than units with no previous combat exposure. He cited the disappointing performance of two armored divisions during the 1944 Normandy campaign, whose men had earlier fought in North Africa, Sicily, and Italy. Their performance was below the standard set by two other divisions previously uncommitted to combat. Only after extensive replacement of leaders and personnel did the veteran organizations again distinguish themselves.[69] Such World War II episodes demonstrated that a point does appear to exist beyond which a man is likely to become a neuropsychiatric casualty. Further, that observation—made in both world wars—strongly suggested that replacements were essential to the continued combat effectiveness of organizations remaining at the front.

Moskos cited the twelve-month rotation policy as the primary cause of high soldier morale during the early years of the Vietnam War, though he simultaneously acknowledged the possibility that it might have less positive effects in the longer term.[70] Moskos concluded that veterans generally did not question the legitimacy of the Vietnam War before the late 1960s, attributing their acceptance to a rotation system that removed them from combat theater before doubts began to arise.[71] Bourne traced a statistical benefit to the fixed-duration tour. Whereas psychiatric casualties at times reached rates of 101 per 1,000 men per year in some areas during World War II and 37 per 1,000 in Korea, his studies of Americans in Vietnam reflected a fairly consistent rate of 12 cases per 1,000. Bourne believed that men's knowledge that they had a legitimate chance to return home without being killed or badly wounded was key to this improvement.[72] Maj. Gen. George I. Forsythe, who commanded the 1st Cavalry Division from August 1968 to April 1969, also felt that the rotation policy was wise, despite the disruptions caused by the constant loss of veterans and introduction of new men. The one-year tour not only sustained morale, Forsythe felt, but it also allowed him to maintain a faster pace of operations than would have been possible if his soldiers had been in combat for the duration of the war.[73] Edward C. Fisher, who commanded B Company, 1/7 Cavalry, in the latter half of 1968, agreed, finding the twelve-month rotation provided a goal on which a soldier could focus to get him through his combat tour.[74] Jones, too, found benefits, concluding that the twelve-month Vietnam tour might have helped to reduce instances of "old sergeants' syndrome."[75]

Addressing the effect of rotation on unit cohesion, Moskos, Savage and Gabriel, and others have argued that the twelve-month rotation undermined the formation of close ties within combat units in Vietnam. However, John H. Faris specifically countered Savage and Gabriel's findings, concluding that there was no evidence to support such claims.[76] After extensive research of soldier performance in World War II, Stouffer similarly observed that rotation had little effect on esprit de corps: "Informal controls based on close personal ties and identifications developed in spite of the influence of the replacement system in the opposite direction."[77]

ARGUMENTS AGAINST THE TWELVE-MONTH VIETNAM TOUR

There is a viable argument that many of the lessons of World War II and Korea were ignored or misapplied in establishing the twelve-month rotation system in Vietnam. The author of *The Personnel Replacement System in the United States Army* wrote after the Korean War that "the army has never entered a war prepared to operate a personnel system built upon the accumulated knowledge of past experience."[78] The U.S. Army Deputy Chief of Staff for Personnel's 1971 "Study of the 12-month Vietnam Tour" judged that "most personnel problems of the past five years are traceable to the twelve-month Vietnam tour."[79] The rotation policy's benefits in reducing some types of neuropsychiatric casualties were noteworthy, but neuropsychiatric casualties were preferable to deaths caused by replacements' inexperience. Stouffer found that, during World War II, "the division with the highest level of anxiety was also the division which had been overseas longest, had the most exposure to combat, had the highest illness rate, especially malaria, and had been subjected to the greatest turnover of officers. On the other hand its battle casualty rate was low in comparison with the other divisions."[80] Surviving long-service noncommissioned officers could have compensated to some extent for the turnover in officers, but that was not possible in Vietnam because of the twelve-month rotation of all personnel. Gen. Bruce Palmer wrote of his experiences with individual rotation. When a

> point system went into effect in the Pacific in May 1945 during World War II, it had a disastrous effect on the division I was serving in, still in active combat against the Japanese in northern Luzon. Rifle companies suddenly lost all their most experienced men, with only green replacements available to bring units up to strength. In my opinion the program resulted in unnecessary casualties among new arrivals because of the dearth of combat-experienced leaders.[81]

Straub concluded that negative effects such as these influenced individual and unit performance well before an individual actually departed. He determined that soldiers became more preoccupied with their personal rotation status than with the welfare of the unit. The result, he believed, was a less cohesive organization.[82]

Stouffer and others also recognized the dangers that a new replacement, inexperienced in combat, posed to himself and other unit members. The shortcomings found most frequently in recent arrivals were bunching up, talking or making noise at night, and shooting before they were able to see their target, all of which could provide an enemy a crucial advantage during an engagement.[83] The costs of these and other mistakes were often high; another study found that new battalions lost over a quarter of their strength in the first fifteen days of combat. The loss rate dropped to twenty-one percent in the next ten days of exposure and stayed at approximately that level until the unit had been in combat for seventy-five days. From that point to three hundred days the percentage of the battalion's strength lost per month gradually decreased to ten percent. The primary causes of the initially high rates of loss were thought to be inexperience and a lack of strong ties between unit members.[84]

Obviously, these effects of inexperience meant that a unit's casualties were likely to be unevenly distributed over time; more losses were generally suffered in the first weeks of action. In his study of 3,047 Illinois men who had died in Vietnam, Roger W. Little found that two-thirds of those killed in "direct combat" died in the first six months of their tours; only 15 percent of those killed died after their ninth month.[85] Some of this can be explained by policies such as not sending "short-timers" on notably high risk missions in their final weeks before rotating and rotating officers out of the line to less dangerous positions in the rear area during the last six months of their tours. Thomas C. Thayer's findings were strikingly similar. He determined that seven of ten army combat deaths occurred during the first six months of a soldier's tour. He further found that an American soldier's chances of being killed during his first three months in Vietnam were nearly as great as in the last nine months combined.[86] These statistics are strikingly similar to those suffered by Dunn's battalion of Royal Welch Fusiliers. A November 1917 group of 240 new arrivals had fewer than forty remaining some six months later.[87] It appears unquestionable that combat experience was a primary factor influencing this timing of casualties.

Neuropsychiatric casualties waxed and waned in a manner similar to physical woundings. The casualty rate was notably high among replacements. In World War II Army Ground Forces, nearly one in five of all losses among those with twenty-five days of service in combat units was due to noncombat causes, the majority of which were neuropsychiatric in character (the "noncombat" label notwithstanding, a soldier or marine's neuropsychiatric problems were very likely influenced by his combat experiences). These losses, Williams found, like those caused by gunfire, were attributable to a lack of group support and failures to adequately prepare new men for the fighting environment. The rate dropped sharply after fifty days, not to rise significantly until the two hundredth day of combat was reached.[88] Williams determined that a combat tour, if short enough, might actually increase neuropsychiatric casualty counts because those unsuitable for combat roles would soon be discovered among new men introduced to combat.

Doubler found that what he called World War II "combat exhaustion casualties" usually fell into one of two broad categories. One group consisted of new soldiers who were either about to first experience combat or were in their first five days on the front lines. The second was veterans who had "endured continuous, severe fighting for four months or more."[89] Again there are similarities between First World War regiments and these later units. Dunn determined that battle exhaustion most severely struck younger men and newly arrived soldiers under shell fire for the first time.[90]

Bradford Perkins personally experienced the lack of a fixed rotation policy as a soldier during World War II. Yet he found it comforting rather than stress-inducing. He and his compatriots knew that unless they were "wounded or killed, we were there for the duration, and in a way this was consoling. In the latter stages of the Korean War and in Vietnam, troops were committed for a fixed period. . . . Men became particularly anxious as their personal calendars ran down. Rotation may have been fair, in a sense democratizing danger, but it exacted a psychological price—and also a bloody one, since it is well known that newcomers to combat are most likely to become casualties. . . . The absence of rotation also meant something else: because those near you were not strangers, you especially did not want to disgrace yourself. I frequently felt this pressure, and I am sure that it was common."[91]

Dowling, while a 1st Cavalry Division psychiatrist in Vietnam, found "pretty much without exception the psychotic patients I have seen have been in the first months of their tour."[92] It follows that the shorter the duration of soldiers' tours, the larger the number of replacements and therefore the higher the number of neuropsychiatric casualties among new men. The assumption that rotation of soldiers out of combat reduces such casualties, especially if the duration of a tour is short, is thus questionable.

Jones, who found new men and those with extensive exposure to combat the most likely to suffer neuropsychiatric problems, provided other possible explanations for Vietnam's low combat-exhaustion casualty rates. These included the absence of prolonged artillery barrages in Vietnam, thorough training of soldiers, confidence in weapons, evacuation of wounded by helicopter, and the episodic character of the combat "that consisted largely of brief skirmishes followed by rests in a secure base camp. Fatigue and anxiety did not have a chance to build up."[93] There is likely a balance between length of tour, combat exposure, and the many other factors that influence combat neuropsychiatric casualties. Finding that balance could conceivably allow military forces to significantly reduce loss rates due to neuropsychiatric problems even below those recorded in Vietnam.

Individual-based rotation systems may in fact undermine the cohesion essential to a unit's success in combat. Despite his conclusion that small group pressures to perform developed in spite of replacement arrivals, Stouffer noted that the number of replacements directly influenced veterans' perceptions of their unit's effectiveness. Long-term members of fighting units who saw the introduction of *limited* numbers of new men were more likely to conclude that teamwork was satisfactory than were those whose organizations had received a greater proportion of those inexperienced in war.[94]

Unit cohesion was difficult to attain even when regular rotation out of the theater was not the norm. Losses due to combat, disease, intratheater rotation, and other causes complicated the process of building unity. The shortfalls of experienced leaders and soldiers with critical combat skills precipitated by the twelve-month rotation in Vietnam further undermined efforts to build cohesion and combat effectiveness. It resulted in soldiers and marines being promoted to officer and noncommissioned officer status prematurely, often before they had acquired the experience critical to successful combat leadership.[95] Addressing the issue of these premature promotions, an officer in A Company, 1/8 Cavalry, noted: "The three-year [staff sergeant] is trouble, and the way I see the trouble, he's made it in a training center or in a job in one of the Fort Benning schools. He comes over here and the first thing he lacks is experience. As an individual soldier he is good and brave. But as a squad leader he just hasn't got it. . . . The men will not respect a man that doesn't have the ability even if he's wearing the stripes."[96] The marines suffered the same problems. They filled extensive shortages in young officer ranks by temporarily commissioning over 5,500 marine NCOs. Small-unit leadership suffered in a war in which small-unit actions predominated.[97]

Richard M. Swain also noted the problems regarding young NCOs arriving from other assignments after accelerated promotions. Swain saw many of these men perform magnificently, but their lack of experience put them in the same difficult situation as was the case with inexperienced platoon leaders arriving to lead men with far more time in combat than themselves.[98] Russell A. Glenn (the author's father) was similarly concerned with captains who arrived during his 1969–1970 Vietnam command of the 816th Engineer Battalion. These dedicated young officers expected to be placed in command positions despite their lack of combat savvy. Glenn, however, found that lieutenants with several months in the theater were far more capable of leading soldiers in such a high-risk environment. He therefore assigned the captains to staff positions in order that they might familiarize themselves with Vietnam and enemy methods of operating before they assumed direct responsibility for men in the field.[99]

Such a policy was by no means uniformly applied. Thayer noted that combat-inexperienced company commanders were more likely to both have higher losses in their units and were more likely to personally suffer death or wounding. Nevertheless, he found that 30 percent of the men who assumed company command positions in Vietnam did so within one month of their arrival in the country.[100]

Further, with virtually every unit suffering a complete replacement of its manpower over a twelve-month period, leaders found it difficult to build and maintain soldiers' pride in their organizations or inculcate performance standards. Jonathan Shay, a psychiatrist who treated veterans of the Vietnam War, concluded that "the individual (as contrasted to unit) rotation policy practiced in Vietnam, which moved individual men in and out of combat units on a preordained time schedule, systematically destroyed the unit cohesion of combat groups."[101]

The difficulty of maintaining combat proficiency and a sense of unity within organizations was heightened by the phenomenon of "short-timer's syndrome," an extraordinary focus on personal safety as a soldier closed to within sixty to ninety days of his tour's end. Toro-Quiñones y Silva found that soldiers in the Pacific in World War II "would lose interest and dedication to their assigned duties and responsibilities" as their tours neared completion.[102] Stouffer had detected a similar reaction in veterans who reported that, after having resigned themselves to endless war escapable only through death or wounding, reawakened to the possibility of surviving as the war approached its end.[103] Ray C. Hunt wrote of a similar redawning of hope as the war neared completion after spending several years as an American guerrilla in the Philippines in World War II: "During most of the war I had assumed fatalistically that I would never live through to the end, but now that the end seemed so near, now that true safety at home again loomed as a distinct possibility rather than a utopian dream, the fear of death flooded my imagination remorselessly."[104] World War II airmen felt a similar trepidation as they approached the number of missions that would send them home, even to the point of wishing that they had not been told how many missions remained before they were due for their return to the United States.[105]

David Hackworth saw the same phenomenon during the Korean War: "Among the other 'good' things the North Koreans were lacking was rotation, an insidious system that caused U.S. troopers to pay more attention to counting days than fighting Reds."[106] Writing of the same war, British historian Max Hastings recorded that

> the American points system was regarded as one of the most pernicious innovations of the campaign: a man needed thirty-six to go home; on line, he earned four a month; in the combat zone, three; in country but beyond reach of enemy action, two. Thus most men serving with an American combat formation might expect to go home after about a year in Korea, while support personnel served eighteen months. It was a discipline which earned intense dislike among professional soldiers and commanders because it caused men to become increasingly cau-

tious and reluctant to accept risk as they grew 'short' and approached release date. [107]

Ebert noted this cohesion-sapping, self-centered focus in Vietnam. Those with little time remaining before rotation became overly cautious and "sought to avoid any condition that might lessen by the smallest fraction their chances of completing their tours intact."[108] Sgt. Gerry Barker of the 1st Cavalry Division related that his men would try to "get out of things toward the end. They made stupid mistakes. . . . Very frequently they got scared. They got real frightened as they got short. . . . I tried to keep them off ambush patrol the last month or so, because everybody thought ambush patrol was the worst. . . . I tried to send them in without warning so nobody knew [when] he was going in."[109]

Anxiety regarding personal safety could directly influence an organization's combat effectiveness. David Hackworth bitterly recalled a personal experience with one of his subordinate commanders when he ordered him

> to set up an ambush on the trail I was sure the enemy would use to withdraw before first light. The Tiger CO started to bitch over the very busy battalion command net that he didn't want to do it. He was close to rotation and didn't want to get knocked off. . . . The ambush was not set, no sack was drawn, and come the dawn many an enemy soldier slipped away down that very trail. . . . I brought the Tigers in and relieved [the commander] on the spot. I didn't give a damn if he was a short-timer. Almost everyone was, and some were well past their rotation dates. The Vietnam one-year rotation policy was already panning out as it had in Korea: when people got short, they just wanted to go back to the base camp and hide under a rock. They were deadweight in an outfit; they didn't do their share, and their lousy attitude was infectious.[110]

Despite the evidence that approaching the end of one's tour caused increased caution, a soldier in the 1/8 Cavalry observed the opposite reaction in 1966 Vietnam. He felt that "what's bad about a soldier here quite awhile is he becomes lax. After awhile his normal instinct is 'Well, I haven't got it, I'm not going to get it now.' So he says, 'Heck with it.' . . . I would say a lot when they get short over here say 'Charlie can't shoot me; I'm too short.'"[111]

Unlike rotation policies in Korea and in World War II, the twelve-month tour in Vietnam made no distinction between tour length for the frontline soldier and for his counterpart in the relative safety of a large base or major city. Equality of treatment for every individual soldier did not equate to fairness; equality implied commonalty of condition, and war discriminates horribly. The infantryman has far greater opportunity to die than a soldier in any other branch. Christopher Straub noted in his study of the American army's rotation policy that soldiers in Vietnam "all faced twelve-month coterminous tours, all would receive the same 'hostile fire' pay, almost all would be honored with the same decorations for 'meritorious service,' but the differences in discomfort and danger would be profound."[112] Moskos found the rotation policy discriminatory because it made no distinction between those whose lives were consistently at greater risk and others in rear areas.[113] Further, soldiers stationed in locations other than Vietnam with no threat of combat shared the twelve-month rotation norm.[114]

It could be argued that one benefit of this universal policy was that there was no need to monitor the points soldiers had acquired toward departure, and no controversy regarding the relative danger of "front" and "rear" in a war that many felt had no proper front in the sense of earlier American conflicts. However, that some men routinely confronted greater risks than others would have been debated by few; Vietnam's marines and soldiers had well-developed views regarding who was forward and who served in rear echelon positions.

Others inside and outside of the army recognized the shortcomings inherent in the system. One author wrote that "the inviolable twelve-month duty concept had several shortcomings. Because it was fixed and inviolable, it led to an inflexible rotation-replacement system. Personnel were shipped back to the continental United States at the completion of the tour regardless of the circumstances. No consideration was given to replacement availability or unit strengths. Combat efficiency of units was disregarded."[115]

He went on to identify a further problem. The drafted soldier, marine, airman, or sailor had to serve but one tour in combat; the career officer or NCO was not so fortunate.[116] One-term enlistees and draftees completed a twelve-month tour and returned to the United States for discharge after a short period. By the time of the American withdrawal, however, some career soldiers had been sent involuntarily to Vietnam two and three times. In this sense, the year-long combat tour worked to the short-term soldier's benefit while causing repeated exposure and family separation for career army personnel.

The personal hardships experienced by those remaining in the army caused further losses of experienced soldiers. A June 1970 army study recognized the cause and effects of the tour duration: "The recurring requirements to sustain the twelve-month tour required individuals to serve unaccompanied overseas tours more frequently than during the period prior to the Vietnam build-up. In subsequent sample surveys, family separation was indicated as the most dissatisfying aspect of military life. . . . Repetitive short tours, or the threat of additional Vietnam tours, adversely affected morale and the individual's attitude toward the military service. . . . The total result was that the various effects of the twelve-month tour upon morale significantly influenced individuals nearing retirement eligibility or expiration of their term of service to leave the service."[117]

The marines suffered the same problem. Their official history notes that few noncommissioned officers given temporary commissions remained in the corps for more than one tour and that, "by 1968, even the prewar senior NCOs began to leave in alarming numbers. Rather than continually adding to its pool of combat-tested leaders, the Marine Corps had constantly to recreate it."[118]

The Australian Army experienced widespread dissatisfaction with its individual rotation policy during the Korean War. The negative effects of personnel turbulence on small-unit morale caused senior army leaders to seek a better means of building cohesion in combat units. It was felt that "members of units who are bonded together during predeployment training and share the experiences of being 'new' together, acclimatizing together, enduring the challenges of operations together, and looking forward to returning home together will perform better than units permanently located 'in country' who receive and shed personnel constantly." The Australian Army therefore adopted a unit rotation policy during the nation's involvement in South Vietnam. Units were in South Vietnam from 1962 to 1972; at its peak the country maintained a brigade-sized organization that included armored vehicles and artillery.

Every Australian who served in Vietnam went through rigorous individual and small-unit training before departing for combat. Many later related that they found this preliminary preparation physically and mentally harder than their service in Vietnam. They departed for combat confident in their skills.[119] Soldiers believed that they understood their individual strengths and weaknesses, and they had learned to depend on their fellow unit members who had accompanied them through the ordeal of jungle training at the hands of Vietnam and Korean War veterans, bolstered by others with experience in the Malayan Emergency.

The Australian Army Doctrine Centre Historian, Garth Pratten, noted that "the unit replacement policy also resulted in periods of lessened activity as units prepared to depart Vietnam and their replacements arrived and [were] given a fortnight to acclimatize. It was on this basis that Westmoreland criticized the Australian system. Australian commanders took no notice of Westmoreland's criticisms and were prepared to trade-off a short period of operational inactivity against the morale, discipline and fighting efficiency achieved through unit relief."[120]

United States military leaders did not find the down time and risks associated with unit rotations practical for American units, however. U.S. organizations therefore retained the individual rotation system despite its drawbacks. Martell D. Fritz, who commanded an artillery battery in support of the 1st Cavalry Division's 1/12 Cavalry, thought these problems were highly significant; he in fact believed that rotation was his unit's greatest problem. During his command tour, "about 70–78 percent of the officers in the battalion rotated in the June–July time frame, and over 50 percent of the en-

listed personnel rotated in that same time frame. So we lost all of the institutional memory and knowledge."[121] Fritz's problems with this bulk turnover
were magnified by his unit's status as an artillery organization. His unit suffered fewer casualties from enemy action. Therefore, a greater percentage
of soldiers remained for the full twelve months of their tour and turnover of
personnel near the anniversary of the organization's arrival in the combat
theater was greater.

One C Company, 2/12 Cavalry, veteran agreed with Fritz: "The major
shortcoming I saw while in Vietnam was the twelve-month tour of duty. It
seemed that just about the time an individual became experienced he
rotated out."[122] Ronald H. Martin of the 2/5 Cavalry found the loss of experienced men frustrating: "When a soldier became a fair soldier, he was to
DEROS—so along comes the new guy. . . . The DEROS thing hurt us more
than the weaponry or being afraid. When you train someone for a year and
replace him with [someone else] you are going to lose more men."[123]

The loss of respected veterans tore at the minds of those left to fight. Marine corporal Jim Howe recalled how he felt when the experienced Cpl.
Jack "Pops" Wandell rotated back to the United States. Howe "was very glad
for him to leave and yet . . . felt that he was abandoning me and that why
should he be the lucky one to go and not I? And also that I knew that I was
more exposed because I didn't have him around to act as a second opinion
or use his judgment."[124]

The 1st Cavalry Division suffered considerably on the first anniversary of
its arrival in Vietnam. Shelby Stanton noted that the rotation "policy constantly refilled the formation with green troops and caused severe personnel
turbulence. The resulting instability was particularly disruptive in late 1966
operations because most division members were lost in a single block of
time as their twelve-month combat tours expired."[125] Stanton concluded
that this "rampant personnel turbulence had the potential of greatly dimin-
ishing the combat proficiency of any unit."[126]

A sense of the problem is evident in looking at the number of soldiers
who passed through the division from January 1966 to the same month the
following year. The 1st Cavalry Division absorbed 19,837 new enlisted replacements and lost 16,173 enlisted veterans due to transfers, injuries, or
death. A brigadier general in the division was angered to hear that replacements arriving to fill the void made by those returning to the United States
were being referred to as "The Second Team," a play on the organization's
moniker as "The First Team." Major General Norton, who assumed command of the 1st Cavalry Division in May 1966, commented that American
forces in Vietnam had not done well in maintaining needed numbers of platoon leaders, key noncommissioned officers, and riflemen. Battalions of 550
men were common.[127] At the time of his remarks, a cavalry battalion had an
authorized strength of 767 men.[128]

Reviewing problems regarding maintenance of unit strengths within the combat theater during future conflicts, the authors of the army's 1971 "Doctrine for Personnel Assignment and Rotation" study recommended that the service "ought to consider very carefully an eighteen-month tour policy to be effective from the beginning of the conflict. However, if this were adopted, a system of relief (point system) for the frontline soldiers would have to be established in order to give them some relief."[129]

The marines found themselves confronted by an additional problem that demanded immediate attention during the conflict. Their service was too small to meet the demands of the war, and the Secretary of Defense denied their requests to increase the total strength of the corps. The problem was in part due to the large number of men who had completed a tour in Vietnam and were due for release to civilian life. As long as they remained in the service, they occupied slots that could otherwise have been filled by new men with eligibility for deployment to Southeast Asia. The typical two-year recruit completed five months of training, went to Vietnam for thirteen months, and therefore returned to the United States with only a few months of duty remaining before separation. Releasing these men early, marine leaders realized, could create vacancies that would be filled by new men who could be trained and sent to Vietnam earlier than if the service waited for the full twenty-four-month tours to expire.[130] In mid-1967 the corps therefore initiated a policy of early release for junior personnel on two-year enlistments.

In war, new men enter the conflict and fight alongside more experienced veterans. A rotation of fixed duration exacerbates the resultant difficulties. Leaders, veterans, and newcomers in future conflicts would benefit from remembering that the sooner a recent arrival is integrated into his combat unit, the better it is for all involved. The payoff is the lives of the initially ignorant and of the experienced men who otherwise would fall because of the replacement's foolish error. Units with a policy of harassing the recent arrival or otherwise delaying the uniting of all their fighting men suffer for such behavior. Athena may favor the veteran with a better chance of survival than she does the neophyte, but her favoritism holds no guarantees. World War II marine James Johnston reminded us that her partners are indistinguishable as they ultimately close ranks:

> I couldn't see any difference between the bravery and competency of men from the old corps and the men who came in at the last. Both groups—the new and the old—served with honor and sacrifice. . . . I saw one hell of a sight up and down the beach. The sand was already littered with dead and mutilated bodies of U.S. marines—bodies of old salts and new selective service recruits lying side by side. You couldn't tell one from the other.[131]

A RETROSPECTIVE CONSIDERATION
OF THE TWELVE-MONTH TOUR

The effects of the twelve-month Vietnam tour were obvious, significant, and ubiquitous. It was credited with being the foundation for good soldier morale. It also had serious personal and institutional drawbacks. The army considered initiating longer tours. The change would have been beneficial from a financial standpoint: longer periods between moves would have reduced training costs, transportation expenses, and the number of personnel moving through the army (and therefore the number of veterans eligible for support after the war). An eighteen-month tour, for example, would also have made better use of the two-year draftee. Those drafted for twenty-four months spent roughly six months in training and eighteen months in Vietnam, only to return to the United States with six months remaining in their obligation. This was hardly enough time to be of value to a new unit stateside, especially after a post-combat tour leave and in-processing at a new installation.[132] Most significantly, casualty statistics demonstrated that longer rotations would very likely have reduced the number of soldiers killed in action. The lessons of World War II and Korea had revealed the dangers of increasing tour lengths for soldiers already in-country, but a decision to lengthen the twelve-month tour could have been implemented for those not yet in Vietnam as units and individuals began the mid-1960s buildup.

The "body of opinion that holds that the one-year tour was one of the main factors responsible for the decrease in psychiatric casualties in Vietnam as compared to World War II and the Korean War" may have been well founded.[133] Yet the focus of most of those whose views comprised that body was the soldier as an individual. Soldiers are by definition members of groups: armies, divisions, battalions, companies, platoons, and squads. The individual welfare of the soldier was inseparable from the welfare of these groups. Eleven perfectly fit, independent, self-centered men did not make a combat-effective squad. The soldier as an individual was safer, more potent, and more confident as he endured the challenges of combat if he had sacrificed some of his independence and self-concern for unity and discipline. "Four brave men who do not know each other will not dare to attack a lion," Du Picq wrote, but "four less brave, but knowing each other well, sure of their reliability and consequently of mutual aid, will attack resolutely. There is the science of the organization of armies in a nutshell."[134]

Various additional factors were thought to have influenced the low Vietnam neuropsychiatric rates, only some of which were related to the twelve-month tour. Less constant exposure to combat, the quality of training, pre-service demographic factors, and sufficiency of medical and psychiatric care were among them.[135] Jones concluded it was a combination of the fixed-length tour and a week of rest and recuperation approximately midway through a soldier's tour that kept rates low.[136]

Numerous studies have considered alternatives to the universal twelve-month tour. One army analysis concluded that rotation of units rather than individuals was deemed "feasible in pure form for relatively short periods. . . . It is not feasible if widely used for long periods of time, or for units subject to extensive battle casualties."[137] Point-based systems were more difficult to implement equitably than it might have appeared at first glance. They proved difficult to administer because of the need for periodic computation. Factors and weighting used to determine point scores were often points of controversy, and replacement requirements were less easily predicted than with predetermined tour lengths.[138]

Many of these considerations had been brought forward just after World War II. A 1946 *Study of Battle Casualties* drew conclusions from a review of losses in the World War II Army Ground Forces and determined that a rotation policy was necessary for combat soldiers. It suggested that frontline service be limited to one year, rotation being based on time in combat rather than time overseas. The study further recommended that replacements not be thrown directly into units during active operations. It concluded that the American soldier fought primarily because of self-respect and group loyalty, that special recognition should be given to frontline soldiers, and that individual rotation was far better than unit rotation. Finally, the report authors suggested that combat divisions should be provided the personnel and equipment necessary to establish and operate rest and recreation centers.[139] These lessons, and those from other nations and other wars, offer a foundation for designing an alternative to the fixed one-year tour.

ALTERNATIVES TO VIETNAM TOUR ROTATION POLICIES

Gen. Donald Bennet concluded that "we wreck ourselves on a six-month rotation or a year's rotation."[140] When possible, leaders and their men should be provided the opportunity to form the bonds critical to combat effectiveness. In Vietnam, the tour-length policy worked against this goal. An ideal solution would have been equitable, kept units together, reduced both battle and neuropsychiatric casualties, and enhanced combat effectiveness. Similarly, an alternative means of integrating replacements and building cohesion would have allowed assimilation into existing groups, provided an opportunity to train new men in critical combat skills before they experienced their first fight, and likewise reduced new soldier losses to combat and neuropsychiatric causes.[141]

Based on observations from World War II, Korea, and Vietnam, several modifications of the Vietnam rotation system suggest themselves which, had they been introduced during that conflict, might well have better met the objectives listed above. First, if avoidable, a replacement should never have been sent to his unit while it was in the field. A combat-inexperienced soldier was more vulnerable to being wounded or killed or to suffering neuropsychiatric injury than a more experienced man, the more so if he encountered the shock of first combat with complete strangers.

On the other hand, introducing small groups of combat-inexperienced soldiers into the combat theater directly from basic or advanced individual training was feasible and effective. This second concept of unit replacement was not unknown to earlier American commanders. Gen. Joseph W. Stilwell, while serving as Commanding General, Army Ground Forces, in February 1945, recommended that infantry training centers in the United States form units of soldiers who were destined for the same division. The soldiers would have maintained their unit organization during training and movement to their combat assignments. Stilwell's concept served as a foundation for later unit-based replacement concepts left untested only because of the early end of the Pacific war.[142]

Leonard Lerwill wrote that many commanders in the European theater "favored individual rotation because they did not believe that relief of divisions would have been practical under World War II conditions. They pointed out that to have changed entire divisions would have been a wasteful, time-consuming process which would have slowed up any momentum that had been gained and which would have nullified the priceless asset of using experienced combat soldiers."[143] Maj. Gen. John S. Wood, who commanded the 4th Armored Division from May 1942 until December 1944, disagreed: "The best system in war is to remove divisions from action and reestablish their combat effectiveness before again committing them. The ability to judge the moment for their withdrawal is one of the marks of a real commander." Wood believed that "individual rotation destroys unit team play and is about as poor a system as has been developed in thousands of years of warfare."[144] Other officers believed that up to a third of a combat division could perhaps be rotated out of the lines, conditions permitting.

Some experimentation was done in World War II Europe with replacing soldiers in small packets. Putting men together in groups of five to nine proved beneficial from a morale standpoint. The groups were kept intact from their creation at overseas replacement depots until arrival at companies in the field, whenever possible.[145] Maj. Gen. Norman Cota, commander of the 28th Infantry Division during the war, believed "American infantrymen should be trained as combat teams. I would have twenty or twenty-five to the group, each under its own sergeant. These teams would be tough, self-sufficient, easily interchangeable battle units. The noncommissioned officer would be a combat veteran who would eat, sleep, and travel with his men. . . . When the time came to rebuild a unit, replacements would come up in teams. They would have confidence in their leader and each other."[146]

A Korean War study on team replacement proposed that "the basic replacement unit be the team; at full strength it will consist of four men," a group that was to "be maintained in all activities including training, billeting, guard duty, and overseas shipment" from "the beginning of training until the unit arrives at its final overseas destination."[147] A student at the United States Army War College in 1960 recommended sending teams "of not less than four men" to their stateside or overseas units to eliminate the "disinterested production line methods of producing replacements."[148]

Still lacking a policy that helped to develop cohesion before new men joined a unit, Vietnam veterans resorted to "buddy training" to build a sense of teamwork while simultaneously easing the replacement integration into their units. A Fort Leavenworth survey respondent emphasized the value in pairing recent arrivals with veteran "buddies"; he also felt that stateside training should better emphasize the responsibilities a man had as a unit member when he entered combat. A 1st Cavalry Division veteran with service in both the 2/7 Cavalry and 1/21 Artillery recalled how his unit ensured new men were made part of their units: "All new guys would be taken in and personally trained. We all felt we were needed and mistakes or misjudgments would be costly but would be absorbed by all. The credit and honor were also shared by all. We walked and flew proud."[149] In B Company of the 1/8 Cavalry, it was standard procedure that a new man was assigned "to a guy who has been on a couple of field problems, probably got three to five months in the country. He'll be assigned to him by name: 'You'll have Joe Doaks with you, and if I come ask you where he is, you better be able to tell me.' And he'll live with him and eat with him, and show him how to cook his C's [C-ration meals]. . . . So the old timer is made kind of responsible for the new man. He's just under his wing and when it looks like he's ready to be cut loose, he is. Of course, he's watched real close."[150]

A third possible modification to the rotation system would have involved altering the tour duration. The length of the Vietnam conflict demanded rotation for humanitarian and family-responsibility purposes and for the long-term retention of career soldiers, but mission accomplishment and saving lives should have taken priority over other considerations. In fact, all of these several factors were mutually served by longer tours in the theater. To a point (one that could have been estimated from the World War II and Korean experiences and then adjusted), rotations of longer than twelve months were the obvious answer. Steps could have been taken to mitigate the stress of combat exposure for the man consistently at risk from enemy fire. Those assigned to positions in which they were less threatened could have, and should have, served longer in Vietnam. These extended tours would very likely have let more fathers, husbands, and sons return home alive or less severely injured, itself a more humane alternative to that which existed. Longer tours would also have reduced the number of repeat rotations for career marines and soldiers.

Fourth, maintaining unit cohesion despite individual rotation should have been the baseline standard for every leader. The welfare of the unit, not that of the individual, had to remain paramount. That principle was frequently overlooked in Vietnam. Determining how to better build unit cohesion is crucial to combat success; it should therefore have been a carefully considered component in the design of any alternative rotation system. Reducing the negative influence of the "short-timer" mind-set on unit morale would have been one positive step. Marines and soldiers should have fully served the duration of their combat tours without exception; to allow those at the end of their rotations to avoid hazardous duty unfairly endangered the whole of which the "short-timer" was supposed to be a part. Such leniency, like establishment of the one-year tour itself, reflected a focus on the individual rather than the fundamental building block of success in combat: the unit.

A system involving a form of intratheater unit rotation that incorporated many of the lessons learned from World War II, Korea, and early Vietnam seems to have been feasible and could have addressed many of these issues. In addition to the once-a-year individual relief provided by rest and recuperation leaves ("R&R"), units could have been periodically moved to rear base camp areas for periods in which to rest, train to upgrade combat skills, disseminate new lessons learned, and out-process unit members due to move on to other assignments. This alternative rotation system should also have (1) favored combat units with more frequent rest and training tours than units with less combat exposure, (2) introduced replacements into units only during a training cycle, and (3) included new personnel in all aspects of training and unit operations so that they could become an effective part of their new organization as rapidly as possible.

Training programs could have been designed to take maximum advantage of opportunities for combat veterans to train replacements assigned to their units. As has been noted, Vietnam veterans recognized the benefits of using experienced soldiers to train new men. One recalled: "The best training I received was from the 'old timers' in my company after I reached the field. They taught the real skills needed for survival. It was not always the best or quickest shots who made it to DEROS. It was knowing how the enemy employed his weapons in the terrain that made the difference. The observant Sky Trooper knew that the VC and NVA built their bunker complexes on reverse slopes near water sources, or [that] the presence of fresh tree stumps in the jungle indicated a bunker complex nearby. Failure to observe such warning signs handed down by years of experience could result in entering the enemy kill zone."[151]

Even these experienced fighters would require refresher training after a stint of rest from the rigors of war, however. Men inevitably fell into bad habits or "lost their edge" during breaks from the field. A veteran of service with A Company, 1/8 Cavalry, noted that "when you come back to base camp, you stay in base camp for maybe a week or two weeks, and you start to get soft."[152] Unit leaders also needed time to pass lessons learned by other units on to veterans and newcomers alike. Procedures like these would have prepared both individual replacements and units for combat, minimized neuropsychiatric casualties, and built both new men's and veterans' confidence.

Some of these unit rotations would also have included periods for rest and recuperation at specified locations in-country, designated Pacific locations outside Vietnam, or in the United States. The duration of rest and recuperation plus training periods could have been determined over time with the goals of minimizing combat and neuropsychiatric casualties and providing a period sufficient for training and team-building without an unacceptable degradation of combat skills.

The 1st Cavalry Division's 3rd Brigade introduced a cycle of rest and recuperation in early 1971 that incorporated some of the points noted above. Companies were on active operations in the "bush" for approximately fifteen days, after which they returned to a fire base and provided security for a five-day period. During this time the unit was refitted, conducted training, and took care of administrative matters. Every forty-five days, rifle companies and reconnaissance platoons went to the "First Team R&R Center" at Vung Tau, Vietnam, that opened in March 1971. The twenty-six men tasked with running the center came "out of hide"; the division went without the soldiers in other, authorized positions in order to keep Vung Tau operating. General Burton, however, concluded that "the degree of morale, spirit, and individual motivation fostered by the Vung Tau R&R was seen to have far outweighed any disadvantages of the program."[153]

The marines had similar periods of well-controlled rest between campaigns during World War II. E. B. Sledge described his regiment's activities on the island of Pavuvu between operations on Peleliu and those on Okinawa. In addition to training, new men and old alike slept on mattresses, wore clean uniforms, and received any decorations and medals earned.[154]

The challenge is determining how to most effectively conduct unit rotations. Kellett and Williams both noted the dangers in not doing so. Kellett found that "the importance of regularly rotating troops out of combat was demonstrated in both world wars, particularly the second. . . . But the American practice of keeping formations constantly in the combat zone, without rotation, while pulling back small groups for occasional rest periods led to exhaustion and resentment."[155] U. P. Williams concluded that the duration of rest periods was also a crucial design element: "No appreciable permanent reduction in the neuropsychiatric casualty rate can be obtained by providing only short periods of relief from the front lines. Important manpower savings can be achieved only by having each and every combat infantryman believe that an honorable *extended* period of relief from combat awaits him."[156] Dowling noted an additional, though not debilitating, problem. He not surprisingly found that after a return from a rest and recuperation period or leave "there is a subsequent week to 10 day depression. Similarly, individuals on emergency leave require a two week convalescence on re-entering the Vietnam scene."[157] Training periods and the subsequent gradual reintroduction to combat as units completed their breaks could have served as a relatively safe convalescence period for such men. An added benefit of scheduling individual leaves just prior to unit breaks would have been the opportunity for returnees to sharpen combat skills during the unit train-up period. Before returning to combat, leaders could mold unit cohesion and build the confidence that new men had in veterans and that the experienced felt for the recently arrived. The unit as a whole, more so than any individual, determined the success or failure of efforts to build cohesion and combat effectiveness in the organization.[158]

The ideal field-rest-train cycle would have gradually worked units back into "full combat." Initial operations for units coming out of a rest and training cycle would have been deliberately designed to ensure success and further build confidence. Such gradual reintroduction to combat had long been recognized as wise. World War I American units trained with the French and later moved into "quiet" sectors for their initial frontline rotation.[159] British soldiers received ten weeks of training in England and were then "given more training at a base camp and were taught new skills such as unarmed combat, which had received relatively little attention in England. Finally they were introduced briefly and in small groups to the front lines, where they were attached to seasoned soldiers to learn the ropes."[160] Great Britain's 1922 Southborough Committee's "Report of the War Office Committee of Enquiry into 'Shell-Shock'" recommended "that troops should, when possible, be entered into battle gradually and not precipitated into the thick of war."[161] British general William Slim applied this method during World War II to restore confidence after his XIV Corps's long withdrawal from Burma to India. He first sent men on patrols to ambush the Japanese and otherwise designed operations to ensure a high probability of success. His focus then turned from individual and small-unit confidence to building faith on a larger scale:

> Having developed the confidence of the individual man in his superiority over the enemy, we had now to extend that to the corporate confidence of units and formations in themselves. This was done in a series of carefully planned minor offensive operations. . . . These were carefully staged, ably led, and, as I was always careful to ensure, in greatly preponderating strength. We attacked Japanese company positions with brigades fully supported by artillery and aircraft, platoon posts by battalions. . . . We could not at this stage risk even small failures. We had very few, and the individual superiority built up by successful patrolling grew into a feeling of superiority within units and formations. We were then ready to undertake larger operations.[162]

Mowat described how a Canadian regimental commander similarly returned his forces to fighting trim in Italy in World War II. Objectives were chosen to ensure success, and extensive, even excessive, planning preceded every attack. The result was virtually a perfect record of success and a corresponding leap in the regiment's confidence in its abilities.[163]

The payoffs from this policy of gradual introduction to combat would likely include fewer neuropsychiatric losses among replacements. Writing after World War II, U. P. Williams concluded that the period during which new men were being introduced to combat required special consideration, "but it is not necessarily true that it need be expensive." He recommended that the "shakedown" period be initially conducted in relatively inactive sectors.[164] Glass described a World War II Southwest Pacific episode in which such a policy was introduced by the American 38th Infantry Division. The commanding general personally briefed the incoming group and assured them of his personal interest in their welfare. New arrivals were assigned according to the specialties for which they were trained whenever possible. Subsequent to arrival in their units, each man was initially assigned simple tasks designed to provide time for him to get to know his fellow soldiers. The men were then gradually introduced to combat. The payoff was a very low number of neuropsychiatric patients from these replacement groups.[165]

There is no reason to believe the lessons of previous wars would not have applied to Vietnam. An intratheater unit rotation system, combined with a longer individual tour, could have reduced both the number of combat casualties and neuropsychiatric losses. Determination of an appropriate individual tour length would have depended on the details of the rotation system's design. Soldiers and marines in combat units should have been rotated out of the combat theater sooner than those in less dangerous positions. Morale implications would have been critical, but unit efficiency and soldier survival should have been principal objectives of any policy.[166] Tour length could have been adjusted during the war. Never, however, should a soldier already in Vietnam have had his tour lengthened. Finally, to avoid the development and tolerance of the "short-timer" syndrome, no man would have rotated except during a cycle out of the lines, and no reprieve from dangerous tasks would have been given as the man approached his departure.

A marine or soldier should have been allowed to leave his unit only after having completed a rest period during which veterans had an opportunity to discuss recent events, receive any awards earned, and be debriefed to determine lessons of value to preparation for future combat. This introductory period for replacements could have simultaneously acted as a decompression period for those departing the combat theater. Such a gradual transition from postcombat environments proved itself a significant step in reducing postconflict psychological problems for New Zealand soldiers returning from Vietnam. The New Zealand Army's Maj. Steve Newman found that his nation's soldiers who returned to civilian society directly from Vietnam tours were more likely to suffer psychiatric problems than soldiers who remained in the army with their units for an extended period.[167] Similarly, Eli

Ginzberg concluded that "one of the more striking findings about the relation between pressure and performance is that a considerable number of men were able to complete their combat tour of duty only to break down after they were out of danger. Apparently they were able to draw on reserves while they were in combat and to gain special support from being a member of a closely knit fighting unit."[168] Initiating decompression prior to departure from the combat theater could have served as the first of several steps to aid men during a controlled return to normalcy.

Some soldiers would have had longer tours under such a rotation policy. This negative aspect (from the individual perspective) would have likely been complemented by reduced numbers of new replacements killed and wounded in action, fewer neuropsychiatric casualties in that group, greater unit cohesion, and a related increase in unit effectiveness. Rotation of units out of the line would have also tended to reduce neuropsychiatric casualties because of the benefits of periodic rests and the opportunity to decompress before rotation to other assignments.

Competent commanders would have remained with their units for the duration of their tours. During periods of intense activity such as Tet 1968, some units might have had to delay rotations out of the line or return to "full combat" prematurely. Such cases would have been unavoidable, but senior leaders would have had to ensure they were minimized if the system were to function effectively.

The requirement that individual replacements not be sent directly into combat except in emergency situations would have been key to success. The lessons of World War II, Korea, and early years in Vietnam had repeatedly demonstrated the costs of ignoring such a policy. Though of little more than academic interest when looking back at Vietnam, such lessons offer far more potential benefit for future generations of American fighting men.

6

The Six-Month Command Tour
Cutting In

I will go with you and suffer whatever I must suffer. For I consider that you are my country and my friends and comrades; and with you, I think I shall be honoured wherever I may be, but without you, I think I am not able either to help a friend or hurt an enemy. Where you go there I will go also: that is my resolve.

Clearchos to his men in Xenophon's Anabasis: The March Up Country, *trans. W. H. D. Rouse*

Problems associated with the twelve-month tour were compounded by a policy of rotating commanders and platoon leaders every six months.[1] Confidence in leaders was critical to a soldier's belief that he would be well led in combat, that the missions he was sent on were worthy of the risk to his life, and that the war itself merited his service. Combat effectiveness was virtually unattainable without this confidence. Baynes argued that the soldier's faith in his officers was the bedrock of unit cohesion, in particular "that the morale of the 2nd Scottish Rifles was so closely bound up with the excellent relationship in the battalion between the officers and the other ranks that anything done to upset that relationship would have upset morale disastrously as well."[2] Ardant Du Picq had, a half-century before, similarly noted that the fighting man needed to have faith in his leaders. That faith existed when the leaders had proved themselves capable over time, but "with his comrades in danger brought together under unknown leaders, he feels the lack of union, and asks himself if he can count on them."[3] Dollard's Spanish Civil War veterans liked "to follow an experienced man. Practically all our informants agree that going into action with a tested man made them better soldiers."[4] Rotation of commanders was one of the primary causes blamed for the 1944 collapse of Merrill's Marauders in the India–Burma theater.[5] Copp and McAndrew also described both the extraordinary influence a very able leader could wield and the difficulty in keeping such men during World War II: "When a soldier served under a trusted and exceptional leader, his loyalty spread farther than his slit trench, but this became increasingly difficult as strangers replaced worn-out unit veterans."[6]

Maintaining consistent officer leadership at lower echelons characteristically has been difficult even without regular rotation. Platoon leaders in particular have tended to suffer high casualty rates. Joe Driscoll commanded Headquarters and Headquarters Troop of the 1st Cavalry Division's 1/9 Aerial Reconnaissance Squadron. He believed that the six-month command tour was too short; it simply compounded what was already a difficult situation as "most of the guys were wounded or killed and taken out of command rather than finishing up the six months."[7] Similarly, William J. Scudder, commander of C Company, 2/12 Cavalry, in the latter half of 1967, "went through several rifle platoon leaders in several different platoons"[8] because of casualties. James O. McKenna, commander of the 3rd Brigade, 1st Cavalry Division, from June to November 1967, found that platoon leaders "are the ones that get hurt the most. This is not because they lack sense or anything like that, but they take charge of the operation and consequently they expose themselves. By doing so, of course, they earn the respect of the platoon, but we lose a lot of platoon leaders that way."[9] The result was that units could expect platoon leaders and commanders to average less than six months in their positions because of casualties, illness, forced rotation, and other causes. The marine corps, often short lieutenants and captains, tended to rotate officers at platoon and company level somewhat less than did the army. At battalion commander level, however, frequent rotations were the norm, much like the policy in its sister service.[10]

U.S. leaders implemented the six-month command rotation policy despite the fundamental linkage between unit success, lower soldier casualties, and consistent, high-quality leadership. Leaders at brigade level and below held their command positions for only half of their tour, serving on staff or in other support positions before or after their "line" experience (time spent at the cutting edge during operations). Soldiers in units under battalion commanders in the first six months of their command tours were half again as likely to be killed in combat as those serving under more experienced commanders who were allowed to command beyond the half-year mark.[11] This was not due to better commanders being allowed to remain in command longer; those with fewer casualties in the latter part of their commands suffered the same rates of loss when they first assumed responsibility for their organizations as did those leaving their units after half a year.

A need to build the U.S. Army's reserve of combat-experienced officers was one of several explanations offered for the frequent rotation of commanders and platoon leaders.[12] The logic seems oxymoronic given that the nation was already at war. It would have been far better to have developed experience among those who demonstrated combat leadership proficiency, retaining those men in command and culling out others who were less able. The result would have been a core of proven leaders rather than many merely familiarized with combat leadership, a large number of whom left the service after one tour in Vietnam or were asked to leave soon after the war during reductions in officer strength.

The costs of officer turnover can be measured in part by losses within the ranks of the leaders themselves. Combat-inexperienced officers lacked the skills critical to their own personal survival, just as did new soldiers serving in their units. Officers from first lieutenant to battalion commander level died in greater numbers relative to their soldiers than was the case in either World War II or Korea (see table 6.1).[13] Thayer demonstrated that the greater number of officer deaths was directly related to their experience levels. A company commander with four or more months in his position was only 60 percent as likely to be killed or seriously wounded in combat as he was in his first four months (see table 6.2).[14] That company commander was also far more likely to be killed or to suffer serious wounds in his third month of command than in any other month.

Several possible explanations exist for the steady increase in casualty rates in the first few months of command and sudden drop thereafter. Battalion commanders may have assigned the least dangerous missions to less experienced company commanders. Officers were perhaps more cautious earlier in

Table 6.1   U.S. Officer Deaths in World War II, Korea, and Vietnam

	World War II		Korean War		Vietnam	
Rank	Total Killed	Off:EM Killed	Total Killed	Off:EM Killed	Total Killed	Off:EM Killed
LTC	338	1:503	21	1:1,246	55	1:495
MAJ	466	1:365	71	1:369	135	1:201
CPT	2,115	1:80	252	1:104	720	1:38
1LT	5,168	1:33	716	1:37	1,206	1:23

where: LTC: Lieutenant Colonel
        MAJ: Major
        CPT: Captain
        1LT: First Lieutenant
        EM: Enlisted man (included ranks of private through sergeant major)

Table 6.2   Company Command Combat Casualties by Experience Levels

Experience of company commander	Percent of company commanders lost due to combat death or serious wounds
Less than one month	2.04
One or more, but less than two months	3.07
Two or more, but less than three months	5.61
Three or more, but less than four months	7.60
Four or more, but less than five months	2.00
Five or more months	2.97

their tours. The sudden drop after four months could be due to savvy coming with increased combat experience, greater caution after near misses or minor wounds, or a commander turnover so high that only the most fortunate or proficient at survival made it beyond their first four months. Regardless of the reasons, the facts are clear: less experienced company commanders both died in greater numbers and lost more men than did those with more time in command positions. One explanation is obvious: the rotation system removed those who had learned hard lessons in combat and replaced them with those who had not.

The significance of leader continuity was influenced by a unit's mission. John E. Robbins's A Battery, 2/19 Field Artillery Battalion, supported the 1st Cavalry Division's 1st Brigade. Robbins felt that "the battery [company] that I took could have functioned under a [month-long] command tour; they didn't really need a commander; they were a pretty stable unit especially with the people that had been there so long."[15] Lenard L. Shlenker, who commanded B Battery in the same battalion from July 1966 to January 1967, likewise "didn't see any effect from a six-month tour. . . . I don't think my leaving my battery after six months had any effect."[16] The nature of command in artillery units helped to explain these attitudes. Though the battery commander's position was critical, providing artillery support involved highly repetitive tasks; once the soldiers had been trained, minimal leadership was needed at commander level to ensure the basic skills were maintained and passed on correctly. Second, many of the technical skills required were concentrated at the NCO level, in particular the "Chief of Smoke" who directed the guns and ensured they were properly readied before fire missions were executed.

Artillery commanders Martell Fritz and Rick Swain distinguished between the effects of rotation on artillery and infantry units. Fritz felt that while his less stressful command tour in charge of a battery could have been longer, the same might not be true for the infantry officer whose job he deemed more demanding. While he thought an eighteen-month tour was appropriate for battery commanders, he questioned the wisdom of extending infantry, armor, or aviation command tours because of what he considered greater "wear and tear" on the latter.[17] Swain's experiences as a forward observer for the 1/5 Cavalry and three Vietnam artillery battery commands supported these observations. From his perspective, most infantry "battalion commanders were up 20 hours a day. . . . Mine had been beat to death by the seven days a week. . . . The tempo of what was going on drove to that. . . . Could platoon leaders have stayed out more than six months? Probably. Company commanders were pretty tired."[18] Swain believed artillery battalion and battery commanders "could have stayed in command forever."[19]

Thomas G. Rhame, infantry commander of B Company, 1/12 Cavalry, from late 1967 to March 1968, disagreed: "I think the six-month tour represented careerism at its worst. I was not tired at the end of six months. . . . I had a good feel for the innovative ways to track down Charlie and how to kill him. . . . Lieutenants were the same way."[20] Harold Moore was also very critical of the short command tours: "Even more devastating [than the twelve-month tour] to the morale and effectiveness of every American unit in combat was the six-month limit on battalion and brigade command. This was ticket-punching: a career officer had to have troop-command time for promotion. The six-month rule meant that twice as many officers got that important punch. It also meant that at just about the time when a commander learned the terrain and the troops and the tricks and got good at the job—if he was going to get good—he was gone. The soldiers paid the price."[21] The problem was compounded for a unit like the 1st Cavalry Division that moved in and out of areas frequently; the constant commander turnover ensured that they knew little of the area in which their units operated when they returned to "familiar" terrain.

Thayer found "no data to indicate that long term commanders 'burn out' or are less effective. This does not mean that the phenomenon of burnout does not exist. However, we cannot prove its existence and we suspect that the present rotation policy may be based more on considerations of providing a wide base of combat experience than on the 'burn out' factors." He went on to state that his works showed "clearly that retention of the best battalion commanders has a real payoff."[22]

It is not surprising that the actions of some enlisted soldiers emulated that of their commanders. Veteran Dan Krehbiel of the 25th Infantry Division recalled that "a lot of guys got out after six or seven or eight months of combat and took jobs in supply, or as a company clerk, or a battalion clerk, or something—anything that got you out of combat so that you could live out your short-timer life in reasonable comfort and security."[23] Ebert found that a man who "secured a rear job was able to justify his actions: things changed; the constant rotation weakened their unit loyalties."[24]

A report looking at the issue of the twelve-month rotation had a similar if more general conclusion: "The rotation system not only affected the experience, expertise, and in some cases goals of officers and senior NCOs. . . . It also encouraged self-centered individualism at all ranks which militated against unit cohesion and the general existence of a favorable command environment."[25] The synergistic effect of the six-month command tour and twelve-month rotation acted to perpetuate an orientation on the self rather than the unit.

Perhaps the most destructive effect of the six-month command tour was the loss of what is best termed leader legitimacy. One cause of this degradation was soldiers' perceptions that officers were moved rapidly through career-enhancing positions merely to improve their professional records.[26] A leader suspected of putting his personal safety or advancement before that of his men could damage morale. This negative effect would be further amplified by convictions that officers (1) failed to fully share in soldier suffering by serving only six months in the field, and (2) unnecessarily caused soldiers' lives to be lost because they took command, one after another, without any prior experience.

The conviction that officer careerism was a problem was by no means restricted to the lower ranks. Retired general Douglas Kinnard surveyed fellow high-ranking officers after the war. Eighty-seven percent considered careerism either "somewhat of a problem" or "a serious problem."[27] One postwar report concluded that careerism "in its various manifestations seems to have been a significant factor in furthering the decline of morale and discipline in the U.S. Armed Forces in Vietnam."[28] A veteran of the 1st Cavalry Division was more pointed:

> Officers leading these men should be experienced prior to combat, as many instances of incompetent, inexperienced command decisions [imposed on] seasoned combat troops caused loss to life which was unnecessary to satiate some idiot who needed some combat time or some medals to make that commander's record look good. Example: A major who was an S-2 [intelligence officer] was sent to command us (the elite unit of the division). Although this man had prior conventional warfare combat experience, he had not seen combat in Vietnam and we greatly suffered at his hand. Our morale went rock bottom as he cared nothing for his men as opposed to gaining personal glory.[29]

Another soldier believed "officers rotated too fast. They covered their asses and punched their tickets. The enlisted men knew what was goin' on. We did a year, period. Officers just went till they got the appropriate shit in their [personnel] file. Once their ticket was punched it was adios grunts. We did resent it but it also caused us to bond tighter. We took care of each other. An officer would have had to be a pretty good leader to just step in and get our respect. Doing a full tour would have been a big step."[30]

It is unfair, however, to harshly judge the entirety of the American officer corps because of the six-month command rotation policy. The vast majority of officers had no control over their abbreviated platoon leader or larger unit leadership experiences. As noted, table 6.1 reflects that more U.S. officers in Vietnam died per enlisted soldier lost than was the case in either World War II or Korea. The rapid rotation of officers undoubtedly contributed to this outcome. Their losses also reflect personal bravery and a willingness to properly lead the subordinates for whom they were responsible, regardless of the risks. Many desired to stay longer out of commitment to their men and belief that theirs should be an equal share of the risk that a Vietnam tour entailed. The decision to move after six months was not theirs. That these leaders recognized the wrongheadedness of the command rotation policy is evident from their post-reassignment comments, their desire to stay in command, and the return of many for repeated combat tours.

Short command tours ensured that few officers realized their full potential as combat leaders. As Harold Moore noted, the six-month tour guaranteed that a commander would be departing for another assignment just as he approached competence. Noncommissioned officers and other enlisted soldiers often possessed more combat savvy than did their officer leaders.[31] One 1st Cavalry Division veteran wrote that the problem was glaringly apparent at the most junior infantry-officer lead position: platoon leader. It "seemed to me that officers (new LTs) were not trained in leadership well enough. They learned how to handle men in the field from the men who were in-country with experience. Then most were moved to the rear in a few months and we had to start over again with a new LT. Problem here was that it greatly endangered the men stuck in the field. It can get a lot of men killed."[32] In Vietnam, as had often been the case in previous American wars, "experience spoke more forcefully than rank."[33]

Australian army commanders, by comparison, joined their units approximately a year prior to their Vietnam deployment to supervise their organizations' formation and preparation. By the time the unit reached Vietnam they were therefore well aware of their men's strengths and weaknesses; they knew their soldiers and were in tune with the temperaments and abilities of their officers.[34] Bob Breen could recall only one infantry battalion commander returning from Vietnam before his unit had completed its twelve-month tour. A back injury, the result of an old rugby injury, caused his early redeployment.[35]

It has been noted that evidence of American officers exhausting themselves during command tours was insufficient to justify the six-month tour. Even if exhaustion had been a problem, senior commanders should have been able to determine when an officer needed to be replaced, assuming they themselves were not being rotated too quickly to develop an ability to gauge their subordinates' conditions.[36] Noncommissioned officers in the field should also have been assigned shorter tours, if fear of exhaustion was a legitimate concern. Corporals and sergeants were less often rotated out of combat positions even if they were serving in a platoon leader position (normally a second lieutenant served as a platoon leader, but it was not unusual for units to have insufficient numbers of these junior officers to fill all platoon leader positions). Whether serving as platoon leaders or in subordinate positions of authority, the NCOs' exposure to danger was at least equal to that of many officer leaders, the stresses on them often as great.

If we return to the argument that the army as an institution benefited from a broader base of combat-experienced officers, there arises the question of why there was not a similar policy in either World War II or Korea, or why a pool of combat-experienced NCOs was not thought to be equally critical. Even had a major conflict broken out soon after the Vietnam War, the applicability of the skills learned in Southeast Asia to combat in another type of war—for example, one in Western Europe—was questionable. A question asked in retrospect should have been considered during development of the six-month command tour policy: Was the marginal difference in officers' development worth the cost in American lives?

7

Conclusion
Last Notes

The history of a battle is not unlike the history of a ball. . . . Then the faults or the misbehavior of some gave occasion for the distinction of others, and perhaps were the cause of material losses; and you cannot write a true history of a battle without including the faults and misbehavior of part at least of those engaged.

The Duke of Wellington, letter to John Wilson Croker dated 8 August 1815, in Wellington at War, 1794–1815, *ed. Antony Brett-James*

Many a brave man, and I believe even some very great men, have been found a little terrified by such a battle as that, and have behaved afterwards remarkably well.

The Duke of Wellington, letter to John Wilson Croker dated 14 November 1815, in Wellington at War

A desire to determine whether American fighting men were willing to fire their weapons in combat originally spurred this undertaking. Had the results even remotely resembled S. L. A. Marshall's World War II findings, dramatic action would have been necessary. Instead, two surveys supported a conclusion that few men hesitated to fire when duty called upon them. In that regard, the nation's soldiers and marines were well prepared for the Vietnam War. As the services' weapons training has changed little since that time, such shortcomings as Marshall warned of are unlikely to reemerge (if, indeed, they ever existed).

However, veterans' comments in the surveys revealed other problems—issues that continued through the Vietnam War's end and could well arise again should the nation find itself in an extended conflict. Their critical observations tended in two directions: (1) Training had other shortfalls, and (2) the adverse effects of individual and command rotation policies were thought to be crippling to morale, effectiveness, and the preservation of American lives.

A man's faith in his training influenced the confidence he had in himself, his unit, and his leaders. It could determine whether he made the right choice in situations in which the wrong one could be fatal. Likewise, experience level could be the difference between a correct decision and a decision of the uninitiated—a decision that a man with twelve, or eighteen, or twenty-four months in Vietnam would not have made. Thus finding solutions to these reported deficiencies remains a significant challenge. Training cannot anticipate every configuration of personnel and weaponry in every battle situation, and properly calibrated tours of duty cannot solve all problems of motivation and morale. We can, however, build on experience to minimize losses by listening to what the survivors of Vietnam have to say about these issues.

As their detailed responses to surveys reflected, many of the men who fought in Vietnam remain intensely dedicated to their army and nation. They defy the grossly unjust stereotype of the Vietnam veteran as a social misfit and malcontent. A small percentage of Vietnam veterans fit that description; a small percentage of veterans from every American war fit that description. However, the vast majority of Vietnam veterans are productive members of society, just as were their predecessors after World War II, Korea, and earlier wars. Vietnam was a significant event in American history, and "it is precisely the mark of great events that their meaning constantly changes, is forever disputed, with the big questions never fully answered."[1] The respondents to the surveys on which this book is based have answered some big questions and raised a number of others.

Combat performance, like many human interactions (including Wellington's ball), is too diverse a phenomenon to be measured by any one factor. Explanations based only on buddy relationships, unit cohesion, leadership, social conditioning, or another single element can only be inadequate. The task of integrating new information about combat performance is further complicated by the nature of combat itself, which is, at best, the realm of complexity; at worst, it is chaos. No combination of factors and events is ever repeated. Weapons, tactics, and organizations change over time. So, too, do the conditions of engagements. Two centuries ago, men standing in disciplined ranks lost sight of the enemy only tens of yards before them; the discharges of their hundreds and thousands of firearms veiled the battlefield in thick smoke. Men in Vietnam similarly could often not see the enemy, but the cause was entirely different. Their adversary used terrain or vegetation for concealment.

Further complicating any effort to understand combat performance is the multifaceted character of the fighting man. Each soldier, marine, sailor, or airman is both an individual and a member of several groups, each group with its own demands on his behavior, formal and informal, clearly articulated and implied. American's Vietnam warrior belonged to a squad, platoon, and larger organizations. He was further grouped by time remaining in-country, his job assignment, the weapon he carried, and any personal relationships he formed. Each of these influenced his attitudes and performance, as did his upbringing and associations with those remaining at home. The amorphous character of his environment and the varied nature of his motivations make comprehending the combat soldier one of a historian's ultimate challenges. Perhaps the best that can be hoped for is to achieve better understanding; complete comprehension is a phantom.

A fundamental truth that helps in this understanding: The warrior is a human being who wants to survive. While the behavior of the few may verge on the bizarre or incomprehensible, while the initial or occasional event may cause inappropriate conduct, fighting men and groups of fighting men tend to respond logically to the conditions of their environments much as human beings in other environments are prone to do. If combat performance does not seem to reflect common sense, the problem is more apt to be a misunderstanding of the man than an inherent deficiency in his behavior. There may be an unseen logic at work that is not at first obvious.

During the American Civil War, Sam Watkins of Company H, First Tennessee Regiment, followed a personal rule of shooting privates; "It was they that did the shooting and killing, and if I could kill or wound a private, why, my chances were so much the better. I always looked upon officers as harmless personages. . . . When we got down to close quarters I always tried to kill those that were trying to kill me."[2] One might argue with Private Watkins's approach to war, but, upon a moment's thought, his motivation seems eminently logical. Had his leaders noticed his failure to fire at officers, a few words to Private Watkins might have converted him to the preferred procedure of shooting those "harmless personages" who led, directed, and motivated his perceived enemies.

In addition to complexities of occasion and person, the historical fate of participants in significant events has forever been tied to the interpretation of the event itself; that of the American fighting man in Vietnam has many facets as yet left virtually untouched. When the war was over, the American public did not want to think about it. The men and women who served in Vietnam deserved better support from those at home; too often the latter confused the war with those who fought it.

Historian Roger Spiller found that "one of the more abiding and interesting questions about the hard-won knowledge of combat soldiering in World War I has to do with its prompt disappearing act after the declaration of peace. Despite the appearance of a formidable body of literature and fiction after the war, much of which contained keen, experienced insights on the behavior of soldiers under fire, one searches in vain for evidence that practicing soldiers took much notice."[3] Perhaps it is simply an institutional habit. Perhaps instead it was a positive impulse: the nation's desire to leave the pain associated with Vietnam in its past. But too many of the problems identified with Vietnam have been relegated to the archives. There are many lessons yet to be learned, and many problems left to be solved. The cost of ignoring them will be unjustly borne by the young men and women whose grandfathers and grandmothers gave so much in Southeast Asia.

Of course, future wars will differ from Vietnam as much as that conflict differed from those earlier and since. The infantryman will soon find his rifle replaced with a weapon that allows him to kill without laying eyes on his target. Yet such changes will not diminish the need to train the man to destroy a fellow human being, to accurately replicate the demands of combat, and to build effective fighting units commanded by dedicated and capable leaders. Though he may watch his target die on a video monitor via fiberoptic cable, the marine or soldier will nonetheless recognize that he is fully responsible for his enemy's death.

Athena has an unquenchable thirst for partners. Men will inevitably find her exciting, exotic, alluring, even magnetic in her attractions. She is also a demanding mistress, unforgiving of missteps and ever changing in her expectations. The nation that sends its youth to her embraces must prepare them well if they are to survive the experience. It is hoped that this offering will help in understanding how and why Americans in Vietnam behaved as they did and that it might also aid in better preparing their grandsons and great-grandsons for future combat, thereby saving the lives of many called to serve. History offers lessons to those willing to learn.

Appendix 1
A Review of Military Surveys

You should have asked questions like this when we first came home. It could have helped a lot more then.

First Cavalry Division respondent 43

Herodotus, often considered the father of history, surveyed Persian War veterans as he reconstructed key battles and analyzed their influence on later events.[1] He interviewed both generals and men who fought in the ranks; his studies thus accounted for the perspectives of common soldiers in addition to those of the leaders who would have attended war councils. Without much exaggeration, one can conclude that Herodotus built his histories on surveys of soldiers, and that surveys of war veterans are therefore as old as Western history itself.

Many of this book's concerns were subjects of reflection prior to the Vietnam War. Soldiers' willingness to fire, the behavior and emotions of a man experiencing first contact with the enemy, the effects of a fixed period before rotation out of the combat zone, the importance of leadership, and the value of the group to its members have all been repeatedly subjected to scrutiny by the professional military man, historian, sociologist, psychiatrist, and other "-ists" interested in understanding man in war. Those who analyze the combat soldier inevitably find him something of a riddle.

Though there is commonalty of experiences, stresses, and reactions, explanations for combat behavior too often suffer from the false premise that soldiers are more alike than different. Commonalties are numerous enough that soldiers and scholars can understand something of today's warrior by reading Xenophon, Julius Caesar, Sun Tzu, or Clausewitz. To truly comprehend him, however, they must understand that even those most alike are more different than similar. Perhaps because armies work to diminish individuality—and are quite successful in doing so if uniformity of appearance alone is considered—analysts presume that the process succeeds at levels below the cloth more extensively than is actually the case. A few weeks of training, even years of active campaigning, cannot eliminate the uniqueness in disposition, attitude, capability, or mental robustness granted by heredity, upbringing, social background, and the myriad other factors that mold human beings. To understand the Americans who fought in Southeast Asia therefore requires that many relate their experiences and someone compose the fragments to construct a whole. Understanding the many helps us to comprehend the individual American fighting man in Vietnam.

Combat-soldier surveys from both Vietnam and earlier wars aid in determining the similarities between those who fought over the last centuries and the men who more recently fought in Southeast Asia. What follows is a sampling of surveys conducted with the intent of understanding men's performance in battle. Objectives differ: some analysts sought to reconstruct historical events, others to fathom the behavior of the soldier himself, still others to determine how past performance could assist in selecting suitable men for soldiering in future wars. Together these efforts demonstrate the similarity of the combat soldier's condition over time and the uniqueness of each warrior as an individual.

TOWARD A BETTER UNDERSTANDING OF MAN AT WAR

Herodotus was not alone in surveying Greek veterans to better understand ancient war. Thucydides wrote in his *History of the Peloponnesian War* that he was present "at the events which I have described or else I heard of them from eyewitnesses whose reports I have checked with as much thoroughness as possible."[2] Thucydides faced the same problems that confronted many later historians attempting to reconstruct military episodes. The Greek discovered that the truth was not easy to determine; he found that eyewitnesses gave "different accounts of the same proceedings, speaking out of partiality for one side or the other or else from imperfect memories."[3] Despite the drawbacks, Thucydides and his successors recognized that surveying participants provided a fuller description of events than memoirs and official records alone could ever provide.

Surgeon Baron Larrey employed similar techniques some two millennia later. Larrey investigated cases of alleged self-inflicted wounds during the 1813 Saxony campaign.[4] Nearly three thousand French soldiers, primarily young recruits, "had their hands run through by balls, or the fingers carried away" during the battles of Lutzen, Bautzen, and Wurchen.[5] Several French commanders insinuated that these men had deliberately wounded themselves in order to avoid further combat. Napoleon was prone to agree; he ordered the men sequestered in a customhouse just outside the village of Bautzen. Two French surgeons "subscribed to the self-mutilation theory, and the principal surgeon of the twelfth corps pointed to the burnt sleeves of those wounded in the forearm and to the scorched and blackened skin of those wounded in the hand as indisputable evidence."[6] An angry Napoleon directed that two of the wounded from each of the twelve corps represented be executed. Larrey, however, at the time serving as surgeon for Napoleon's Guard, disputed the finding, prompting the emperor to direct that he establish a board of inquiry consisting of five surgeons and three other officers.[7] The board spent three days examining each of the 2,632 soldiers,

> all of them wounded in the hands or fingers. . . . After a most detailed review of the wounds, the board reported that most of them had been caused by firearms, but that in the majority of cases the men had other wounds as well, or else multiple tears in their clothing due to the passage of bullets, and finally that the few to whom this did not apply were old soldiers whose devotion to duty could not be doubted. They went on to say that they believed that lack of experience in handling arms was a main reason for the high incidence of wounds in the hands in the young conscripts.[8]

Larrey's investigation did not end with an inspection of wounds, however. "Each wounded soldier made his report. The inquiry was rigid, and the result was a proof beyond doubt that all the wounds in the hands were received involuntarily."[9] The board found that as units advanced in three ranks and received the order to fire, soldiers in the second and third ranks had prematurely discharged their muskets as they raised them to engage the enemy. These early discharges struck the hands and arms of comrades in ranks to the immediate front. The board further pointed out that when assaulting heights, the hands and arms of advancing French troops were the first parts of the body exposed to fire from defenders above.[10] The condemned soldiers were spared; Larrey received the thanks of his emperor.

Two years later, Napoleon was defeated at Waterloo in a battle that would become the focus of the most extravagant effort to reconstruct a single military event in the history of war to that time.[11] The British Army granted its Lt. William Siborne an extended leave during which he gathered information for the building of two Waterloo battlefield models.[12] His research included a survey of all the battle's surviving British officer participants. This effort, completed by mail, asked respondents to identify the type of formation in which their units were formed at a precise instant in the event. Respondents were additionally asked to describe the French forces' formations at that same moment in time. Officers were further requested to draw these formations on a sketch that accompanied the questionnaire. Finally, those surveyed were provided an opportunity to include "any remarks which you may consider likely to conduce to the accuracy and fidelity of the Model."[13] Siborne received over seven hundred responses.

His first model took eight years from inception to completion. It originally appeared on display in the Egyptian Hall, Piccadilly, on October 4, 1838. William Siborne subsequently published his findings in the two-volume *History of the War in France and Flanders in 1815*. He subsequently published a detailed atlas depicting each engagement in the campaign, and in 1845 the first model was joined by a second rendition that showed another critical moment in the battle but on a larger scale.[14]

Siborne's survey procedures and his use of its responses quickly drew criticism. He was faulted for too greatly relying on British sources alone, his having not polled any of Britain's allies from Prussia, Belgium, the Netherlands, Hanover, Nassau, or Brunswick, and having contacted only one Frenchman. Perhaps most damaging were accusations of inaccuracies linked to Siborne's personal financial problems. In his analysis of Siborne, David Hamilton-Williams noted that government funding for the project was terminated in 1833 when it became apparent that Siborne intended to use its results for personal profit. The British officer thereafter secured a substantial loan of £1,500; as a result he was in "an extremely embarrassed financial situation" by 1836. Hamilton-Williams concluded that "from now on the objectivity which had marked Siborne's approach to his project became a luxury he could no longer afford. He felt constrained to enlarge the roles played by his benefactors, and correspondingly to suppress the evidence of other officers that tended to contradict those who had paid."

Hamilton-Williams backed his accusations with substantial evidence based on a review of the over seven hundred responses received by Siborne. He also provided an explanation for the lack of earlier investigations into the correspondence despite the criticisms of Siborne's contemporaries, noting that "during Siborne's lifetime, and that of his son, no one in that more honour-conscious age would have presumed so far as to ask to inspect the letters in Siborne's collection. After all, Siborne had solicited the letters with the blessing of the army Commander-in-Chief, and, as a serving officer, Siborne was a gentleman, as were all the men with whom he had corresponded. One gentleman would not seek to read the correspondence of another."[15]

Later in the nineteenth century, Col. Ardant Du Picq conducted a similar survey of his fellow French army officers. His purpose, however, was not to recreate combat events but rather to fathom the motivations underlying men's willingness to fight. Du Picq understood that it was not the nature of soldiers to confront death without reservation simply because they were ordered to do so. He believed that "absolute bravery [in the face of death] is not natural in man,"[16] and he sought to determine what factors motivated men in battle. His ultimate purpose was to train France's military leaders in the belief that "the best masters are those who know man best."[17] Du Picq recognized that his own experiences, like those of any other individual, were too limited to serve as the basis for understanding war and its impact on soldiers. He therefore created a questionnaire and distributed it to fellow combat-experienced officers of equal or subordinate rank.[18] His survey sought to determine the behavior of men in combat and the factors that influenced leaders' control over their soldiers. Among the questions used to make these determinations:

- "What happened when the troops came within the range of the enemy's cannon and rifle bullets?"
- "What was the attitude and the behavior (that is, order, disorder, cries, silence, excitement, or composure) of the officers and the soldiers on our side and on the enemy side before, during, and after the charge?"
- "Were the soldiers always manageable, had they always acted upon orders, or did they, at some moments, show a tendency to leave the ranks, either lagging behind or plunging forward?"[19]

Du Picq combined the responses to his many detailed questions with a study of history to identify what he thought were the key elements of victory in battle:

> To insure success in the rude test of conflict, it is not sufficient to have a mass composed of valiant men. . . . The mass needs . . . leaders who have the firmness and decision of command proceeding from habit. . . . We add good arms. We add methods of fighting suitable to these arms and those of the enemy and which do not overtax the physical and moral forces of man. We add also a rational decentralization that permits the direction and employment of the efforts of all even to the last man. We animate with passion . . . an iron discipline. . . . A wise organization insures that the personnel of combat groups changes as little as possible, so that comrades in peace time maneuvers shall be comrades in war.[20]

Experienced officers and maintenance of soldier relationships were essential to unit cohesion. Unit cohesion was in turn critical to battlefield success: "Soldiers, no matter how well drilled, who are assembled haphazard into companies and battalions will never have, have never had, that entire unity which is born of mutual acquaintanceship. . . . It is the infantryman on whom the battle has the most violent effect, for he is always most exposed; it is he therefore who must be the most solidly supported. Unity must be secured by a mutual acquaintanceship of long standing between all elements."[21]

The enigma of soldiers' motivations similarly spurred John Baynes to investigate the performance of men in the British army's Second Scottish Rifles (2nd Battalion, the Cameronians) during the World War I Battle of Neuve Chapelle. Baynes believed that "too few have troubled themselves overmuch with the minds and spirits of the men involved [in that war], and those who have done so have tended to simplify, and thus distort, complex motives, beliefs, aspirations, anxieties and aims in order to argue a case and bolster a prejudice. The soul of man, in all its majesty and mystery, has been dwarfed by the war game."[22]

Baynes's references included books that appeared to him "to cover aspects common to all units and men serving in the War"[23] and both published and unpublished manuscripts regarding the Cameronians. A third source of material was "the letters, notes, answers to questionnaires, and spoken comments sent or given to me by all the different people to whom I have turned for help and advice."[24] Baynes's research led to his recognition that a soldier's view regarding war varied over time, a factor critical to fully understanding man in battle: "There is the awkward fact that those who fought in the War varied in their reactions to it from sharp and real enjoyment through different frames of mind to utter loathing of every moment. . . . They probably varied within themselves many times during the course of each week they were in France. . . . Within an hour a man could easily say 'This is fun,' and 'This is hell,' and genuinely mean it both times."[25] His studies and surveys led to the conclusion that the high morale of the Second Scottish Rifles had five "main ingredients":

> First, I would place Regimental loyalty; the pride in belonging to a good battalion, in knowing other people well and being known by them; in having strong roots in a well-loved community.[26] Second, the excellent officer–other rank relationship; the high quality of the leaders, and the trust placed in them by their men; the mutual confidence and goodwill which developed in the harsh life of the trenches. Third, strong discipline; the balance between self-discipline and the imposed sort. Fourth, the sense of duty of all ranks; highly developed in the officer by his training and background; developed in the soldier both by his training and by the realization that someone else would have to do his job if he failed to do it properly himself. Fifth, sound administration, so that in spite of many difficulties the battalion was well provided with the necessities of war such as rations and ammunition. Here was the essence of the battalion's morale.[27]

Akin to Baynes's focus on a single unit was John Dollard's study of Abraham Lincoln Brigade veterans after that unit's fighting in the Spanish Civil War.[28] The "object of the research [was] to offer data which may be useful to the authorities in the American Army concerned with the fear problem."[29] Dollard's *Fear in Battle* was primarily a presentation of data regarding the sources and effects of fear on men in combat. His findings were compiled from a forty-four-page questionnaire completed by three hundred Abraham Lincoln Brigade veterans.[30] Dollard found that "seven out of ten men reported experiencing fear when going into first action" and that this "fear is greatest just before action."[31] As the soldier gained experience in combat, however, the nature of this fear changed; fear of "being a coward" in particular decreased rapidly.[32] Other fears, however, increased as a man spent more time under fire. A veteran's fear of being captured or tortured was more than twice that of the soldier in combat for the first time; the veteran feared crippling or disfiguring wounds far more than his novice associate.[33] Dollard identified the specific types of wounds men feared most (abdomen, eyes, brain, genitals), the most discomforting enemy weapons, and conditions that enhanced the effects of fear (hunger, thirst, fatigue, ignorance of plans, and idleness).[34]

Those who answered his questions firmly believed that recognizing the likelihood that one will be afraid and determining a course of action to deal with that fear better prepared a man for combat, as did realizing that others in his unit were also afraid.[35] Good leadership, understanding war aims, and self-discipline were other keys to performing well under fire.[36]

Dollard addressed several characteristics of his sample that cast doubts as to "whether these findings could be transferred from the sample at hand to a similar sample of troops in the Army of the United States"—a matter that "could be finally determined only by a parallel study of American troops after they had spent a period of time in combat."[37] These elements included (1) the all-volunteer nature of the Abraham Lincoln Brigade, (2) the related "strong sense of 'cause'" that volunteering implied, (3) the brigade's having had to fight as part of "a technically inferior army," (4) the suffering of "defeats and retreats, and heavy casualties" inflicted on its soldiers, and (5) the primarily urban background of most unit members.[38]

However, Dollard believed several conditions supported the universality of the findings drawn from his research: (1) "Fear in the face of danger is presumably a common human emotion," (2) "The fundamentals of modern war are presumably alike everywhere," and (3) "The sample is composed of very experienced men from a military standpoint. Seventy-four per cent of them had more than six months front-line experience, and fifty-eight per cent had been wounded at least once."[39]

World War II precipitated a plethora of survey efforts undertaken to understand combat performance. Within the American military the most influential of these works was that done by S. L. A. Marshall. Marshall was initially assigned to the Pacific Theater as a combat historian; later studies took him to Europe. He developed his original survey techniques during efforts to reconstruct late 1943 and early 1944 battles in the Southwest Pacific. While attempting to determine the sequence and character of events comprising a battle on Butaritari in the Gilbert Islands, Marshall at first found that "there was a general doubt that the tactical confusions of that strange night of combat would ever be clarified. Few of those who were closest to it, including the actual commanders in the battle, knew much more about it than that our men had behaved well in a difficult situation. None knew the relationship of any one combat episode to another. Even in these first hours after the fight we were already mixing up parts of the story, and as rumor got about over the island, fable was rapidly being substituted for fact."[40]

Marshall responded by developing his post-combat interview technique. Entire units were brought together and queried to reconstruct events. In his *Island Victory: The Battle for Kwajalein*, Marshall described the procedure that was to be adapted in numerous forms for later research by himself and others:

> For four days we went over and over that one night of battle, reconstituting it minute by minute from the memory of every officer and enlisted man who had taken an active part. By the end of those four days, working several hours every day, we had discovered to our amazement that every fact of the fight was procurable—that the facts lay dormant in the minds of men and officers, waiting to be developed. . . . We found that the memory of the average soldier is unusually vivid as to what he has personally heard, seen, felt and done in the battle. . . . In four days we were able to reconstruct the story of that Makin night defense.[41]

All witnesses were put on an equal footing during the interviews—an important point given that Marshall was working with a military hierarchy. Any participant could substantiate or counter any comment made during a session, and the record was not "regarded as closed at any time. If, upon being given time to refresh his memory on an incident which has already been recorded, any witness says that he recalls some new and vital fact, the record would be amended."[42]

In *Men against Fire: The Problem of Battle Command in Future War* (1947), Marshall used his post-combat interview results and personal observations to go beyond battle reconstruction. *Men against Fire* included discussion of primary group influences on men's motivations to fight, the effects of cohesion on soldier performance, and the value of weapons firing and talking as stimuli in inspiring unit effectiveness. Marshall also addressed contradictions between training, in which the enemy was generally visible when engaged, and actual fighting, during which time the adversary was, more often than not, invisible due to his efforts to avoid being shot.

Marshall's most controversial finding, however, concerned what he called the "ratio of fire," the percentage of men in a unit who used their weapons against the enemy. According to one author, the problem of men hesitating to fire had surfaced early in World War II; "reports of problems with small arms volume of fire existed as early as the Tunisian campaign [1942–1943]. Such reports increased in frequency as the fighting moved to Sicily, Italy, and into France."[43] Marshall, however, went further than identifying the problem; he quantified the shortcoming with his estimate that, on average, not more than 15 percent of a unit's soldiers ever fired their weapons and that even under the best of conditions this value never exceeded 25 percent.[44]

Marshall's ratio of fire values gained widespread acceptance outside and within the military. In addition to the use of his estimates by civilian historians, the U.S. Army adopted several of Marshall's training recommendations in the late 1950s so as to improve soldier participation. Anthony Standish cited Marshall's work frequently in his 1952 effort to determine "What makes a man a fighter or a nonfighter?"[45] Standish concluded by recommending "everything [Marshall] has devised should become standard training doctrine."[46]

As late as 1986, David Rowland used evaluations of historical battles and British training in an attempt to extend the applicability of Marshall's findings beyond World War II, noting that "there has been no general acceptance that his findings for GIs in the Second World War applied to other situations—for example modern British troops."[47] Rowland's work was "analytical, as distinct from being based on interviews," but he found the "ratio between [training] trials' results and the results of the wars studied is consistent with Marshall's participation factor of at most 15 per cent for rifle degradation."[48]

Others have more recently taken issue with Marshall's statistics. The most thoroughly researched assessment of his work is that by Roger J. Spiller. Spiller determined that the issue of ratio of fire was never directly addressed during Marshall's interviews. None of Marshall's personal correspondence provided evidence of his having collected supporting statistics. Further, John Westover, Marshall's assistant, who was normally present during the interview sessions conducted in the European theater of operations, did not remember the issue of refusal to fire ever having been addressed.[49] Spiller concluded that "the 'systematic collection of data' that made Marshall's ratio of fire so authoritative appears to have been an invention."[50]

Spiller concluded that, although Marshall believed his ratio of fire values were correct, they had their basis more in the latter's personal estimates than rigorous statistical analysis.[51] In 1993, Marshall's grandson, whom S. L. A. Marshall disowned after the younger man became a conscientious objector during the Vietnam War, wrote of a conversation between himself and Dr. Hugh Cole, a historian who had served with S. L. A. Marshall in World War II Europe. The younger Marshall described Cole's reaction to a question regarding the ratio of fire. During an interview with the historian, John Marshall asked,

> "Did Sam [Samuel L. A. Marshall] ever talk to you about how he came up with that 25 percent firing finding, where he got that number?"
> "Christ, I warned Sam!" Doc snaps. "I said to him, 'You're out of your fucking mind to pick out a percentage like that?' Sam replied, 'You don't understand. I'm just making a point.'"
> All of my senses suddenly kick in. I feel as though someone has just plugged me into an electric socket. "You mean," I say, "he didn't really have any statistics to back up that percentage?"

"No, he agreed that he didn't. He picked out something, some figure; he was making a point. He had a perception of things that other people lacked, but he was not trained in that kind of research. . . . He did what a lot do—he gave a number and believed people would believe him. And maybe he wouldn't have gotten as far without that number."[52]

In an interview some years later, Cole stated his belief that "Sam had no idea as to what precise percentage actually fired their weapons in their first engagement. . . . He was trying to make a point and the point needed making, that was clear. . . . Incidents like this had occurred and had affected the outcome of small unit engagements" in both Europe and the Pacific.[53]

Marshall may have invented his numbers, yet there was further evidence of hesitation to fire both during World War II and Korea. The Australian Army's J. O. Langtry cited S. L. A. Marshall's values and noted that "German troops during World War II and Commonwealth troops in Korea also displayed this deplorable but characteristically human failing. It was not unusual to find that up to 40–50 percent of the individuals in night ambushes in Korea failed to fire at all or produced ineffective fire as a result of firing their weapons in such a way that their position was not betrayed to the enemy by the muzzle flash of their personal weapon. The underlying reason for this apparent defection was simply active expression of the desire for self-preservation in the more psychologically inadequate individuals."[54] Maj. Gen. Hans Kissel, retired from the German Army, was another who read of Marshall's findings; he wrote that "there were also numerous 'nonshooters' in the German infantry. . . . Their percentage is unknown."[55] Whether the actual numbers of soldiers who failed to fire during World War II were close to those Marshall proposed, however, and whether those who did not fire habitually failed to do so, will likely remain a mystery.

As noted in the introduction, Marshall continued to use his post-combat interview technique during the Korean and Vietnam Wars. He concluded that improvements in the numbers of American soldiers using their weapons in Korea were in considerable part attributable to his World War II studies.[56] Using the same procedures in Vietnam, Marshall observed, "According to the data basis, the U.S. infantry line in Vietnam requires no stimulation whatever to its employment of organic weapons when engaged. The fire rate among patrols in heavy, if brief, contact is not infrequently 100 percent. Within the rifle company, during engagement prolonged for several hours, the rate will run 80 percent or more and the only nonfirers will be the rearward administrative element or the more critical cases among the early wounded."[57]

The most extensive surveys of World War II military personnel were those done under the direction of Samuel A. Stouffer.[58] One scholar has written: "Perhaps the most valuable source of information on the World War II serviceman is found in the volumes of *The American Soldier* by Samuel A. Stouffer and his associates. Never before or since have so many aspects of military life been studied so systematically."[59] The surveys included responses from over a half million soldiers; survey samples included both army ground force and air corps personnel.[60]

The results of the work completed by Stouffer and his associates were published in four volumes. The first, *The American Soldier: Adjustment to Army Life,* assessed soldier adaptation to the military environment. This initial volume considered attitudes toward service based on a soldier's preentry background, service experience, job assignment, race, and views regarding discipline and the war effort. Volume II, *The American Soldier: Combat and Its Aftermath,* was an investigation of combat performance. The analysis considered the relationships between actions in combat and soldiers' precombat attitudes, motivation, and reactions to fear, among a myriad of other factors. Additional studies regarded combat replacements, rotation issues, adaptation to post-service life, and frontline soldier attitudes toward rear-echelon personnel and civilians in the United States. In Volume III, *Experiments on Mass Communication,* the authors looked into the army's use of film. The final of the four volumes was *Measurement and Prediction,* a summary of the techniques used in the conduct of the study.

Americans were not alone in administering surveys during the Second World War. The Japanese conducted a study of their soldiers repatriated from the Chinese captivity and of deserters returned to Japanese control. Their objective in interrogating the returnees was determination of the causes of capture or of the factors that underlay breakdowns in morale and discipline that had precipitated desertion.[61]

Edward Shils and Morris Janowitz interrogated World War II prisoners of war to determine the role of unit and primary group cohesion on German Army stability.[62] Their results showed that deserters were often men who had been unable to assimilate themselves into their primary groups.[63] Factors influencing primary group solidarity included isolation (diminished face-to-face contact with other unit members), preoccupation with family, concerns for physical survival, and the weakening of Hitler as a symbol.[64] Other factors of importance were perceptions of soldierly honor, the honor of officers, and an infantry soldier's honor. Political factors were notable only in "the case of the 'hard core' minority of fervent Nazis in the German Army."[65]

World War II confirmed the value of surveys in combat-related studies. The Korean War provided further opportunity. S. L. A. Marshall's work during that conflict has been mentioned. A direct extension of his post-combat interview technique was used by G. N. Donovan, who surveyed 636 enlisted personnel representing every regiment in Korea.[66] His extensive study sought to determine "how the infantryman used his . . . weapons in Korea;

what difficulties he experienced either because of the characteristics of the weapon itself or because he was insufficiently or improperly trained; and what load of clothing and equipment he carried. . . . Half the men had come from the front lines in Korea but a few days before and were returning home on rotation; the other half were going back to Korea following hospitalization in Japan."[67] The average duration of his respondents' Korean combat service was 6.7 months.[68]

While "riflemen felt they had been adequately trained in the use of their weapons . . . men who operated crew-served weapons did not feel adequately trained."[69] Particular problems existed in matching assigned soldiers to the jobs for which they had been prepared. "A 57-mm RR [recoilless rifle] section leader said that in the six months he was in Korea only one of the 30 replacements received in his section had ever had any previous training on the 57-mm RR."[70] Donovan additionally found that procedures used in combat often varied from those taught during training in the United States. He recommended modification of stateside training to reflect the actualities of combat.

Donovan also assessed soldier combat performance. "Only one-quarter of the men questioned felt that all new men could give effective support their first time in combat. One-third of the men felt that 50 percent or more of the new men could not give effective support in their first engagement. . . . Half the men interviewed believed that in the average squad at least one man would not be fighting when he should be. . . . All agreed that if a man was close to rotation he would keep his head down the whole time."[71] A questioning of World War II officer veterans reflected a belief that the percentage of men using their weapons in combat was higher in Korea, but many agreed that at least some soldiers did not engage the enemy when they had the opportunity and responsibility to do so.[72]

Robert L. Weislogel and John C. Flanagan conducted surveys of Korean War combat veterans "to obtain data necessary for establishing standards of effective combat performance for infantry personnel for use in developing objective methods of assessing the proficiency of soldiers during . . . training, in determining troops' combat readiness, and in evaluating training."[73] The authors "collected more than 9700 factual reports of effective and ineffective combat behaviors from combat-experienced infantrymen in Korea, Japan, and the United States."[74] Their conclusions included observations that "behaviors contributing to the development and maintenance of morale and *esprit de corps* are seen as important for effective job performance at all levels" and that ineffective behaviors generally reflected deficiencies in motivation. They also concluded that their results provided a basis for establishing infantry squad job requirements for training and combat purposes.[75]

Robert L. Egbert's study to determine the causes "for the varying performance of infantrymen in combat" was another influenced by S. L. A. Marshall's work.[76] Egbert's conclusions were based on a forty-hour battery of tests administered during the autumn of 1953 to 310 combat infantrymen in Korea. The men had been designated "as good or poor combat performers" so as "to develop complete psychological descriptions of a sample of fighters and of non-fighters who served in Army combat units during the Korean hostilities."[77] A fighter tended to be:

    (1) more intelligent
    (2) more masculine
    (3) a "doer"
    (4) more socially mature
    (5) preferred socially and in combat by his peers, and tended to have
    (6) greater emotional stability
    (7) more leadership potential
    (8) better health and vitality (larger and heavier)
    (9) a more stable home life
   (10) a greater fund of military knowledge
   (11) greater speed and accuracy in manual and physical performance.[78]

Roger W. Little applied an alternative survey methodology in his Korean War study of primary groups.[79] Little limited his sample to members of a single rifle platoon—the platoon with which he lived from November 1952 through February 1953. During that period, the unit "covered three consecutive tactical situations: (1) a reserve bivouac with intensive patrol activity in forward areas; (2) a defensive position on the forward edge of the battle area with intermittent patrolling; and (3) withdrawal into reserve for retraining and the reception of replacements."[80]

Little noted the dissimilarities between the Korean War American soldier and his World War II predecessors: "First, there was a higher degree of youthful homogeneity among these troops. Ninety per cent of the platoon that the author observed were twenty-three years of age or less. . . . Second, the duration of membership in the organization was determined by a concrete measure of individual experience rather than a national goal (such as 'Victory' in World War II). . . . Third, almost one-fourth of the platoon consisted of native Korean soldiers."[81] Of the thirty-nine men in the platoon, nine were Korean soldiers who were not included in the study; the thirty Americans were interviewed and observed.

Little "talked to each [platoon member] alone at least twice, and subsequently in the presence of his companions at their positions, in the bunkers, or at chow. In the solitary interviews, he encouraged each man to talk about his 'best friends' and asked him which, if any, he considered a buddy. The men were reluctant to designate one or more specific persons as a buddy. . . . Everyone was a buddy, but one man was usually more so. . . . Buddy choices were private decisions and consequently never threatened the solidarity of the squad or platoon" though "in a crisis and if forced to make a choice, a man would think first of his loyalty to a buddy, and second of his obligations to the organization."[82] Little concluded that "buddy relationships were the basic element of infantry social organization in the Korean Conflict."[83] Interestingly, however, Little found that a man selected by another as a buddy "rarely reciprocated the choice" during private interviews.[84]

Stanley W. Davis used "psychiatric and general interviewing" in conjunction with physiological (blood, urine, and saliva) tests in the Korean autumn of 1952 "to examine the kinds and degree of physiological and psychological changes that occur as a result of the stress placed on the infantrymen by combat."[85] His team of thirteen physiologists, psychologists, and psychiatrists concluded that "the most important aspects of stressful combat experiences [were:] (1) fear of physical injury; (2) unpleasant effects associated with the unavoidable physical discomforts of battle; (3) empathy with other unit members leading to vicarious experiences of mutilation or death; (4) fear of social disapproval; (5) fear of official disapproval and its attendant punishment; and (6) fear of damage to one's self-picture."[86] "Major modifying factors" regarding stress over which the military had some element of control included leadership quality, combat experience, the soldier's ability, his morale, and interpersonal relationships within the unit.[87]

Two survey-based studies by D. G. Severin and associates sought to determine the characteristics of good combat performance.[88] The Severin research team surveyed platoon and squad noncommissioned officers regarding subordinates' aggressiveness and performance.[89] Unsurprisingly, the results reflected that both aggressiveness and quality of performance in combat were positively related to rank; in other words, the higher the rank of the enlisted man, the higher his ratings by platoon members with respect to both aggressiveness and performance in combat.[90]

The United States also conducted surveys of North Korean and Chinese prisoners of war to enhance understanding of the enemy, as had been done with captured enemy during World War II. Lessing A. Kahn used a questionnaire, albeit "a rough and ready instrument designed to elicit information on the background data of the respondent and the general effects of weapons and types of fighting on the respondent."[91] Samples included 288 Chinese and 71 North Korean enlisted men, all of whom were interviewed from twelve to twenty-four hours after capture. Air- and artillery-delivered weapons were found to "evoke the greatest number of fear reactions in the two sample groups."[92]

Harley O. Preston and his associates conducted a similar study involving interviews with 856 enemy prisoners of war and 260 American soldiers.[93] Preston studied "the general problem of psychological effects of weapons fire on Chinese Communist Forces (CCF) and North Korean Army (NKA) personnel, and specifically to discover the relationship between the performance of soldiers in Korea and their exposure to fire from different types of UN weapons. Some consideration is also given to the performance of U.S. soldiers under effective enemy fire."[94] Conclusions regarding weapons effects were analogous to those in the Kahn study: artillery, bombs, napalm, and strafing were "outstanding in producing a significant psychological effect in terms of ineffective performance by enemy soldiers."[95] The study also looked at behavioral responses to fire, one of which was surrender.

A third survey of seventy-three North Korean and forty-five Chinese prisoners of war used interviews in an effort to determine "the process by which ['small, formally organized Communist and anti-Communist groups'] were formed and how they could become so significant in the life of the prisoners and to the UN Command."[96] Survey controls were limited by the need to complete the interviews quickly; the research team arrived the day after the truce was signed on 27 July 1953. Samplings of prisoners were non-random and interview questions were not standardized. The chief of the research team, William Bradbury, "concluded that in spite of the shortcomings of the data, other available knowledge of the events under study was so meager that any information ought to be disseminated, although not of course without qualification and caution."[97]

The interviews were used in conjunction with existing U.S. Army prisoner administration and behavior reports, essay petitions from prisoners, and other pertinent written materials.[98] Researchers found that soldiers' fear of immediate punishment, their leaders' use of positive persuasion, and self-interest were of only secondary importance in explaining North Korean and Chinese courage in combat and generally disciplined behavior as prisoners of war. Interrogation and post-capture incidents, however, demonstrated that despite there positive traits, "dissatisfaction was widespread and disaffection serious" among Chinese Communist Forces in the field.[99] Analysts concluded that primary groups were a significant factor underlying these apparent contradictions. While the earlier studies of German soldiers by Shils and Janowitz involved "spontaneously interacting members," here "intra-group relations were carefully nurtured, monitored, and channeled by the Communist hierarchy through the use of a well-trained, militant cadre of activists. . . . This control of primary groups by the Communist hierarchy, coupled with the traditional way the Chinese related to those in authority, made for a highly effective and cohesive military organization."[100]

Fighting among prisoners in compounds was attributed to struggles for camp control between Communist and anti-Communist elements. "The data clearly showed that when the Chinese and for that matter the North Koreans became captives of the United Nations force, the Communist system of control had been seriously disrupted. This disruption of Communist control permitted elements hostile to Communism to emerge within the prison compounds."[101] Anti-Communist leaders used the same cohesion-building techniques that had earlier been practiced on them. In the ensuing camp struggles, "Communists were successful in gaining control in some compounds, anti-Communists in others. But whatever the political coloration of the successful leadership, the prisoners were once again transformed into cohesive and effective units."[102]

Charles Moskos used data taken from the 1964 National Opinion Research Center (NORC) to conduct a broadly based study of the Vietnam era enlisted man. This survey was "based on a 10 per cent sample of all officers and a 5 per cent sample of all enlisted men on active duty at that time, and a national sample of civilian men, 16–34 years of age."[103] Questionnaire respondents numbered over 110,000. Survey questions included items regarding "personal background, military occupation and training, occupational values, future career plans, and attitudes towards military service and the draft."[104] Queries also solicited views on volunteering for the armed forces, race relations, officer-enlisted relations, attitudes of soldiers stationed overseas, and opinions regarding Vietnam, all part of a review of selective service policies ordered by President Johnson.

Among Moskos's findings was a uniformity of views regarding Vietnam's rotation policy. He concluded that the war's fixed tour lengths led men to make personal concerns paramount, regardless of whether they were in frequent contact with the enemy or assigned to a rear area.[105] He also concluded that despite American soldiers' "general aversion to . . . overt patriotic appeals," any study of the Vietnam fighting man should not ignore the motivational power of his belief in the inherent good of American society.[106] Moskos additionally forwarded a pragmatic explanation for men's attitudes regarding buddy relationships and other primary groups. He considered them a form of "rudimentary social contract; a contract which is entered into because of advantages to individual self-interest."[107]

George A. Clum and Jack L. Mahan used questionnaires to collect data from 224 marines in basic training and 137 in their second year of service to determine predictors of combat effectiveness. They cited Stouffer, "who found that Army personnel who anticipated success in combat and who harbored little concern for being injured had high combat ratings when compared to men who doubted their ability to perform effectively and who had a great deal of apprehension about personal injury."[108] Clum and Mahan sought "to determine if attitudes can be used to predict combat effectiveness beyond the prediction afforded by background demographic information."[109] They found that marines rated highly in combat preferred infantry or reconnaissance positions, held moderate views (they neither completely agreed nor disagreed with statements regarding the Marine Corps), and felt that more individual recognition for achievement was in order. The study concluded that "attitudinal data in combination with biographical data afforded better prediction than biographical data considered alone."[110]

In addition to his finding a dramatic increase in the "ratio of fire" during post-combat interviews in Vietnam, Marshall also made observations regarding other aspects of American soldier performance. His results were published in a "Vietnam Primer: Lessons Learned" compilation of observations designed to promulgate pertinent information to U.S. forces throughout the theater. Marshall, accompanied by Lt. Col. David Hackworth, provided a summary of interview observations on fourteen topics. All had direct application to battlefield actions (e.g., "The Direct Assault," "Contending with Jungle," and "Ruses, Decoys, and Ambushes") or preparation for hostilities ("Training").[111]

George A. Magner and associates similarly sought to "make available to appropriate U.S. Army agencies information of current interest on small-unit combat actions in Vietnam."[112] Findings based on "182 detailed interviews with 471 members of twenty-nine rifle companies at company commander, platoon leader, squad leader, and fire team leader levels" covered observations on the combat environment, preparing for missions, movement to areas of operations, movements to contact, actions on enemy contact, and other topics.[113] The United States Army Military History Institute similarly interviewed selected officers regarding many aspects of their war experiences as they completed instruction at the Army War College in Carlisle Barracks, Pennsylvania. Unlike Magner's interviews, which took place in Vietnam during the war, the Military History Institute sessions were conducted several years later. The war college officers served their tours in Vietnam as lieutenants and captains; by the time of their assignment to the war college they had been promoted to lieutenant colonel.

Peter R. Prunkl and Wiley R. Boyles sought "to describe the ways in which ineffective aviators cope with combat stress."[114] Their sample included sixty-two aviators, all of whom had flown combat missions in Vietnam. Objectives of the 1968 study were to "begin developing measures of overall aviation combat effectiveness" and to test the Kern performance model, which postulated that

> after the initial period of adjustment to combat, there occurs a period of maximum effectiveness during which the individual carries out his combat missions smoothly and efficiently. After a further period of time in combat, we begin to see lapses in efficient job performance, and as time passes, these lapses become more frequent and of longer duration. As exposure continues, the individual increasingly responds to internal anticipation of bodily damage. Feelings of hopelessness for ever getting out of the situation alive become evident at this point. Physical harm threat stimuli overwhelm the individual's ability to control his environment, and he takes action to escape.[115]

The researchers concluded that Kern's model had some application to aviators if modifications were made for differences between the continuous exposure to danger for which Kern developed his model and the intermittent nature of aviator exposure. They also developed a list of factors that reflected a progression toward ineffectiveness. The list included:

(a) Number of missions aborted (air or ground)
(b) Number of unconfirmed reports of engine malfunction
(c) Number of visits to the flight surgeon in which no diagnoses could be made
(d) Isolation on a sociometric rating as an indication of withdrawal from the group[116]

CONCLUSION

Surveys of fighting men have long served to provide the details essential in reconstructing an accurate depiction of combat, establishing a basis for better understanding of why men conducted themselves as they did in that life-and-death environment, and in developing means to better prepare soldiers to fight. The result in sum has been a better understanding of how that prominent, undesirable, yet undeniable element of social intercourse called war has influenced the soldier.

> Man is the fundamental instrument in battle. Nothing can wisely be prescribed in an army—its personnel, organization, discipline and tactics, things which are connected like the fingers of a hand—without exact knowledge of the fundamental instrument, man. . . . Let us then study man in battle.[117]

Ardant Du Picq, *Battle Studies*

Appendix 2
The Survey Questionnaires

1ST CAVALRY DIVISION SURVEY

INSTRUCTION: Fill in the blanks or check the appropriate box as necessary. If you desire to make comments on a specific question and insufficient space is available, continue at the end of the survey or on additional sheets of paper. Please specify which question you are continuing by putting the number of the question where the comment started.

IMPORTANT PRELIMINARY CONDITION: If you were never stationed in Southeast Asia during the Vietnam War, or if you did not serve in a position where exposure to enemy direct fire was <u>possible</u>, check the "Does not apply" block below. You need not complete the remainder of the survey; please put it in the envelope provided and mail it. All other persons please continue with the remainder of the survey.

[ ] Does not apply
1) With what unit(s) did you serve in Vietnam (e.g., 1/18 Inf Bn, 1st Inf Div)?
2) What was your MOS/job specialty (enlisted) or branch (officer)?
3) What job assignments(s) did you hold while in Vietnam?
4) When did you serve in Vietnam (e.g., June 1965–June 1966)?
5) How did you enter the service prior to your assignment to Vietnam?
   [ ] Voluntary enlistment   [ ] Drafted
6) Where did you receive your basic training (officers give source of commission)?
7) Where did you receive your advanced individual training (enlisted only)?
8) What was <u>your</u> primary direct fire weapon during your service in Vietnam?

[ ] M16   [ ] M203   [ ] M60   [ ] .45 pistol   [ ] other (please specify)

9) How many times during your tour(s) in Vietnam did you fire your weapon to engage the enemy with direct fire?
[ ] 0   [ ] 1-5   [ ] 6-10   [ ] 11-15   [ ] 16-20   [ ] more than 20 (please specify your best estimate: ____)

10) How many times were you in a life-threatening situation due to enemy <u>direct</u> fire?
[ ] 0   [ ] 1-5   [ ] 6-10   [ ] 11-15   [ ] 16-20 [ ] more than 20 (please specify your best estimate: ____)

11) What percentage of the number of times that you were in the life-threatening situations described in question 10 did you engage the enemy with your direct fire weapon? (Place check mark or X at your estimate)
[Respondents either checked "I was never in such a situation" or marked a horizontal percentile scale.]

12) If there were times when you were in a life-threatening situation and did not fire your weapon, what were your reasons for not firing?
[ ] Does not apply   [ ] Comments follow

13) If you carried a M16 or M203, what percentage of the time did you fire in the full automatic mode? (Place check mark or X at your estimate)
[Respondents either checked "I did not carry either weapon" or marked a horizontal percentile scale.]

14) If you never engaged the enemy with your weapon, why did you not do so?
[ ] never in a situation where it was appropriate   [ ] other (please explain)

15) What type of terrain were you in when you engaged the enemy with your direct fire weapon? (Check all that apply)
[ ] I never engaged enemy   [ ] jungle   [ ] rice paddy or open area
[ ] civilian built-up area   [ ] fire base or military installation   [ ] other (please specify)

16) Did you ever see another soldier not fire his weapon in combat when he should have?
[ ] Yes   [ ] No

17) Why do you think he/they failed to fire the weapon(s) (Check all that apply)
[ ] I never saw such a situation   [ ] I don't know   [ ] fear (the soldier "froze")   [ ] moral conviction   [ ] other (please explain)

18) In situations where fellow soldiers should have placed direct fire on the enemy with <u>individual</u> weapons, what percentage normally did put out such fire? (Place check mark or X at your estimate)
[Respondents either checked "I was never in such a situation" or marked a horizontal percentile scale.]

19) In situations where fellow soldiers should have placed direct fire on the enemy with <u>crew-served</u> weapons, what percentage normally did put out such fire? (Place check mark or X at your estimate)
[Respondents either checked "I was never in such a situation" or marked a horizontal percentile scale.]

20) What percentage of the soldiers in your unit <u>regularly</u> wasted ammunition through poor fire discipline or because they were "trigger happy?" (Place check mark or X at your estimate)
[Respondents marked a horizontal percentile scale.]

21) Do you have any suggestions/comments pertaining to this questionnaire? Continue your comments on the reverse side or add sheets as necessary.
[ ] No, I have no comments   [ ] Yes, comments follow

22) Do you have any comments on how the armed services can better train its soldiers to use their weapons in combat? Continue your comments on the reverse side or add sheets as necessary.
[ ] No, I have no comments   [ ] Yes, comments follow

FORT LEAVENWORTH SURVEY

INSTRUCTION: Fill in the blanks or check the appropriate box as necessary. If you desire to make comments on a specific question and insufficient space is available, continue at the end of the survey or on additional sheets of paper. Please specify which question you are continuing by putting the number of the question where the comment started.

IMPORTANT PRELIMINARY CONDITION: If you were never stationed in Southeast Asia during the Vietnam War, or if you did not serve in a position where exposure to enemy direct fire was <u>possible</u>, check the "Does not apply" block below. You need not complete the remainder of the survey; please put it in the envelope provided and mail it. All other persons please continue with the remainder of the survey.

[ ] Does not apply

1) With what unit(s) did you serve in Vietnam (e.g. 1/18 Inf Bn, 1st Inf Div)?
2) What was your branch while assigned in Vietnam?
3) What job assignments(s) did you hold while in Vietnam?
4) When did you serve in Vietnam (e.g., June 1965–June 1966)?
5) Did you ever see a soldier not fire his weapon in combat when he should have?
   [ ] I never saw a soldier in combat (Go to question 14)   [ ] Yes   [ ] No
6) Why do you think he/they failed to fire the weapon(s)? (Check all that apply)
   [ ] I do not know   [ ] fear (the soldier "froze")   [ ] moral conviction
   [ ] other (please explain)
7) In situations where your men should have placed direct fire on the enemy with <u>individual</u> weapons, what percentage normally did put out such fire? (Place check mark or X at your estimate)
   [Respondents either checked "I never saw my men in such a situation" or marked a horizontal percentile scale.]
8) In situations where fellow soldiers should have placed direct fire on the enemy with <u>crew-served</u> weapons, what percentage normally did put out such fire? (Place check mark or X at your estimate)
   [Respondents either checked "I never saw my men in such a situation" or marked a horizontal percentile scale.]
9) During engagement, what percentage of fire can be expected from a normal body of well-trained infantry under average conditions of combat? (Place a check mark or X at your estimate)
   [Respondents either checked "I do not know" or marked a horizontal percentile scale.]

10) What type of terrain was your unit in when you engaged the enemy with direct fire weapons? (Check all that apply)

[ ] My unit never engaged the enemy with direct fire [ ] jungle [ ] rice paddy or open area [ ] civilian built-up area [ ] fire base or military installation [ ] other (please specify)

11) How many times did you see your men in a life-threatening situation due to enemy <u>direct</u> fire?

[ ] I never saw my men in such a situation (Go to question 13)

[ ] 0 [ ] 1-5 [ ] 6-10 [ ] 11-15 [ ] 16-20 [ ] more than 20 (please specify your best estimate: ___)

12) While in the life-threatening situations(s) described in question 11, what percentage of your men engaged the enemy with their direct fire weapons at least once during each such situation? (Place a check mark or X at your estimate)

[Respondents marked a horizontal percentile scale.]

13) What percentage of the soldiers in your unit <u>regularly</u> wasted ammunition through poor fire discipline or because they were "trigger happy?" (Place check mark or X at your estimate)

[Respondents marked a horizontal percentile scale.]

14) Do you have any suggestions/comments pertaining to this questionnaire? Continue your comments on the reverse side or add sheets as necessary?

[ ] No, I have no comments [ ] Yes, comments follow

15) Do you have any comments on how the armed services can better train its soldiers to use their weapons in combat? Continue your comments on the reverse side or add sheets as necessary.

[ ] No, I have no comments [ ] Yes, comments follow

Appendix 3
Selected Survey Statistics

CONTENTS

Frequency of Firing in Combat (1st Cavalry)

Training Suggestions or Comments

INTRODUCTION

The twenty-nine tables and charts that follow establish basic background data and then show, statistically, the surveyed veterans' recollections of selected aspects of combat. The final section records the surveyed veterans' observations and recommendations for improvements in training.

The survey groups are identified by the name of the survey to which they responded. Responses from Fort Leavenworth veterans who served with the 1st Cavalry Division are included only in the Fort Leavenworth statistics.

Percentages may total less or more than one hundred in the tables because of rounding or because the respondent could give to more than one response to a question (e.g., more than one type of terrain, duty position, or weapon might apply).

"Unit of service" (table 1) refers to the first combat unit to which the respondent was assigned for Fort Leavenworth veterans. In the case of 1st Cavalry Division respondents, it refers to the first combat unit in which they served with that division.

"Duty position" (tables 2 and 9c and 9d) refers to the senior or final position (e.g., squad leader if individual served as rifleman and squad leader; machine gunner if soldier had been rifleman and later transferred to machine gunner) in which the veteran served. "Enlisted—Combat Position" includes only rifleman, grenadier, assistant machine gunner, or ammunition bearer and excludes the other enlisted functions shown in table 2. Enlisted positions in which firing a weapon was not the primary task include medic, artilleryman, and engineer. Officers may have held both platoon leader and company commander positions, so the Fort Leavenworth percentages for duty position total more than one hundred.

Tours of duty (charts 4 and 5) are expressed as one calendar year or as an inclusive period of two years; a veteran who served only in 1965, for example, would be counted in the "1965 or 1965–1966" column.

Figures shown in table 10 regarding recommendations for improvements in training indicate the number of times each topic was cited by at least two respondents (by one respondent, for some selected topics).

"Other reason" entries in tables 7 and 8 refer to written-in comments.

BACKGROUND DATA

Table 1   Unit of Service

1a. 1st Cavalry Division Veterans

Unit	Number (%) of Respondents
1st Battalion/5th Cavalry	10 (4)
2nd Battalion/5th Cavalry	14 (5)
1st Battalion/7th Cavalry	27 (10)
2nd Battalion/7th Cavalry	27 (10)
5th Battalion/7th Cavalry	11 (4)
1st Battalion/8th Cavalry	25 (10)
2nd Battalion/8th Cavalry	25 (10)
1st Battalion/12th Cavalry	23 (9)
2nd Battalion/12th Cavalry	31 (12)
1st Squadron/9th Cavalry	34 (13)
Other or No Response	30 (12)

1b. Fort Leavenworth Officer Veterans

Unit	Number (%) of Respondents
1st Cavalry Division	9 (20.5)
101st Airborne Division	9 (20.5)
1st Infantry Division	4 (9.1)
4th Infantry Division	4 (9.1)
9th Infantry Division	3 (6.8)
Americal Division	3 (6.8)
25th Infantry Division	3 (6.8)
173rd Airborne Brigade	3 (6.8)
82nd Airborne Division	1 (2.3)
198th Brigade	1 (2.3)
7/17th Cavalry	1 (2.3)
1-44 Artillery	1 (2.3)
46th Engineer Battalion	1 (2.3)
169th Engineer Battalion	1 (2.3)

Chart 1   Branch or Specialty, 1st Cavalry Division Respondents

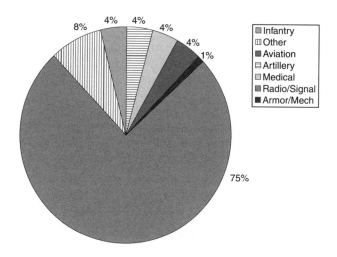

- Infantry
- Other
- Aviation
- Artillery
- Medical
- Radio/Signal
- Armor/Mech

Chart 2   Branch, Fort Leavenworth Respondents

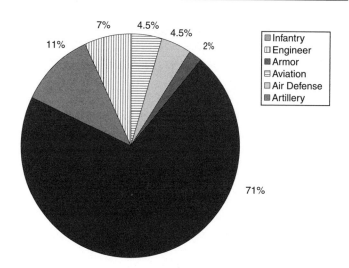

- Infantry
- Engineer
- Armor
- Aviation
- Air Defense
- Artillery

Table 2   Duty Position

Senior or final position, if veteran served in more than one (e.g., squad leader if served as rifleman and squad leader; machine gunner if rifleman later transferred to machine gunner).

2a. First Cavalry Division Veterans

Duty Position	Number (%) of Respondents
Enlisted, combat position (rifleman, grenadier, assistant machine gunner, ammunition bearer)	74 (30)
Enlisted, squad leader or platoon sergeant	70 (28)
Enlisted, machine gunner	8 (3)
Enlisted, aviation	10 (4)
Warrant officer, aviation	6 (2)
Officer, other than aviation	28 (11)
Officer, aviation	5 (2)
Enlisted, non-combat or position in which firing weapon not the primary task (e.g., medic, artilleryman, engineer)	47 (19)
No response	10 (4)

2b. Fort Leavenworth Officer Veterans

Duty Position	Number (%) of Respondents
Platoon Leader	26 (59.1)
Company Commander	31 (70.5)

Chart 3   Voluntary or Draft Enlistment, 1st Cavalry Division Respondents

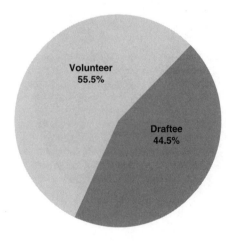

Volunteer 55.5%

Draftee 44.5%

Chart 4 Period of First Vietnam Tour, 1st Cavalry Division Respondents

Number of respondents

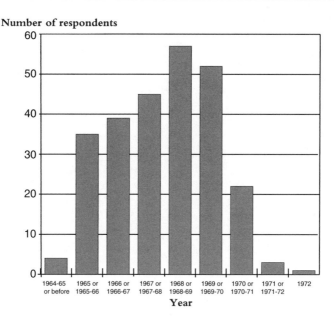

Year

Chart 5 Period of First Vietnam Tour, Fort Leavenworth Respondents

Number of respondents

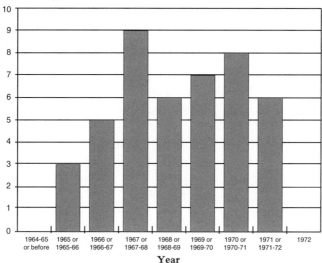

Year

Table 3   Location of Basic Training/Source of Commission, 1st Cavalry Division Respondents

Military bases where enlisted and warrant officer veterans received BCT and the sources of officer veterans' commissions. Some percentages are shown as zero due to rounding.

Location	Number (%) of Respondents
Fort Dix, New Jersey	28 (10)
Fort Leonard Wood, Missouri	26 (10)
Fort Knox, Kentucky	24 (9)
Fort Campbell, Kentucky	21 (8)
Fort Polk, Louisiana	20 (8)
Fort Benning, Georgia	19 (7)
Fort Jackson, South Carolina	18 (7)
Fort Lewis, Washington	15 (6)
Fort Ord, California	13 (5)
Fort Bliss, Texas	12 (5)
Fort Gordon, Georgia	12 (5)
Fort Bragg, North Carolina	7 (3)
Fort Carson, Colorado	3 (1)
Fort Wolters, Texas	2 (1)
Camp Chafee, Arkansas	1 (0)
Fort Hood, Texas	1 (0)
Keesler Field, Mississippi	1 (0)
Sheppard Field, Texas	1 (0)
Fort Sill, Oklahoma	1 (0)
Commission from Officer Candidate School	16 (6)
Commission from ROTC	8 (3)
Commission from United States Military Academy, West Point	2 (1)
Direct Commission	2 (1)
Commissioned in Reserves	1 (0)

Table 4   Location of Advanced Individual Training (AIT), 1st Cavalry Division Respondents

Location	Number (%) of Respondents
Fort Polk, Louisiana	64 (26)
Fort Ord, California	25 (10)
Fort Gordon, Georgia	20 (8)
Fort Jackson, South Carolina	17 (7)
Fort Lewis, Washington	14 (6)
Fort Dix, New Jersey	12 (5)
Fort Knox, Kentucky	11 (4)
Fort Sam Houston, Texas	9 (4)
Fort McClellan, Alabama	8 (3)
Fort Benning, Georgia	7 (3)
Fort Lee, Virginia	4 (2)
Fort Rucker, Alabama	4 (2)
Aberdeen Proving Grounds, Maryland	2 (1)
Fort Carson, Colorado	2 (1)
Fort Eustis, Virginia	2 (1)
Fort Leonard Wood, Missouri	2 (1)
Fort Bliss, Texas	1 (0)
Fort Bragg, North Carolina	1 (0)
Fort Campbell, Kentucky	1 (0)
Camp Holabird, Maryland	1 (0)
Fort Hood, Texas	1 (0)
Fort Monmouth, New Jersey	1 (0)
Scott Field, Illinois	1 (0)
No Response	13 (5)
Not Applicable[1]	27 (11)

[1]Most officers did not undergo AIT. Some percentages are shown as zero due to rounding.

Chart 6   Primary Weapon Carried, 1st Cavalry Division Respondents

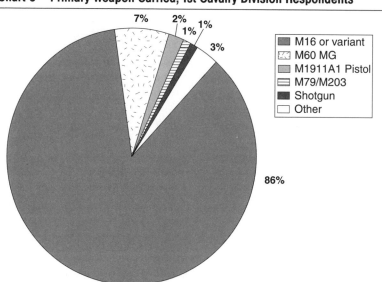

7%   2%   1%   1%   3%   86%

- M16 or variant
- M60 MG
- M1911A1 Pistol
- M79/M203
- Shotgun
- Other

Table 5   Type of Vietnam Terrain in Which Respondents Fought

Many respondents fought in more than one type of terrain.

5a. 1st Cavalry Division Respondents

Type of Terrain	Number (%)
Jungle	231 (89.5)
Rice paddy or other open terrain	189 (73.3)
Military installation or fire base	169 (65.5)
Civilian village, town, or city	85 (32.9)
Other	73 (28.3)

5b. Fort Leavenworth Respondents

Type of Terrain	Number (%)
Jungle	35 (79.5)
Rice paddy or other open terrain	29 (65.9)
Military installation OR fire base	27 (61.4)
Civilian village, town, OR city	11 (25.0)
Other	9 (20.5)

THE "NO-FIRE" ISSUE

Table 6   Responses to question: "Did veteran ever see another American soldier not fire in a situation when the fellow soldier should have fired?"

6a. 1st Cavalry Division Respondents

Saw Other Soldier Not Fire?	Number (%)
Yes	126 (48.8)
No	130 (50.4)

6b. Fort Leavenworth Respondents

Saw Other Soldier Not Fire?	Number (%)
Yes	23 (52.3)
No	18 (40.9)
Not applicable (not in position to see such an event)	3 (6.8)

Table 7　1st Cavalry Division Respondents—Reasons for veteran himself or other soldiers not firing

Percentages are based on the number of respondents who answered that they had observed another soldier not fire; some gave more than one reason.

Reason for Veteran Himself or Other Soldiers Not Firing	Number (%) Times Cited
Fear	101 (80.2)
Moral	19 (15.1)
Do Not Know	12 (9.5)
Other Reason(s)	51 (40.5)
Incoming rifle, machine gun, mortar, or other enemy fire pinned down soldier or made it impossible to return fire	39 (31.0)
Did not know where enemy was/Had no visible target	33 (26.2)
Weapon malfunction	32 (25.4)
Did not want to reveal position	29 (23.0)
Friendly forces or civilians in line of fire	28 (22.2)
Leader of unit performing other duties	20 (15.9)
Medic performing duties	10 (7.9)
Radio operator performing duties	9 (7.1)
Soldier confused or did not recognize danger	9 (7.1)
Artillery forward observer performing duties	7 (5.6)
Soldiers performing other duties (e.g., passing ammunition, resupplying machine gun; advisor, photographer)	7 (5.6)
Conscientious objector	6 (4.8)
Ran out of ammunition	5 (4.0)
Conserving ammunition	5 (4.0)
Used other means to engage enemy (e.g., artillery, helicopter fires, jet aircraft, bayonet, claymore mine, hand grenade)	4 (3.2)
"Short-timer" would not expose himself to enemy fire	3 (2.4)
Changing position or running for cover	3 (2.4)
Under influence of drugs	2 (1.6)
In a no-fire zone	2 (1.6)
In a helicopter as operator or passenger with doors closed	2 (1.6)
Did not want to attract enemy fire	2 (1.6)
Directed not to fire unless ordered or given permission to do so	2 (1.6)
Doing maintenance work while protected by infantry soldiers	1 (0.8)
Weapons locked up while soldier was in rear area	1 (0.8)
Man was a coward	1 (0.8)
Did not fire at woman in spite of her being armed	1 (0.8)
Saw enemy for first time, asked if he should fire. Subsequently was too late	1 (0.8)

Table 8   Fort Leavenworth Respondents—Reasons for another soldier not firing

Percentages are based on the number of respondents who answered that they had observed another soldier not fire; some gave more than one reason.

Reason for Other Soldiers Not Firing	Number (%) Times Cited
Fear	11 (47.8)
Moral	1 (4.3)
Do not know	1 (4.3)
Other reason(s)	15 (65.2)
Did not know where enemy was/Had no visible target	11 (47.8)
Did not want to attract enemy fire	2 (8.7)
Incoming rifle, machine gun, mortar, or other enemy fire pinned down soldier or made it impossible to return fire	1 (4.3)
Attempted to get enemy to surrender and was killed in effort	1 (4.3)

FREQUENCY OF FIRING IN COMBAT—1ST CAVALRY DIVISION

Table 9   Engaged Enemy with Personal Weapon or Machine Gun

9a. By Branch or Specialty

Branch or Specialty	Number of Times Enemy Engaged				
	0–15	16–50	51–84	85–100	>100
Infantry	62	86	12	13	12
Administration	9	6	2	1	1
Aviation	2	1	1	2	5
Medical	6	5	—	—	—
Field Artillery	5	5	1	—	—
Radio Operator/Signal	8	1	—	—	—
Armor/Mechanized	1	—	1	—	—

9b. By Branch or Specialty—Life-Threatening Situation

Values indicate the number of veterans who fired that percentage of times in life-threatening situations.

Branch or Specialty	Percentage of Times Enemy Engaged			
	0–15	16–50	51–84	85–100
Infantry	16	30	52	83
Administration	3	5	4	6
Aviation	2	—	1	8
Medical	3	1	4	2
Field artillery	1	1	3	5
Radio operator/signal	4	1	2	1
Armor/mechanized	—	1	—	1

9c. By Duty Position

Duty Position	Number of Times Enemy Engaged				
	0–15	16–50	51–84	85–100	>100
Enlisted, combat position	27	34	2	6	5
Enlisted, squad leader or platoon sergeant	18	35	7	7	3
Enlisted, machine gunner	1	5	1	—	1
Enlisted, aviation	3	2	1	1	3
Warrant officer, aviation	1	—	1	1	3
Officer, other than aviation	17	8	1	1	1
Officer–aviation	1	2	1	—	1
Enlisted, non-combat or position in which firing weapon not the primary task (e.g., medic, artilleryman, engineer)	26	19	2	—	—

9d. By Duty Position—Life-Threatening Situation

Percentage of times veteran himself engaged enemy with personal weapon or machine gun when in life-threatening situation. Values indicate the number of veterans who fired that percentage of times in life-threatening situations.

Duty Position	Percentage of Times Enemy Engaged			
	0–15	16–50	51–84	85–100
Enlisted, combat position	9	11	24	29
Enlisted, squad leader or platoon sergeant	3	11	19	36
Enlisted, machine gunner	—	1	—	6
Enlisted–Aviation	—	—	2	8
Warrant officer, aviation	1	—	—	5
Officer, other than aviation	5	4	10	9
Officer, aviation	1	—	1	3
Enlisted, noncombat or position in which firing weapon not the primary task (e.g., medic, artilleryman, engineer)	10	11	12	10

9e. By Primary Weapon Carried

Primary Weapon Carried	Number of Times Enemy Engaged				
	0–15	16–50	51–84	85–100	>100
M16 (or early variant)	86	99	12	12	10
M60	2	6	3	3	4
M1911A1 .45 caliber pistol	5	—	—	—	1
M79/M203	1	1	—	1	—
Shotgun	1	1	—	—	1
Other	2	1	1	1	2

9f. By Primary Weapon Carried—Life-Threatening Situation

Percentage of times veteran himself engaged enemy with personal weapon or machine gun when in a life-threatening situation. Values indicate the number of veterans who fired that percentage of times in life-threatening situations.

Primary Weapon Carried	Percentage of Times Enemy Engaged			
	0–15	16–50	51–84	85–100
M16 (or early variant)	25	39	61	88
M60	—	—	3	15
M1911A1 .45 caliber pistol	3	2	1	—
M79/M203	—	—	—	3
Shotgun	1	—	1	1
Other	1	—	1	4

9g. By Enlistment as Volunteer or Draftee

	Number of Times Enemy Engaged				
Voluntary Enlistment or Drafted	**0–15**	**16–50**	**51–84**	**85–100**	**>100**
Volunteer	54	62	8	9	9
Draftee	43	46	8	8	9

9h. By Enlistment as Volunteer or Draftee

Percentage of times veteran himself engaged enemy with personal weapon or machine gun when in a life-threatening situation. Values indicate the number of veterans who fired that percentage of times in life-threatening situations.

	Percentage of Times Enemy Engaged			
Voluntary Enlistment or Drafted	**0–15**	**16–50**	**51–84**	**85–100**
Volunteer	16	19	38	96
Draftee	14	22	30	46

9i. By First Vietnam Tour

	Number of Times Enemy Engaged				
Period of First Tour	**0–15**	**16–50**	**51–84**	**85–100**	**>100**
1964–65 or before	1	3	—	—	—
1965 or 1965–66	13	16	—	2	4
1966 or 1966–67	20	14	2	2	1
1967 or 1967–68	19	14	5	5	2
1968 or 1968–69	11	30	5	3	7
1969 or 1969–70	18	24	3	4	3
1970 or 1970–71	13	7	2	1	—
1971 or 1971–72	1	1	—	—	1
1972	1	—	—	—	—

9j. By First Vietnam Tour

Percentage of times veteran himself engaged enemy with personal weapon or machine gun when in a life-threatening situation. Values indicate number of veterans who fired that percentage of times in life-threatening situations.

	Percentage of Times Enemy Engaged			
Period of First Tour	**0–15**	**16–50**	**51–84**	**85–100**
1964–65 or before	1	1	2	—
1965 or 1965–66	4	7	7	17
1966 or 1966–67	3	10	7	17
1967 or 1967–68	5	6	10	22
1968 or 1968–69	6	7	18	24
1969 or 1969–70	5	8	18	20
1970 or 1970–71	5	2	6	9
1971 or 1971–72	1	—	—	2

TRAINING SUGGESTIONS OR COMMENTS

Table 10   Training Suggestions or Comments—1st Cavalry Division and Fort Leavenworth Respondents

A synthesis of training suggestions and comments by both survey groups, the table includes all suggestions cited two or more times and selected topics cited once. Values indicate the total number of times a suggestion or comment relating to the topic was made.

	Survey	
Training suggestion or comment	1st Cavalry Division	Fort Leavenworth
Stress basic marksmanship training and/or fire discipline	28	5
Train with weapons other than soldier's own personal weapon [include training with enemy weapons]	19 [7]	—
Train in more than weapons use (e.g., map reading, call for artillery fire, tactics, patrolling, target location)	14	—
Train in similar terrain or environment	13	4
Provide better leader training	12	4
Train in "quick kill" techniques (e.g., hip shooting); use pop-up targets, reaction drills, or live fire courses	11	5
Emphasize weapons and ammunition maintenance	11	1
Train as a unit; use squad drills	9	9
Training as provided was sufficient	9	—
Use combat veterans as trainers	8	—
Simulate firing at or actually fire toward soldiers during training	7	3
Train with proper weapon in Basic and AIT (comment primarily from soldiers trained on M14 in U.S. but issued M16 on arrival in Vietnam)	5	—
Include mental preparation for combat	5	—
Use MILES during training	5	1
Stress importance of keeping fire low when putting out high volume of fire (train soldiers to use "grazing fire")	4	—
Restrict or do not use full automatic	4	2
Train more in methods to clear jammed weapons, to include training when visibility limited or when blindfolded	4	—
Better train rear area soldiers in weapons use and how to suppress enemy fire	4	—
Provide more refresher training for units or newly arrived soldiers	4	—
Replace units, not individuals, after training	3	1
Better train for night combat	3	—
Use known distance ranges[1]	3	1
Train in enemy soldier identification	3	—
Use more rounds for weapons qualification and other weapons training	2	—
Teach soldiers to beat enemy, not fear him	1	—
Provide refresher training for soldiers changing jobs (especially those from rear area)	1	—
Train soldiers in proper actions to take when front of column is attacked (Do not fire to front and hit fellow soldiers)	1	—
Train to engage targets at longer ranges	1	1
Better training in placement of crew-served weapons during fire fights	1	—

[1]Known distance ranges were used for weapons qualification prior to the introduction of pop-up targets. A target positioned at a known distance was raised. The soldier fired to hit a bull's-eye. Thereafter the target was lowered and the soldier was shown his results.

Notes

CHAPTER 1. Introduction: Your presence is requested . . .

1. S. L. A. Marshall, *Men Against Fire: The Problem of Battle Command in Future War* (Glouces-ter, Mass.: Peter Smith, 1978), 78.

2. For example, see Russell F. Wrigley, *Eisenhower's Lieutenants: The Campaign of France and Germany, 1944–1945* (Bloomington: Indiana University Press, 1981), 26; and John En-glish, *On Infantry* (New York: Praeger, 1984), 145 and 154.

3. Frederic Smoler, "The Secret of the Soldiers Who Didn't Shoot," *American Heritage* 40 (March 1989): 45.

4. George MacDonald Fraser, *Quartered Safe Out Here: A Recollection of the War in Burma* (London: Harvill, 1993), 118.

5. Roy E. Moore, "Shoot, Soldier," *Infantry Journal* 56 (December 1945): 21; and Milton H. Mater, "If Shooting Is a Problem, Forces Should Find Out Why," *Army* 39 (September 1989): 17–18.

6. For example, Lucian Truscott noted hesitancy to fire in his World War II memoir *Command Missions* (Novato, Calif.: Presidio, 1990).

7. Marshall's ratio of fire values appeared in periodical and book form that year.

8. Russell W. Glenn, "Men Against Fire in Vietnam." Monograph, School of Advanced Mili-tary Studies, Fort Leavenworth, Kans., 1987. Articles drawing on this research appeared as "Men and Fire in Vietnam," *Army* 39 (April 1989): 18–27, and "Men and Fire in Vietnam: Why They Didn't Shoot," *Army* 39 (May 1989): 38–45.

9. See S. L. A. Marshall, "Commentary on Infantry Operations and Weapons Usage in Ko-rea," Operations Research Office, The Johns Hopkins University, 27 October 1951; and S. L. A. Marshall, "Vietnam Primer" (Sims, Ark.: Lancer Militaria), undated, 15.

10. Spiller's findings were published in 1988. See Roger J. Spiller, "S. L. A. Marshall and the Ratio of Fire," *Journal of the Royal United Service Institution* 133 (December 1988): 63–71. Dr. Spiller's findings are discussed in greater detail in appendix 1.

11. Craig M. Cameron, *American Samurai: Myth, Imagination, and the Conduct of Battle in the First Marine Division, 1941–1951* (New York: Cambridge University Press, 1994), 249.

12. Paul Fussell, speaking at Fort Leavenworth, Kans., 7 April 1995.

13. The veterans sought were those who were regularly with infantry units during operations away from firebases and base camps.

14. The author does not distinguish between "officers" and "soldiers" or "marines" in this manuscript. All members of the army were soldiers; all those in the Marine Corps were marines. The 1st Cavalry Division survey is reproduced in appendix 2.

15. Richard M. Swain interview with author at Fort Leavenworth, Kans., 20 December 1996.

16. Anne Firor Scott, "One Woman's Experience of World War II," *The Journal of American History* 77 (September 1990): 561.

17. Tim Millar of the 1st Cavalry Division Association supplied the names of his organization's members who had served with combat units during the Vietnam War. From this list, five hundred names were randomly selected to receive the survey mailing. Just under 52 percent responded. A handful of the responses could not be used. Three were from veterans who had not served with the 1st Cavalry Division in Vietnam. Two others were not completed in a manner that allowed use. Statistics derived from both the 1st Cavalry Division survey and the Fort Leavenworth officer survey (see note 18) differed slightly from those cited in earlier works by the author. This study incorporates late responses not included in those efforts.

18. The Fort Leavenworth survey is reproduced in appendix 2.

19. See chart 3, appendix 3.

20. Paul L. Savage and Richard A. Gabriel, "Cohesion and Disintegration in the American Army: An Alternative Perspective," in *The Military in America: From the Colonial Era to the Present,* ed. Peter Karsten (New York: The Free Press, 1980), 418–19.

21. Some of these tours were cut short by wounds received in action and other injuries, illness, or causes.

22. The total exceeds 100 percent because some officers served both as platoon leaders and as company commanders.

23. The following description of the 1st Cavalry Division's evolution as an airmobile unit is largely taken from Shelby L. Stanton, *Anatomy of a Division: The 1st Cav in Vietnam* (Novato, Calif.: Presidio, 1982), 27–40.

24. Men who had served prior tours in Vietnam in many cases were not eligible for reassignment to the theater at the time of the division's deployment.

25. Pilot shortages were not limited to army units. The marines were similarly plagued with a lack of those qualified to operate aircraft. See Jack Shulimson, Leonard A. Blasiol, Charles R. Smith, and David A. Dawson, *U.S. Marines in Vietnam: The Defining Year, 1968* (Washington, D.C.: Headquarters, United States Marine Corps, 1997), 570.

26. Stanton, *Anatomy of a Division,* 37.

27. J. D. Coleman, ed., *1st Air Cavalry Division: Memoirs of the First Team, Vietnam, August 1965–December 1969,* undated, 26.

28. Stanton, *Anatomy of a Division,* 43.

29. Information in this table is taken from J. D. Coleman, *Pleiku: The Dawn of Helicopter Warfare in Vietnam* (New York: St. Martin's Press, 1988), 36 and 279–81, and Stanton, *Anatomy of a Division,* 253–55.

30. Harold G. Moore and Joseph L. Galloway, *We Were Soldiers Once . . . And Young: Ia Drang: The Battle That Changed the War in Vietnam* (New York: Random House, 1992), 51.

31. Moore and Galloway, *We Were Soldiers Once,* 63.

32. Joseph L. Galloway, "Vietnam Story," *U.S. News & World Report,* 29 October 1990, 47.

33. "Operation Report on Lessons Learned, Headquarters, 1st Cavalry Division (Airmobile) for period ending 31 Oct 66," 22 November 1966, 21–22; "Operational Report—Lessons Learned, HQ, 1st Cavalry Division (Airmobile)," 20 April 1967, 22; and "Seven Month History and Briefing Data (September–March 1966)," Headquarters, 1st Air Cavalry Division, 9 June 1967, 12.

34. Shulimson et al., *U.S. Marines in Vietnam, 1968,* 108.

35. Phillip B. Davidson, *Vietnam at War: The History 1946–1975* (Novato, Calif.: Presidio, 1988), 625; and Stanton, *Anatomy of a Division,* 177–78.

36. Ibid.

37. "Operational Report—Lessons Learned, Headquarters, 1st Cavalry Division (Airmobile), for period ending 31 January 1969," 6 June 1969, 33.

38. "After Action Report—Keystone Robin Charlie," Headquarters, 1st Cavalry Division (Airmobile), 15 April 1971, cover letter and pages 1–2.

39. Ibid., D-1-1; and Stanton, *Anatomy of a Division*, 241.

40. The number of personnel had to be reduced in accordance with the prevailing national troop reduction policy. "After Action Report—Keystone Robin Charlie," D-1. Squad strength from "Rifle Co, Inf Bn, Airmobile Div or Rifle Co, Airborne Inf Bn, Airmobile Div (TOE 7-57T)," undated. Provided to author by Lt. Gen. Harold G. Moore, USA (ret.).

41. Ibid., 244.

42. Vietnam casualty statistics were provided by Arthur J. Junot, Executive Director, 1st Cavalry Division Association, during a telephone conversation with the author, 17 July 1995. The exact number of 1st Cavalry Division soldiers wounded in action during the Vietnam War was 20,070; another 4,469 men were killed in combat.

    For information regarding 1st Cavalry Division casualties during the Korean War, see "Battle Casualties of the United States Army," Office of the Assistant Chief of Staff, G-1, Department of the Army, 31 March 1954. The division lost 2,812 KIA and 12,374 WIA in that conflict.

43. Between 18 September 1965, when the division was committed to action, and 26 June 1972, when its 3rd Brigade left Vietnam—a total of 2,475 days—4,469 1st Cavalry Division soldiers were killed in action. Thus the average number of deaths per day caused by enemy action was 1.81—nearly two men per twenty-four-hour period. These values do not include soldiers who died of nonbattle causes, such as disease, accidents, or other events not directly attributable to enemy action.

44. Thomas C. Thayer, *War Without Fronts: The American Experience in Vietnam* (Boulder, CO: Westview Press, 1985), 11–13. The lack of records available at the time of writing made it impossible to determine trends in NVA and Vietcong casualties.

45. Ibid., 116.

46. Ibid., 34 and 37; and "Study of the 12-month Vietnam Tour," Office of the Deputy Chief of Staff for Personnel, Washington, D.C., 7 June 1974, 2.

47. Thayer, *War Without Fronts,* 119.

48. Shulimson et al., *U.S. Marines in Vietnam, 1968,* 572 and 756.

49. Thayer, *War Without Fronts*, 33. The formal name of the People's Republic of Vietnam regular army was the People's Army of Vietnam (PAVN). The author has chosen to use the term used by most American soldiers during the war, North Vietnamese army (NVA).

50. The 1st Cavalry Division, however, met North Vietnamese army forces very soon after arriving in South Vietnam, fighting such a force during the Ia Drang campaign in November 1965.

51. Thayer, *War Without Fronts,* 44–45. Vietcong and NVA attacks in the period 1965–72 were as follows:

Type of attack	1965	1966	1967	1968	1969	1970	1971	1972
Battalion-size or greater	73	44	54	126	34	13	2	106
Total ground attacks	685	906	1538	1500	1615	1770	1615	2429
% ground attacks greater than battalion strength[a]	10.7	4.9	3.5	8.4	2.1	0.7	0.1	4.4
Mortar or artillery attacks[b]	—	32	992	2410	2237	1630	1009	4074

[a]The increase in large-scale attacks during 1968 was due to enemy attacks during the Tet offensive of that year. The upsurge in battalion-size or larger attacks in 1972 came as American forces were leaving Vietnam and enemy forces stepped up assaults on Republic of Vietnam units.

[b]"Mortar or artillery attacks" values include enemy attacks during which only indirect fire weapons were used and twenty or more rounds were fired. As this definition of "attack" was adopted late in 1966, many such attacks in 1965 and 1966 went unrecorded.

52. Thayer, *War Without Fronts,* 117.
53. Spurgeon Neel, *Medical Support of the U.S. Army in Vietnam, 1965–1970* (Washington, D.C.: Department of the Army, 1973), 173.
54. Guenter Lewy, *America in Vietnam* (New York: Oxford University Press, 1978), 82–83 and Thayer, *War Without Fronts,* 91–93.
55. Robert Thompson, *No Exit From Vietnam* (New York: David McKay, 1969), 135.
56. Department of State response to Question 7, National Security Study Memorandum 1, 21 January 1969.
57. Shulimson et al., *U.S. Marines in Vietnam, 1968,* 576.

F. J. West, writing for RAND, disagreed with the conclusion that U.S. casualties were dictated by the enemy's willingness to fight. He concluded that

it has frequently been asserted without proper qualification that the enemy can control both its own and U.S. levels of fatalities. . . . However, at least 80 percent of U.S. fatalities are associated with U.S. offensive actions. This point has been refuted by the assertion that the enemy can engage or disengage at its choosing even when we are on an offensive operation, thereby controlling our fatalities. Empirical evidence from the Quang Nam case study, however, has indicated that for a sample of 1,154 fighting engagements, U.S. fatalities occurred in 58 situations, whereas enemy fatalities occurred in 211. The hypothesis is offered that the enemy cannot be credited with unilateral control of fatalities: In 198 of those situations the enemy was attrited without inflicting any fatalities on U.S. troops.

See F. J. West, "U.S. Fatalities during Vietnamization: Part I, Overview," prepared by the RAND Corporation for the Advanced Research Projects Agency, June 1970, 10. It should be noted that West's analysis was based on his study of a single province (Quang Nam, which ranked second in U.S. combat deaths between January 1967 and December 1972) during seven months of 1969. His conclusions were therefore (1) based on observations made after 1968, during the period when Thayer concluded that American forces had begun to erode the enemy's disproportionate advantage in initiating engagements, and (2) limited to a single geographic area and relatively short time span.

58. Thayer, *War Without Fronts,* 113. Soldiers' deaths in combat during their first three months in-country were 11,502 for the period considered; 14,248 members of the U.S. Army were killed in action during the final nine months of their tours in Vietnam. Therefore 45 percent of soldier deaths in combat were during the first quarter of a twelve-month tour.
59. Many veterans have been quoted in the following pages. Their exact words were modified only in cases where grammar, spelling, or structure were such that they would have interfered with the reader's understanding or unduly embarrassed the original writer.

CHAPTER 2. Soldiers and Their Weapons: Choose Your Partners

1. First Cavalry Division respondent 123. Emphasis in original.
2. Despite the shortcomings sometimes associated with carrying the longer weapon, many in positions authorized a .45-caliber pistol opted to carry the M16 instead of, or in addition to, the sidearm.
3. "Tactical Employment of the M79 Grenade Launcher," Developmental Bulletin No. 2-62, United States Marine Corps Schools, undated, 1; and Weapons Department, United States Army Infantry School, "The M79." *Infantry* 53 (March–April 1963): 31–40.
4. Jac Weller noted the close-range ineffectiveness of the M79 with the high-explosive round due to its 15-meter arming distance. He also commented that "buckshot rounds are the obvious answer, but for some reason, they have not been as efficient as they should be. I opened several in Vietnam and always found only 20 pellets, size number 4 buckshot. The *Remington* 12-gauge, three-inch Magnum cartridge has 41. The *M79* has more than twice the bore diameter of a 12-gauge shotgun. . . . Some arrangement for delivering more number 4 buckshot pellets, limited only by the recoil that a man could stand, would

appear to be desirable." See Jac Weller, "Good and Bad Weapons for Vietnam," *Military Review* 48 (October 1968): 57–58.

5. First Cavalry Division respondent 198.

6. "Interviews on Small Unit Combat Actions in Vietnam, Annex H: Interviews with Members of Cavalry Battalion No. 8," prepared by the Human Resources Research Office, The George Washington University, for the Department of the Army, fall 1966, 365.

7. United States Army Military History Institute, Company Commander in Vietnam Collection, Carlisle Barracks, Pa. Interview with Thomas G. Rhame, conducted by Michael E. Ekman, 1981.

8. First Cavalry Division respondent 160.

9. First Cavalry Division respondent 144.

10. "Interviews on Small Unit Combat Actions in Vietnam, Annex I: Interviews with Members of Cavalry Battalion No. 9," prepared by the Human Resources Research Office, The George Washington University, for the Department of the Army, fall 1966, 34.

11. M16/grenade launcher combinations such as the XM-148 or M203 were nicknamed "Over and Unders," the "over" referring to the M16 rifle barrel above, the "under" to the grenade launcher attached beneath.

12. "Final Report: XM-148 Grenade Launcher." Report prepared by the Department of the Army, Army Concept Team in Vietnam, 8 May 1967, 23 and 27–28. Responses regarding weapons combinations preferred were:

	M16/ XM-148	CAR15/ XM-148	M79/ .45	M79/ Other Wpn	M16/ Hand Grenade
In thick vegetation:					
Officer	3	2	8	0	2
NCO	10	1	22	3	2
Grenadier	59	8	43	11	20
Other	2	0	2	1	1
In open terrain:					
Officer	2	1	9	1	0
NCO	10	3	14	8	1
Grenadier	90	1	27	21	2
Other	2	0	2	0	0

13. "Final Report," 23.

14. See Thomas M. Johnson, "The Contenders," *Infantry* 56 (July–August 1966): 44, for a comparison of M14 and M16 characteristics.

15. Henry R. Shelton, "The M-16 Rifle: Decade of Evolution 1957–1967," U.S. Army War College Research Element, 3 March 1969, 28.

16. Shelton, "M-16 Rifle," 8. The rifle went through several changes in name and modifications in design that were typical for new weapon systems. The AR15 was followed in turn by the following nomenclatures: XM16E1, M16A, and M16A1; however, the weapon was generally known simply as the M16 after its adoption as the basic rifleman's weapon. See "Report of the Special Subcommittee on the M-16 Rifle Program," prepared by the Committee on Armed Services, House of Representatives, Ninetieth Congress, 19 October 1967, 5321.

17. "Report of the Special Subcommittee on the M-16 Rifle Program," 5322.

18. "Report of the Special Subcommittee on the M-16 Rifle Program," 5327, and Thomas L. McNaugher, *The M16 Controversies: Military Organizations and Weapons Acquisition* (New York: Praeger, 1984), 31.

19. "Rifle Evaluation Study," United States Army Infantry Combat Developments Agency, Fort Benning, Ga., 8 December 1962, II-E-8.

20. Thomas L. McNaugher, "Marksmanship, McNamara and the M16 Rifle: Organizations, Analysis and Weapons Acquisition," The RAND Corporation, March 1979, 34–35; and "Report of the Special Subcommittee on the M-16 Rifle Program," 5329–30.

21. Thomas L. McNaugher, "Marksmanship, McNamara and the M16 Rifle," 36.

22. Shelton, "M-16 Rifle," 33–34.

23. Thomas L. McNaugher, "Marksmanship, McNamara and the M16 Rifle," 44.

24. James R. Ebert, A Life in a Year: The American Infantryman in Vietnam, 1965–1972 (Novato, Calif.: Presidio Press, 1995). 68. Ebert states that the division was "issued M16 rifles only ten days prior to its departure."

25. The "Report of the Special Subcommittee on the M-16 Rifle Program" noted this point in its findings. Included in the many deficiencies it identified with regard to fielding and maintaining the weapon was the "shortage of officers and NCOs who knew anything about maintenance of the rifle," 5344.

26. Quoted in Moore and Galloway, We Were Soldiers Once, 197–98. William C. Westmoreland wrote that Moore's words were "Brave soldiers and the M16 brought this victory." William C. Westmoreland, A Soldier Reports (New York: Dell, 1980), 205.

27. "Report of the Special Subcommittee on the M-16 Rifle Program," 5370. Also see Shelton, "M-16 rifle," 29.

28. First Cavalry Division respondent 96.

29. First Cavalry Division respondent 245.

30. "The first USAWECOM [United States Army Weapons Command] survey team stayed in Vietnam from 21 October 1966 until 2 December 1966. . . . The team taught maintenance in every major USARV [United States Army, Vietnam] unit except the 1st Air Cavalry Division." The report provided no explanation for the failure to visit the 1st Cavalry Division. "Report of the M16 Rifle Review Panel: History of the M16 Weapon System," Office of the Director of Weapons Systems Analysis, Office of the Chief of Staff of the Army, 1 June 1968, D-77. See also Shelton, "M-16 Rifle," 34.

31. Franklin D. Miller, Reflections of a Warrior (Novato, Calif.: Presidio, 1991), 21. Emphasis in original.

32. Keith William Nolan, The Magnificent Bastards: The Joint Army–Marine Defense of Dong Ha, 1968 (New York: Dell, 1994), 105.

33. Shulimson et al., U.S. Marines in Vietnam, 1968, 202.

34. First Cavalry Division respondent 181. The veteran meant magazines rather than "clips."

35. First Cavalry Division respondent 194.

36. Ibid.

37. First Cavalry Division respondent 29.

38. First Cavalry Division respondent 223.

39. Steve Siegel telephone interview with author, 17 December 1996.

40. "Rifle Evaluation Study," II-E-8.

41. Paddy Griffith, Forward into Battle: Fighting Tactics from Waterloo to Vietnam (Chichester, UK: Antony Bird, 1981), 31. Bruce W. Farcau cited interesting evidence that the soldiers of at least one side preferred the rifles of their adversaries during the 1932–35 Chaco War. When a Paraguayan commander visited the front lines he "noted that beside each Bolivian body had been laid a Paraguayan Mauser rifle. He thought this odd until a staff officer explained that his men much preferred the Bolivian Vickers rifle." Bruce W. Farcau, The Chaco War: Bolivia and Paraguay, 1932–1935 (Westport, Conn.: Praeger, 1996), 134.

42. Machine gun ammunition bearers generally carried an M16, while the assistant gunner, as has been noted, generally carried the .45-caliber pistol. Material regarding rifle platoon organization from "Rifle Co, Inf Bn, Airmobile Div or Rifle Co, Airborne Inf Bn, Airmobile Div (TOE 7-57T)," undated.

43. First Cavalry Division respondent 204. Emphasis in original.

44. J. D. Coleman telephone interview with author, 7 October 1996.

45. A starter belt was a short belt of ammunition carried with its first round chambered in the M60. The gun was therefore ready for immediate firing should an enemy be confronted unexpectedly.

CHAPTER 3. Engaging the Enemy: Allow me to introduce . . .

1. Faris R. Kirkland et al., "The Human Dimension in Force Projection: Discipline under Fire," *Military Review* 76 (March–April 1996): 62.

2. Truscott, *Command Missions,* 534–35. Truscott first published his book in 1954, after S. L. A. Marshall published articles and a chapter in *Men Against Fire* on the subject of hesitancy to fire. Whether Marshall's work is what Truscott referred to as "our investigation" is unknown; *Command Missions* had no footnote on the issue nor was it published with bibliographic references.

3. Marshall, *Men Against Fire,* 54 and 57.

4. Ibid., 57.

5. Ibid., 71.

6. Ibid., 78.

7. Samuel A. Stouffer et al., *The American Soldier: Combat and its Aftermath,* vol. 2 (Princeton, N.J.: Princeton University Press, 1949), 283.

8. Martin Blumenson, "Did 'Slam' Guess at Fire Ratios? Probably: A Legend Remembered," *Army* 39 (June 1989): 16–21.

9. Francis C. Steckel, "Morale and Men: A Study of the American Soldier in World War II." Dissertation, Temple University, Philadelphia, 1990, 216.

10. Spiller, "S. L. A. Marshall and the Ratio of Fire," 69. See also Smoler, "The Secret of the Soldiers Who Didn't Shoot," *American Heritage* 40 (March 1989): 36–45, and letters regarding the Smoler article in the May/June, July/August, and September/October issues of that publication.

11. Ebert, *Life in a Year,* 111.

12. Ibid., 138 and 111.

13. S. W. Ranson, "The normal battle reaction: Its relation to pathologic battle reaction," *The Bulletin of the U.S. Army Medical Department* 9 (1949): 4.

14. Ibid.

15. Dave Grossman, *On Killing: The Psychological Cost of Learning to Kill in War and Society* (New York: Little, Brown, 1995), 10 and 19.

16. Ibid., 19.

17. Ibid., 10.

18. Jay Luvaas, ed., *Frederick the Great on the Art of War* (New York: The Free Press, 1966), 77.

19. Ardant Du Picq, *Battle Studies: Ancient and Modern Battle,* trans. John N. Greely and Robert C. Cotton (Fort Leavenworth, Kans.: Combat Studies Institute, 1946), 245–48.

20. Earl J. Hess, *The Union Soldier in Battle: Enduring the Ordeal of Combat* (Lawrence: University Press of Kansas, 1997), 23.

21. Steckel, "Morale and men," 213.

22. Robert Mason, *Chickenhawk* (London: Corgi, 1984), 63.

23. D. E. Bonsper, "The LP Doesn't Answer," *Marine Corps Gazette* 69 (August 1985): 27.

24. Perry D. Jamieson, *Crossing the Deadly Ground: United States Army Tactics, 1865–1899* (Tuscaloosa: The University of Alabama Press, 1994), 147–48.

25. George S. Patton, *War As I Knew It* (New York: Bantam, 1981), 321.

26. J. Glenn Gray, *The Warriors: Reflections on Men in Battle* (New York: Harper & Row, 1970), 51, 54–55, and 56–57.

27. Ernie Pyle, *Brave Men* (New York: Henry Holt, 1944), 135.

28. Gray, *Warriors*, 102.

29. John Ellis, *Sharp End: The Fighting Man in World War II* (New York: Charles Scribner's Sons, 1980), 102.

30. Steckel, "Morale and men," 210.

31. Bradford Perkins, "Impressions of Wartime," *The Journal of American History* 77 (September 1990): 566.

32. John Dollard, *Fear in Battle* (Washington, D.C.: The Infantry Journal, 1944), 48 and 50.

33. Gray, *Warriors*, 137.

34. E. B. Sledge, *With the Old Breed at Peleliu and Okinawa* (New York: Bantam, 1983), 37–38.

35. Benjamin de Leon. Session with Seminar Four, School of Advanced Military Studies, Command and General Staff College, Fort Leavenworth, Kans., 29 April 1996.

36. Jones, *War Psychiatry*, 301.

37. Farley Mowat, *The Regiment* (Toronto: McClelland and Stewart, 1973), 83–84. Emphasis in original.

38. First Cavalry Division respondent 81.

39. Du Picq, *Battle Studies*, 250.

40. Ibid., 71–72.

41. Maurice de Saxe, "My Reveries upon the Art of War," in *Roots of Strategy: The Five Greatest Military Classics of All Time*, ed. and trans. Thomas R. Phillips (Harrisburg, Pa.: Stackpole, 1985), 190.

42. Dollard, *Fear in Battle*, 9.

43. Marshall, *Men Against Fire*, 71.

44. Ebert, *Life in a Year*, 234.

45. Detailed statistics are in appendix 3. The nine who did not fire during their time in Vietnam held the following positions: medic (2), aircraft mechanic, legal clerk, chaplain, radioman (in a headquarters), an artillery forward observer, an infantry squad leader, and an infantry platoon leader.

46. "Interviews on Small Unit Combat Actions in Vietnam, Annex G: Interviews with Members of Cavalry Battalion No. 7." Prepared by the Human Resources Research Office, The George Washington University for the Department of the Army, fall 1966, 175.

47. For respondents who had carried the M16 as their primary weapon, 185 of 219 fired their weapons fifty or fewer times in Vietnam combat (84 percent). The corresponding values for all veterans, regardless of primary weapon carried, were 206 of 258 (80 percent). Not all opportunities to engage the enemy were in situations during which the 1st Cavalry Division veteran considered his life endangered.

48. The three interview collections pertaining to the 1st Cavalry Division were "Interviews on Small Unit Combat Actions in Vietnam, Annex G: Interviews with Members of Cavalry Battalion No. 7"; "Interviews on Small Unit Combat Actions in Vietnam, Annex H: Interviews with Members of Cavalry Battalion No. 8"; and "Interviews on Small Unit Combat Actions in Vietnam, Annex I: Interviews with Members of Cavalry Battalion No. 9."

49. J. D. Coleman telephone interview with author, 7 October 1996.

50. See Daryl G. Severin et al., "Measures of Combat Performance in Korea, I. Criterion Measures for Enlisted Men" (Washington, D.C.: The Adjutant General's office, 7 April 1952), and Daryl G. Severin et al., "Measures of Combat Performance in Korea, II. Criterion Measures for Officers and Squad Leaders" (Washington, D.C.: The Adjutant General's Office, 10 June 1952).

51. Moore and Galloway, *We Were Soldiers Once*, 73. Emphasis in original.

52. The study apparently did not address how many carried weapons but never used them. See Grant Willis, "Chaplains Fired Weapons, Researchers Report: Despite Prohibitions Against Doing So, 8 Percent of Those in Vietnam Report Using Weapons," *Army Times*, 15 April 1988, 17.

53. Curtis Bowers telephone interview with author, 12 November 1996, and e-mails to author dated 5 and 8 March 1999.

54. For the Fort Leavenworth survey, 52.3 percent responded that they had seen another soldier fail to fire in situations where he should have used his weapon. Of this group who had seen a failure, 47.8 percent considered fear a cause.

55. First Cavalry Division respondent 65.

56. First Cavalry Division respondent 69.

57. First Cavalry Division respondent 193.

58. First Cavalry Division respondent 49.

59. Coleman interview with author.

60. Lawrence A. Palinkas and Patricia Coben, "Psychiatric Casualties among U.S. Marines in Vietnam." Prepared by the Naval Health Research Center, October 1985, 13.

61. "Unit Historical Reports," Headquarters, 1st Cavalry Division (Airmobile), 7 June 1967, 9. John E. Kelly wrote of the difficulty of getting soldiers to act under fire in "Shoot, Soldier, Shoot," *Infantry Journal* 58 (January 1946): 47–48.

62. "Unit Historical Reports," Headquarters, 1st Cavalry Division (Airmobile), 15 August 1967, 22.

63. Lawrence C. Vetter, Jr., *Never Without Heroes: Marine Third Reconnaissance Battalion in Vietnam, 1965–70* (New York: Ivy, 1996), 30.

64. First Cavalry Division respondent 173.

65. First Cavalry Division respondent 241.

66. Fort Leavenworth respondent 55.

67. First Cavalry Division respondent 228. Emphasis in original.

68. First Cavalry Division respondent 116. Emphasis in original.

69. First Cavalry Division respondent 100. Emphasis in original.

70. First Cavalry Division respondent 156. An "FNG" was a "f——ing new guy," a term used for inexperienced replacements.

71. First Cavalry Division respondent 127.

72. First Cavalry Division respondent 113.

73. First Cavalry Division respondent 127.

74. First Cavalry Division respondent 26, 30, and 144 respectively.

75. First Cavalry Division respondent 22.

76. Fort Leavenworth respondent 43.

77. First Cavalry Division respondent 129.

78. Ebert, *Life in a Year,* 230 and 235–36.

79. Otto J. Lehrack, *No Shining Armor: The Marines at War in Vietnam* (Lawrence: University Press of Kansas, 1992), 44.

80. First Cavalry Division respondent 163.

81. First Cavalry Division respondent 95.

82. Eli Ginzberg, *The Ineffective Soldier: Lessons for Management and the Nation: Patterns of Performance* (Westport, Conn.: Greenwood, 1975), 41.

83. First Cavalry Division respondent 41.

84. First Cavalry Division respondent 175. Emphasis in the original.

85. First Cavalry Division respondent 176.

86. Moore and Galloway, *We Were Soldiers Once,* 205.

87. "Study of Strategic Lessons," 7-7.

88. Ben Shalit, *The Psychology of Conflict and Combat* (New York: Praeger, 1988), 11.

89. S. L. A. Marshall, *Men Against Fire,* 75–76.

90. Ebert, *Life in a Year,* 114. Ebert added: "Not surprisingly, the job often fell to men of large stature."

91. Fort Leavenworth respondent 24.

92. First Cavalry Division respondent 59.

93. "Interviews on Small Unit Combat Actions in Vietnam, Annex I: Interviews with Members of Cavalry Battalion No. 9," 39.
94. Ibid.
95. James W. Johnston, *The Long Road of War: A Marine's Story of Pacific Combat* (Lincoln: University of Nebraska Press, 1992), 84.
96. First Cavalry Division respondent 205.
97. "Interviews on Small Unit Combat Actions in Vietnam, Annex I: Interviews with Members of Cavalry Battalion No. 9," 39.
98. During the American Civil War, the Medal of Honor was bestowed for actions involving either Union or Confederate colors a striking number of times. Of the 1,200 Union veterans who earned a Medal of Honor, 136 were cited for seizing friendly unit colors either to save them from falling into enemy hands or to inspire other soldiers during battle. Another 315 were awarded the medal for capturing enemy colors. Thus 451, over a third, of all Medal of Honor awards to soldiers for actions during the Civil War were related to saving or seizing colors. Such men recognized the rallying power of a unit's colors for their comrades under fire, as did the enemy who attempted to bring the bearer to ground. (Actually 318 were cited for seizing enemy colors, but three of these men, Charles H. Pinkham, 57th Massachusetts Infantry; James C. Walker, 31st Ohio Infantry; and Christopher W. Wilson, 73rd New York Infantry, earned the medal for actions involving both friendly and enemy colors and were not double-counted here.) Committee on Veterans' Affairs, United States Senate, *Medal of Honor Recipients, 1863–1978* (Washington, D.C.: GPO, 1979), pages 18–267.
99. Holding a leadership position did not ensure reduced participation in firefights. Nor did Vietnam results parallel those of Severin, who found Korean War NCO leaders more aggressive with their weapons than were their subordinates (see appendix 1).

CHAPTER 4. Training: Learning the Steps

1. Carl von Clausewitz, *On War* (Princeton, N.J.: Princeton University Press, 1989), 122.
2. Discussions of new methods and the importance of ensuring training met the demands of combat environments include Anthony Kellett, *Combat Motivation: The Behavior of Soldiers in Battle* (Boston: Kluwer-Nijhoff, 1984), 85; Edward N. Luttwak, *The Pentagon and the Art of War* (New York: Simon and Schuster, 1984); Frank Kitson, *Warfare as a Whole* (London: Faber and Faber, 1987), 154 and 157; and Richard E. Simpkin, *Race to the Swift: Thoughts on Twenty-First Century Warfare* (London: Brassey's Defence: 1985), 314–15.
3. "Study of the 12-month Vietnam Tour," D-1 to D-2.
4. Shulimson et al., *U.S. Marines in Vietnam, 1968*, 561–62. Marines did not designate their training "BCT" or "AIT." Rather, their preparation began with Marine Recruit Training ("boot camp"), was followed by Individual Combat Training (undergone by all marines, regardless of specialty), and then either the above-mentioned period of on-the-job training with a unit or, beginning in September 1965, a centralized training program called Basic Specialist Training. Some marines additionally attended formal schools for selected specialized skills. Before being sent to Vietnam, lance corporals and below also received Southeast Asia Orientation Training that included acclimatization.
5. First Cavalry Division respondent 202. The veteran likely meant "efficient" rather than "effective."
6. Du Picq, *Battle Studies*, 47.
7. This is an example only. Units each had their own standing operating procedures that specified the responsibilities of soldiers in given positions. Dictated actions might differ according to the terrain, mission, and other factors.
8. Lehrack, *No Shining Armor*, 49.
9. Stouffer, *American Soldier*, vol. 2, 91–94.

10. Michael D. Doubler, *Closing with the Enemy: How GIs Fought the War in Europe, 1944–1945* (Lawrence: University Press of Kansas, 1994), 277.

11. Tom Hamrick, "Compared to Today's Sophisticated Basic Trainees 'Dad Was a Dud,'" *Army* 21 (September 1971): 37.

12. Ibid., 36.

13. Material regarding Vietnam-era Basic Combat and Advanced Individual Training is surprisingly sparse. Course schedules were destroyed by training centers after the war. Although only five weeks of the course's schedule were available, a review of an infantry AIT training schedule from a late 1967–early 1968 course at Fort Gordon, Georgia demonstrated the emphasis given to weapons training. Trainees attended formal instruction six days weekly; the five weeks of the schedule available included twenty-eight training days due to a two-day holiday period. For riflemen, ten days were spent on individual or crew-served weapons training [M16 (3 1/2 days), M60 machine gun (5), grenade launcher (1/2), M1911 .45-caliber pistol (one day familiarization)] and two days on "techniques of fire" at the squad level that entailed firing and maneuvering as a unit during an attack and a defense. Mortar crewmen had eleven and a half days of mortar instruction, one day with the M16, a half day with the grenade launcher, and a day of pistol familiarization. The mortar men also participated in the squad techniques of fire instruction. Both groups had two days of land navigation (map and compass training) during the five weeks. The foregoing is from the Advanced Individual Training schedule for Company A, 7th Battalion, 3rd Training Brigade (Infantry), Fort Gordon, Georgia (provided by William J. Jones; 6 December 1996, fax to author). The schedule weeks available were Week 1 (4–9 December 1967), Week 3 (3–6 January 1968), Week 4 (8–13 January 1968), Week 6 (22–28 January 1968), and Week 7 (29 January–3 February 1968). See also Creighton W. Abrams, "Basic Facts on Basic Training," *Army Digest* 21 (July 1966): 9; and Warren J. Le Mon, "This Is Basic!" *Army Digest* 21 (June 1966): 44.

14. Sixty-four veteran respondents, 26 percent of the total, attended AIT at Fort Polk.

15. "An Oral History of Fort Polk, Louisiana with Mr. T. L. Berry, Civilian Aide to the Secretary of the Army, 1940–1990." Military History Institute, Carlisle Barracks, Pa., undated, 16.

16. Abrams, "Basic Facts on Basic Training," 9.

17. Le Mon, "This Is Basic!" 44.

18. First Cavalry Division respondent 50. Emphasis in original.

19. J. C. Dunn, *The War the Infantry Knew, 1914–1919* (London: Cardinal, 1989), 245.

20. James Cooke, "The American Soldier in France, 1917–1919," in *Facing Armageddon: The First World War Experienced,* ed. Hugh Cecil and Peter H. Liddle (London: Leo Cooper, 1996), 243.

21. David M. Kennedy, *Over Here: The First World War and American Society* (New York: Oxford University Press, 1980), 199.

22. Ellis, *Sharp End,* 5.

23. Doubler, *Closing With the Enemy,* 282.

24. Ibid.

25. Ellis, *Sharp End,* 11.

26. Ibid., 131.

27. United States Army Military History Institute, Company Commander in Vietnam Collection, Carlisle Barracks, Pa., John A. Fesmire interview.

28. First Cavalry Division respondent 91. For further discussions of the division's replacement training program, see "Seven Month History and Briefing Data (September–March 1966)" and "Senior Officer Debriefing Program: Report of Major General John J. Tolson." Office of the Adjutant General, 15 July 1968, 5.

29. First Cavalry Division respondent 124.

30. First Cavalry Division respondent 103.

31. Shulimson et al., *U.S. Marines in Vietnam, 1968,* 559–60.

32. Ebert found that new-arrival training throughout Vietnam was different in each unit; "there was no apparent consistency in these schools, apart from an attempt to instill in each new man respect for the enemy and teach him to listen to experienced people." *Life in a Year,* 98.

33. First Cavalry Division respondent 130. S. L. A. Marshall noted that World War II soldiers also had problems adjusting to the differences between marksmanship training and combat. See *Men Against Fire.*

34. First Cavalry Division respondent 112.

35. Ebert, *Life in a Year,* 55.

36. "Interviews on Small Unit Combat Actions in Vietnam, Annex G: Interviews with Members of Cavalry Battalion No. 7," 152–53.

   Richard M. Swain had two tours with the 1st Cavalry Division, the first as a forward observer and battery commander with the 1st Battalion, 77th Artillery, from 1967–1968, the second from 1969–1970 with the 1/21 Artillery as an assistant operations officer and battery commander. When he went through the division school during his first tour, officers completed a one-week version separate from the instruction provided to enlisted soldiers. The last night of the course for enlisted soldiers involved going outside the perimeter at An Khe and establishing a night defensive position. Richard M. Swain interview.

37. Rhame, interview.

38. United States Army Military History Institute, Company Commander in Vietnam Collection, Carlisle Barracks, Pa., John E. Robbins interview, XXXIX-9 to XXXIX-10.

39. First Cavalry Division respondent 205.

40. United States Army Military History Institute, Company Commander in Vietnam Collection, Carlisle Barracks, Pa., Joe Driscoll interview.

41. Fesmire, interview, II-14 to II-16.

42. United States Army Military History Institute, Company Commander in Vietnam Collection, Carlisle Barracks, Pa., James E. Tindall interview, XLIII-10.

43. "Study of the 12-month Vietnam Tour," D-2.

44. First Cavalry Division respondent 205.

45. Fort Leavenworth respondent 254.

46. First Cavalry Division respondent 224.

47. Rhame, interview, 23–24.

48. United States Army Military History Institute, Company Commander in Vietnam Collection, Carlisle Barracks, Pa., John D. Fuller interview, 23.

49. Nolan, *Magnificent Bastards,* 34.

50. "Interviews on Small Unit Combat Actions in Vietnam, Annex I: Interviews with Members of Cavalry Battalion No. 9," 147–48.

51. J. O. Langtry, "Tactical Implications of the Human Factors in Warfare," *Australian Army Journal* 107 (April 1958): 9–10.

52. William L. Hauser, "The Will to Fight," in *Combat Effectiveness: Cohesion, Stress, and the Volunteer Military,* ed. Sam C. Sarkesian (Beverly Hills, Calif.: Sage), 189.

53. Ebert, *Life in a Year,* 221.

54. Ibid.

55. Miller, *Reflections of a Warrior,* 15.

56. First Cavalry Division respondent 205.

57. "Winning in the Jungle for Squad through Battalion Operations," Center for Army Lessons Learned, Fort Leavenworth, Kans., May 1995, II-7. Emphasis in original.

58. For example, see Barry Broadfoot, *Six War Years, 1939–1945: Memories of Canadians at Home and Abroad* (New York: Doubleday & Company, 1974), 149.

59. Ebert, *Life in a Year,* 128; and Kellett, *Combat Motivation,* 82.

60. United States Army Military History Institute, Company Commander in Vietnam Collection, Carlisle Barracks, Pa., George F. Smith interview, 2.

61. Ibid., 11.

62. "Interviews on Small Unit Combat Actions in Vietnam, Annex G: Interviews with Members of Cavalry Battalion No. 7," 113.

63. Ebert, *Life in a Year*, 57.

64. First Cavalry Division respondent 88.

65. First Cavalry Division respondent 133.

66. First Cavalry Division respondent 160.

67. First Cavalry Division respondent 226.

68. Combat medic, e-mail letter to author.

69. First Cavalry Division respondent 176.

70. First Cavalry Division respondent 69.

71. First Cavalry Division respondent 70.

72. G. N. Donovan, "Use of Infantry Weapons and Equipment in Korea." Prepared by the Operations Research Office, The Johns Hopkins University, for the United States Army, 13 May 1952, 30.

   According to Donovan, 270 soldiers he questioned (56 percent) used only one weapon; 162 (34 percent) used two; 42 (9 percent) used three; 6 (1 percent) used four; and only three (less than 1 percent) used as many as five weapons.

73. First Cavalry Division respondent 81.

74. First Cavalry Division respondent 211.

75. Moore and Galloway, *We Were Soldiers Once*, 99–100.

76. Ibid.

77. See Marshall, *Men Against Fire*, 10.

78. Jamieson, *Crossing the Deadly Ground*, 56. By "open order" Jamieson meant tactical formations in which soldiers were dispersed rather than in ranks, as had long been the norm.

79. First Cavalry Division respondent 164.

80. First Cavalry Division respondent 170.

81. First Cavalry Division respondent 127. The value of these "quick kill" techniques was widely recognized; such methods were taught in training throughout the army during the Vietnam War. See E. O. Reusse's recommendation that the Marine Corps adopt such training in his "Quick Kill vs. Marksmanship," *Marine Corps Gazette* 53 (December 1969): 38–40.

82. First Cavalry Division respondent 93.

83. "Operational Report—Lessons learned, Headquarters, 1st Cavalry Division (Airmobile), for period ending 31 January 1970." 12 June 1970, 51.

84. First Cavalry Division respondent 226.

85. Fort Leavenworth respondent 26. By "integrated fire" the veteran meant coordinating fire so as to gain a better combined effect than was possible if every soldier engaged targets independently.

86. Vetter, *Never Without Heroes*, 111.

87. Dollard, *Fear in Battle*, 7.

88. F. M. Richardson, *Fighting Spirit: A Study of Psychological Factors in War* (New York: Crane, Russak & Company, 1978), 47.

89. Richard Holmes, *Firing Line* (London: Jonathan Cape, 1985, uncorrected proof), 67.

90. Roy L. Swank and Walter E. Marchand, "Combat Neuroses: Development of Combat Exhaustion," in *Archives of Neurology and Psychiatry* (Chicago: American Medical Association, 1946), 238.

91. Johnston, *Long Road of War*, 147.

92. Ibid., 238–39.

93. Elmar Dinter, *Hero or Coward: Pressures Facing the Soldier in Battle* (New York: Frank Cass, 1985), 98.

94. Herbert Gardiner Lord, *The Psychology of Courage* (Boston: John W. Luce, 1918), 115–16.

95. Hans Kissel, "Panic in Battle," translated and digested in *Military Review* 36 (July 1956): 100.

96. Kellett, *Combat Motivation*, 82.

97. Ibid. German units used live machine-gun fire, artillery, and half-strength hand grenades during World War I storm trooper training. See Thomas Nevin, "Ernst Jünger: German Stormtrooper Chronicler," in *Facing Armageddon: The First World War Experienced,* ed. Hugh Cecil and Peter H. Liddle (London: Leo Cooper, 1996), 269 and 274.

98. Lord Moran, *The Anatomy of Courage* (Garden City Park, N.Y.: Avery, 1987), 46–47.

99. Keith Simpson, "Dr. James Dunn and Shell-shock," in *Facing Armageddon: The First World War Experienced,* ed. Hugh Cecil and Peter H. Liddle (London: Leo Cooper, 1996), 514 and 516.

100. Ibid., 514.

101. Ellis, *Sharp End,* 9–10. For perhaps the most comprehensive overview of British battle schools and their use of inoculation, see Denis Forman, *To Reason Why* (London: Andre Deutsch, 1991).

102. Stouffer, *American Soldier,* vol. 2, 223.

103. Ibid., 229–30. See also Holmes, *Firing Line,* 53, and Doubler, *Closing With the Enemy,* 284 and 290.

104. Stouffer, *American Soldier,* vol. 2, 231.

105. Ibid., 199.

106. Robert H Ahrenfeldt, *Psychiatry in the British Army in the Second World War* (New York: Columbia University Press, 1958), 198.

107. Ibid., 202–3.

108. Forman, *To Reason Why,* 201.

109. Robert H. Ahrenfeldt, *Psychiatry in the British Army,* 203–4.

110. Sledge, *With the Old Breed,* 28–29.

111. Truscott, *Command Missions,* 534.

112. Ibid.

113. Terry Copp and Bill McAndrew, *Battle Exhaustion: Soldiers and Psychiatrists in The Canadian Army, 1939–1945* (Montreal: McGill–Queen's University Press, 1990), 132.

114. Stouffer, *American Soldier,* vol. 2, 232 and 234–35. However, Stouffer noted that British reports concluded that experience led to the opposite reaction in their soldiers (235 n).

115. Dollard, *Fear in Battle,* 14.

116. Of 476 soldiers responding to the question of what weapon they feared most, 338 cited the mortar. Other weapons and the number of soldiers choosing them were:

Burp gun (feared because of its noise):	65
Artillery:	47
Land mines:	12
Machine gun:	8
Bren gun:	3
Grenades:	3

From Donovan, "Use of Infantry Weapons and Equipment in Korea," 33.

117. Swank and Marchand found that "the large majority of men achieved adequate adjustment [to combat] in approximately five to seven days." Swank and Marchand, "Combat Neuroses," 239.

118. Ahrenfeldt, *Psychiatry in the British Army,* 201–2.

119. Ebert, *Life in a Year,* 140 and 149.

120. First Cavalry Division respondent 84.

121. First Cavalry Division respondent 133.

122. John Purdy telephone interview with author, 3 December 1996.

123. William J. Jones, respondent to 1st Cavalry Division survey, who served with both B and C Companies, 1/8 Cavalry, in 1968–69. Author telephone interview, 6 December 1996.

124. Fort Leavenworth respondent 30.

125. Bob Breen e-mail letter to author.

126. First Cavalry Division respondent 5.

127. Dollard, *Fear in Battle,* 24.

128. Richardson, *Fighting Spirit,* 138.

129. Ahrenfeldt, *Psychiatry in the British Army,* 200–201.

130. Moran, *Anatomy of Courage,* 156.

131. John Baynes, *Morale: A Study of Men and Courage, The Second Scottish Rifles at the Battle of Neuve Chapelle, 1915* (New York: Frederick A. Praeger, 1967), 43 and 88.

132. For example, see Sledge, *With the Old Breed,* 101.

133. Ellis, *Sharp End,* 98.

134. Ernst Jünger, *Copse 125* (Zimmermann & Zimmermann, 1985), 228.

135. Ginzberg, *Ineffective Soldier,* 43.

136. Sledge, *With the Old Breed,* 59.

137. The quotation is taken from Thomas B. Buell, *The Warrior Generals: Combat Leadership in the Civil War* (New York: Three Rivers, 1997), 18.

138. James M. McPherson, *For Cause & Comrades: Why Men Fought in the Civil War* (New York: Oxford, 1997), 48.

139. "Interviews on Small Unit Combat Actions in Vietnam, Annex G: Interviews with Members of Cavalry Battalion No. 7," 183.

140. First Cavalry Division respondent 120. Emphasis in original.

141. Fort Leavenworth respondent 261.

142. First Cavalry Division respondent 27. Emphasis in original.

143. First Cavalry Division respondent 25.

144. First Cavalry Division respondent 43.

145. Dunn, *War the Infantry Knew,* 353–54.

146. Kellett, *Combat Motivation,* 324.

147. Stouffer, *American Soldier,* vol. 2, 224 and 227.

148. Ahrenfeldt, *Psychiatry in the British Army,* 204–5. Also cited in Kellett, *Combat Motivation,* 84.

149. "Study of Strategic Lessons," 7–16.

150. Richard Kern and Howard McFann, "The Trumpet Sounds: Can Our Troops Be 'Battle-proofed?'" *Army Information Digest* 20 (December 1965): 25–26. Emphasis in original.

151. Ahrenfeldt, *Psychiatry in the British Army,* 208.

152. David R. Livingston, "Jungle Reaction Course," *Infantry* 56 (September–October 1966): 48.

153. Abrams, "Basic Facts on Basic Training," 10.

154. Fort Leavenworth respondent 1. Emphasis in original.

155. First Cavalry Division respondent 173.

156. First Cavalry Division respondent 55.

157. Clausewitz, *On War,* 122.

158. Dollard, *Fear in Battle,* 7.

159. Ardant Du Picq, *Battle Studies,* 231.

160. Stouffer, *American Soldier,* vol. 2, 468.

161. Ibid., 480.

162. Abrams, "Basic Facts on Basic Training," 8.

163. Moore and Galloway, *We Were Soldiers Once,* 344.

164. Paul D. Richard, "Realism Into Readiness," *Army Digest* 24 (January 1969): 57; and John S. Gregory, "Returnees Put Experience to Work," *Army Digest* 24 (July 1969): 45–46. Ebert also noted that "as the war progressed, veterans provided an ever increasing percentage of the training staff." Ebert, *Life in a Year,* 26–27.

165. First Cavalry Division respondent 144.

166. Lehrack, *No Shining Armor,* 301.

167. As has been noted, soldiers going to Vietnam did get some training on map reading and compass use. Hamrick quoted a drill sergeant who stated trainees in basic training "get at least six hours of it in the classroom and then go out into the field and orient themselves on the ground." Hamrick, "Sophisticated Basic Trainees," 37. Ahrenfeldt noted

that the same problem hindered the Wingate Expedition of 1943 in the India-Burma theater: "Some of the causes of low morale in the force were: inadequate selection of the original force, and lack of training in this specific type of warfare (*map reading,* river-crossing, etc.). . . ." (emphasis added) Ahrenfeldt, *Psychiatry in the British Army,* 208.

168. First Cavalry Division respondent 64.

169. First Cavalry Division respondent 57.

170. First Cavalry Division respondent 204.

CHAPTER 5. The Twelve-Month Tour: Home by Midnight

1. Ardant Du Picq, *Battle Studies,* 96.

2. General officers and colonels in selected positions were to serve longer tours. However, Douglas Kinnard noted: "Of the 183 generals who commanded in Vietnam, over half served there . . . for less than a year, and a quarter for less than eight months." Kinnard went on to state that these moves between jobs were likely unavoidable to some extent due to promotions, creation of new positions, and the force reductions toward the war's end. *The War Managers* (Hanover, N.H.: University Press of New England, 1977), 115.

3. Shulimson et al., *U.S. Marines in Vietnam, 1968,* 569.

4. A "butt" was some fraction of a whole. The day the soldier was scheduled to leave did not count as a full day because he was gone before its completion; it was thus the "butt" of a day.

5. Jerome Dowling, "Psychologic Aspects of the Year in Vietnam," *United States Army, Vietnam Medical Bulletin* (May–June 1967): 45.

6. Correlli Barnett, *Britain and Her Army* (London: Allen Lane The Penguin Press, 1970), 176.

7. Baynes, *Morale: A Study of Men and Courage,* 149.

8. Elbridge Colby, "Replacements for a Field Army in Combat," *Infantry Journal* (March 1947): 15–16.

9. Ellis, *Sharp End,* 187.

10. Forman, *To Reason Why,* 190.

11. Copp and McAndrew, *Battle Exhaustion,* 47.

12. Ibid.

13. Quoted in Ellis, *Sharp End,* 205.

14. Leonard L. Lerwill, *Department of the Army Pamphlet No. 20-211: The Personnel Replacement System in the United States Army* (Washington, D.C.: Department of the Army, 30 August 1954), 328.

15. Ibid., 330.

16. Stouffer, *American Soldier,* vol. 2, 102. The study was conducted from 9 September 1943 to 4 April 1944.

17. U. P. Williams, "They May Not Die—But They Wither Fast," *Military Review* 30 (July 1950): 16. Casualties from the U.S. Army Air Corps were not included.

18. "Study of AGF Battle Casualties," Headquarters, Army Ground Forces Plans Section, 25 September 1946, 8.

19. Ibid., 17. Emphasis in original. It is important to note that some authors wrote of the number of "combat days" (days in which a soldier was exposed to the direct effects of fighting), while others used calendar days, the number of days a soldier served in the theater, whether exposed to combat or not. Problems in analysis can arise as authors' definitions of combat days differed. For example, had a soldier experienced a combat day if in a position behind the front lines but still exposed to long-range artillery? Or must he have spent the day at the front, exposed to the enemy's direct fire? Similarly, authors did not always use the same formula for translating combat days into calendar days; many estimates of calendar-day limits (how long a soldier could withstand the pressures of service in a

combat theater measured in the actual passage of time, rather than the number of days a man was "in combat") were the result of multiplying the number of combat days by an author's factor that was dependent on frequency and intensity of combat, fighting conditions, and other variables (see, for example, "Study of AGF Battle Casualties," page 5, in which "ten combat days are equivalent to 17 calendar days"). Often the definitions of combat days and translation factors for determining calendar day limits were unstated.

In the eight months between early November 1944 and the end of the war in Europe, G Company, 328th Infantry Regiment, 26th Infantry Division had 625 men serve in its ranks, over three times its initial strength of 193 personnel. Its losses to enemy action (201 killed in action or wounded such that they were permanently lost to the unit) alone exceeded its original manning. Bruce E. Egger and Lee MacMillan Otts, *G Company's War: Two Personal Accounts of the Campaigns in Europe, 1944–1945,* ed. Paul Roley (Tuscaloosa: The University of Alabama Press, 1992), 261.

20. Ibid., 16. James Cooke noted a similar turnover in excess of 100 percent in the U.S. Army's 1st Infantry Division during World War I. During its time in France, "the 1st Infantry Division had an authorized strength of 28,000 officers and men. By the Armistice, 30,206 replacements had passed through the division." "American Soldier in France," 242–43.

21. Johnston, *Long Road of War,* 46.

22. "Rotation Policy." Surgeon General, United States Army, 12 July 1949, 1.

23. Lerwill, *Army Pamphlet No. 20-211,* 331.

24. Ibid., 332.

25. Albert J. Glass, ed., *Neuropsychiatry in World War II,* vol. 2, *Overseas Theaters* (Washington, D.C.: Office of the Surgeon General, 1973), 811. Glass wrote that after one such change "the neuropsychiatric hospital admission rate went from 23 per 1,000 to 31 per 1,000 in 3 months."

26. Francisco Toro-Quiñones y Silva, "Rotation of Combat Personnel within the United States Army." Unpublished thesis, United States Army Command and General Staff College, Fort Leavenworth, Kans., 1972, 1.

27. "Analytical Studies: The Army Replacement System," Command and Staff College, Fort Leavenworth, Kans., 21 June 1946, B-5. See also Lerwill, *Army Pamphlet No. 20-211,* 330.

28. "Analytical Studies: The Army Replacement System," A-V-1.

29. "Logistics in the Korean Operations, Volume I." Headquarters, United States Army Forces, Far East and Eighth United States Army (Rear), 1 December 1955, 66.

30. "Officer and Enlisted Rotation," Headquarters, 1st Cavalry Division, 10 April 1951, 1. Emphasis in original.

31. Charles G. Cleaver, "Personnel Problems," in "History of the Korean War, Volume III, Part 2," Office of the Chief of Military History, Department of the Army, 15 August 1952, 96.

32. "Officer and Enlisted Rotation," Headquarters, 1st Cavalry Division, 1.

33. Cleaver, "Personnel Problems," 98.

34. Ibid., 97–98. The requirement to return reservists involuntarily recalled to active duty did not apply to officers.

35. Ibid., 101–3.

36. Quoted in Cleaver, "Personnel Problems," 105.

37. One such problem was the simultaneous attainment of rotation eligibility by many unit members, especially national guard and reserve organizations. Cleaver, "Personnel Problems," 109.

38. Ibid., 110. See also "Rotation for period 1–15 July 1951." Headquarters, 2nd Infantry Division, 28 June 1951, 1.

39. Ibid., 111; and Toro-Quiñones y Silva, "Rotation of Combat Personnel," 28–33.

40. "Army Rotation Study, 20 February 1953." Assistant Chief of Staff, G-1, Department of the Army, 23 March 1953, 1 and Tab E.

41. D. J. Chester and N. J. von Steenberg, "Effect on Morale of Infantry Team Replacement and Individual Replacement Systems," *Sociometry* 18 (1955): 597.
42. "Army Rotation Study, 20 February 1953," 6.
43. "Study of the 12-month Vietnam Tour," A-1.
44. Ibid.
45. Ibid. The recommended tour length was twenty-four months for those with families, fifteen months for others in Saigon, and twelve months for "all others outside of Saigon."
46. "Study of the 12-month Vietnam Tour," A-1. These tour lengths also applied to personnel under the Commander, United States Military Assistance Command, Vietnam (COMUS-MACV) in services other than the army. With respect to the actual length of general officer tours, see the second note for this chapter.
47. Ibid., A-2. This request was initiated by the secretary of the army. The supporting study noted that approval would have reduced the demand for replacements by 20 percent in Vietnam while increasing unit effectiveness.
48. Westmoreland, *Soldier Reports,* 386.
49. "Study of the 12-month Vietnam Tour," A-2. The U.S. Marine Corps tour—thirteen months before the change in policy—was to have included two weeks processing in Okinawa en route to and after departure from Vietnam. Not all marines processed through Okinawa on their way to Vietnam, however; some therefore served in Vietnam for nearly the full thirteen-month period prior to the reduction in tour length.

Tours for marines serving with Fleet Marine Forces (FMF) in the Far East was reduced from fifteen to thirteen months in October 1960. The twelve-month tour for FMF marines serving in Vietnam and other Western Pacific (WestPac) areas was established in November 1969 "to standardize the 12-month Vietnam tours and to better control assignments to FMF personnel between Vietnam and other WestPac areas." "FMFPAC Tours," news release, United States Marine Corps, 28 June 1973. See also "Tour for Marines with Far East Combat Units Cut to 13 Months," news release, Department of Defense, Office of Public Affairs, 3 October 1960; David A. Dawson, "The Impact of Project 100,000 on the Marine Corps," occasional paper published by the History and Museums Division, Headquarters, U.S. Marine Corps, 1995; and Jack Shulimson, "Men and Material," in *U.S. Marines in Vietnam: An Expanding War, 1966* (Washington, D.C.: History and Museums Division, Headquarters, U.S. Marine Corps, 1982).
50. Charles C. Moskos, *The American Enlisted Man: The Rank and File in Today's Military* (New York: Russell Sage Foundation, 1970), 141–42.
51. Westmoreland, *Soldier Reports,* 387.
52. Dowling, "Psychologic Aspects of the Year in Vietnam," 45.
53. Moskos, *American Enlisted Man,* 142–43.
54. Glass, *Overseas Theaters,* 1002.
55. Albert J. Glass and Robert J. Bernucci, eds., *Neuropsychiatry in World War II,* vol. 1, *Zone of Interior* (Washington, D.C.: Office of the Surgeon General, 1966), 406–7.
56. Edwin A. Weinstein and Calvin S. Drayer, "A Dynamic Approach to the Problem of Combat-Induced Anxiety," in "Combat Psychiatry: Experiences in the North African and Mediterranean Theaters of Operation, American Ground Forces, World War II," ed. Frederick R. Hanson, *The Bulletin of the U.S. Army Medical Department* (November 1949): 25.
57. Gilbert W. Beebe and John W. Appel, "Variation in Psychological Tolerance to Ground Combat in World War II," prepared by the National Academy of Sciences for the Medical Research and Development Board, Office of the Surgeon General, Department of the Army, 10 April 1958, 166.
58. Franklin D. Jones et al., eds., *War Psychiatry* (Washington, D.C.: Office of the Surgeon General, 1995), 14; see also 54.
59. Raymond Sobel, "Anxiety-Depressive Reactions after Prolonged Combat Experience— the 'Old Sergeant Syndrome,'" in "Combat Psychiatry: Experiences in the North African and Mediterranean Theaters of Operation, American Ground Forces, World War II," ed.

Frederick R. Hanson, *The Bulletin of the U.S. Army Medical Department* (November 1949): 137–39.

60. Franklin D. Jones et al., eds., *Military Psychiatry: Preparing in Peace for War* (Washington, D.C.: Office of the Surgeon General, 1994), 42.

61. William M. Hughes, "Rotation of Combat Personnel," monograph, United States Army Command and General Staff College, Fort Leavenworth, Kans., January 1973, 28.

62. Copp and McAndrew, *Battle Exhaustion,* 153, 155, and 191.

63. Mowat, *Regiment,* 231–32.

64. Baynes, *Morale: A Study of Men and Courage,* 100–101.

65. Stouffer, *American Soldier,* vol. 2, 284.

66. Ibid., 280.

67. Ibid., 289.

68. Ellis, *Sharp End,* 217.

69. Holmes, *Firing Line,* 223.

70. Moskos, *American Enlisted Man,* 12.

71. Ibid., 163.

72. Peter G. Bourne, *Men, Stress, and Vietnam* (Boston: Little, Brown and Company, 1970), 74–75.

73. "Senior Officer Debriefing Report: MG George I. Forsythe, CG, 1st Cavalry Division (Airmobile)," period 19 August 1968 to 23 April 1969, 15 May 1969.

74. Edward C. Fisher interview in the United States Army Military History Institute, Company Commander in Vietnam Collection, Carlisle Barracks, Pa., XXII-8 to XXII-9.

75. Jones et al., *Military Psychiatry,* 42.

76. John H. Faris, "An Alternative Perspective to Savage and Gabriel." *Armed Forces and Society* 3 (spring 1977): 457–62.

77. Stouffer, *American Soldier,* vol. 2, 104.

78. Lerwill, *Army Pamphlet 20-211,* 477.

79. "Study of the 12-month Vietnam Tour," 2.

80. Stouffer, *American Soldier,* vol. 2, 451.

81. Bruce Palmer, *The 25-Year War: American's Military Role in Vietnam* (New York: Touchstone, 1984), 204–5.

82. Christopher C. Straub, *The Unit First: Keeping the Promise of Cohesion* (Washington, D.C.: National Defense University Press, 1988), 28–29.

83. Stouffer, *American Soldier,* vol. 2, 282–83.

84. Williams, "They May Not Die—But They Wither Fast," 17.

85. Roger W. Little, "Social and Psychological Differentials in Combat Survival," prepared by the University of Illinois for the U.S. Army Research Institute for the Behavioral and Social Sciences, July 1981, 11. Of the 3,047 records, 1,962 were those of army personnel.

86. Thayer's findings were based on data collected between January 1967 and December 1972, *War Without Fronts,* 113.

87. Dunn, *War the Infantry Knew,* 414.

88. U. P. Williams, "They May Not Die—But They Wither Fast," 20–21. Williams wrote that "the nonbattle loss rate curve discloses that the rate started off at approximately 15 percent per month, had an abrupt rise to 19 percent per month at about 25 days, and then dropped to 6 percent at 50 days. After 50 combat days, the rate rose gradually to 11 percent at 200 days, and then rose more sharply to 24 percent of remaining strength per month at 300 days."

89. Doubler, *Closing with the Enemy,* 271.

90. Simpson, "Dr. James Dunn and Shell-shock," 513.

91. Perkins, "Impressions of Wartime," 566.

92. Dowling, "Psychologic Aspects of the Year in Vietnam," 46. Jones also found "a soldier new to battle is more likely to break down than an experienced soldier; however, a soldier exposed to combat for a long period of time is also likely to be a stress casualty." Jones, *War Psychiatry,* 14.

93. Jones, *War Psychiatry,* 17–18.
94. Stouffer, *American Soldier,* vol. 2, 258.
95. "Study of Strategic Lessons," 3-12.
96. "Interviews on Small Unit Combat Actions in Vietnam, Annex G: Interviews with Members of Cavalry Battalion No. 7," 31.
97. "Study of Strategic Lessons," 4-38.
98. Richard M. Swain interview with author, 20 December 1996.
99. Russell A. Glenn interview with author, 24 January 1998.
100. Thomas C. Thayer, "A Systems Analysis View of the Vietnam War, 1965–1972, Volume 8: Casualties and Losses." Prepared by the OASD(SA)RP Southeast Asia Intelligence Division, Washington, D.C., 18 February 1975, 228.
101. Jonathan Shay, *Achilles in Vietnam: Combat Trauma and the Undoing of Character* (New York: Atheneum, 1994), 61.
102. Toro-Quiñones y Silva, "Rotation of Combat Personnel," 11.
103. Stouffer, *American Soldier,* vol. 2, 189.
104. Ray C. Hunt and Bernard Norling, *Behind Japanese Lines: An American Guerrilla in the Philippines* (New York: Pocket, 1988), 264.
105. Ibid., 385 and 410. Emphasis in original.
106. David H. Hackworth and Julie Sherman, *About Face: The Odyssey of an American Warrior* (New York: Touchstone, 1989), 243.
107. Max Hastings, *The Korean War* (New York: Simon & Schuster, 1987), 284.
108. Ebert, *Life in a Year,* 112 and 319.
109. Ibid., 320–21.
110. Hackworth, *About Face,* 537–38.
111. "Interviews on Small Unit Combat Actions in Vietnam, Annex G: Interviews with Members of Cavalry Battalion No. 7," 219.
112. Straub, *Unit First: Keeping the Promise,* 21.
113. Moskos, *American Enlisted Man,* 142.
114. "Doctrine for Personnel Assignment and Rotation," 1.
115. Toro-Quiñones y Silva, "Rotation of Combat Personnel," 35.
116. Ibid.
117. "Study of the 12-month Vietnam Tour," P-1.
118. Shulimson et al., *U.S. Marines in Vietnam, 1968,* 565.
119. Bob Breen e-mail letter to author, 13 January 1997.
120. Garth Pratten e-mail letter to author, 20 December 1996.
121. Interview of Martell D. Fritz, United States Army Military History Institute, Company Commander in Vietnam Collection, Carlisle Barracks, Pa.
122. First Cavalry Division respondent 112.
123. First Cavalry Division respondent 190.
124. Lehrack, *No Shining Armor,* 347.
125. Stanton, *Anatomy of a Division,* 212.
126. Ibid. The low esteem with which new arrivals were regarded was not new to Vietnam. Bell Irvin Wiley quoted a letter from a American Civil War Union soldier who had recently joined his Massachusetts regiment: "We recruits are getting kicked around pretty well now; we do all the duty in our company, and they call us d—d recruits." Bell Irvin Wiley, *The Life of Billy Yank: The Common Soldier of the Union* (Baton Rouge: Louisiana State University Press, 1989), 54. While a historical constant, such treatment does little to speed the integration of recent arrivals into combat teams.
127. Quoted in Stanton, *Anatomy of a Division,* 197.
128. Ibid. In August 1967 the cavalry battalion authorized strength was increased to 920 men in a headquarters and headquarters company, four rifle companies, and a combat support company.

129. "Doctrine for Personnel Assignment and Rotation," 1.
130. Shulimson et al., *U.S. Marines in Vietnam, 1968,* 558–59.
131. Johnston, *Long Road of War,* 72 and 74.
132. For a fuller discussion of these issues see "Study of the 12-month Vietnam Tour," 2–5 and Appendices A–C. During future contingencies, an alternative to tailoring the combat tour length to the term of enlistment would be to adjust enlistment obligations to the duration of combat tours. When "optimal" combat tour lengths were determined, soldiers and marines could be enlisted for a period equal to initial training, plus their combat tour, plus outprocessing. If combat tours were of different lengths for different specialties, individual enlistments could be adjusted to account for the variations. Similarly, men and women assigned to locations other than the combat theater could be retained on duty for longer periods, a "payback" for their not having been exposed to the dangers of the conflict.
133. "Study of Strategic Lessons," 8.
134. Du Picq, *Battle Studies,* 110.
135. "Study of Strategic Lessons," 10–25.
136. Jones, *War Psychiatry,* 479.
137. Hughes, "Rotation of Combat Personnel," 110–11. See also David W. Gray, "Is Unit Replacement *Really* the Way to Go?" *Army* 32 (June 1982): 56. Nevertheless, the army seems to have attempted unit replacement at the company level during Vietnam. Circa 1967–68, a trial AIT program at Fort McClellan, Alabama, provided units a nine-month period to train together as a company before deploying the unit as a whole to the combat theater. In the instance of which this author is aware, the only officer with combat experience was the company commander (a captain). Senior noncommissioned officers had served in Vietnam with the 1st Cavalry Division. Unfortunately the individual who provided this information left the unit for Officer Candidate School during the AIT phase; further details of this program could not be obtained. Author interview with Ernie Gurany, Santa Monica, California, 16 October 1997.
138. Hughes, "Rotation of Combat Personnel," 114.
139. Cited in Toro-Quiñones y Silva, "Rotation of Combat Personnel," 20.
140. "Study of Strategic Lessons," 4–36.
141. Stouffer, *American Soldier,* vol. 2, 242.
142. Lerwill, *Army Pamphlet No. 20-211,* 303–4.
143. Ibid., 337.
144. Ibid., 337–38.
145. Ibid., 476.
146. Colby, "Replacements for a Field Army in Combat," 16.
147. "Staff Study: Team Replacement." Originating organization unknown, undated, 1.
148. George R. Sedberry, "Army Replacements." United States Army War College, Carlisle Barracks, Pa., 25 January 1960, 16.
149. First Cavalry Division respondent 163.
150. "Interviews on Small Unit Combat Actions in Vietnam, Annex G: Interviews with Members of Cavalry Battalion No. 7," 281.
151. First Cavalry Division respondent 205.
152. "Interviews on Small Unit Combat Actions in Vietnam, Annex G: Interviews with Members of Cavalry Battalion No. 7," 113.
153. "Senior Officer Debriefing Report: 3d Brigade (Separate), 1st Cavalry Division (Airmobile), Period 10 April 1971 to 13 December 1971." 3 May 1972, 11.
154. Sledge, *With the Old Breed,* 172.
155. Kellet, *Combat Motivation,* 323.
156. U. P. Williams, "They May Not Die—But They Wither Fast," 23. Emphasis in original.
157. Dowling, "Psychologic Aspects of the Year in Vietnam," 47.

158. Jones, *Military Psychiatry*, 2.

159. Cooke, "American Soldier in France," 248.

160. Kellett, *Combat Motivation*, 81–82.

161. Ahrenfeldt, *Psychiatry in the British Army*, 198.

162. William Slim, *Defeat into Victory* (London: The Reprint Society, 1957), 192.

163. Mowat, *Regiment*, 289.

164. Williams, "They May Not Die," 18.

165. Glass, *Overseas Theaters*, 634.

166. Obviously morale, unit efficiency, and soldier survival were interrelated. Consideration of this relationship should have been a part of any rotation system's design.

167. Author telephone interview with Maj. Stephen Newman, New Zealand Army, 21 November 1996.

168. Ginzberg, *Ineffective Soldier*, 42.

CHAPTER 6. The Six-Month Command Tour: Cutting In

1. Platoon leaders, like officers in command positions senior to them, were rotated after six months when possible. Higher level U.S. Army leaders stated that the reasons behind moving company grade (lieutenant and captain) infantry officers was based less on career enhancement than on avoiding "burnout." Battalions did not have sufficient positions to absorb all those who completed a half-year tour, however. Though some remained in platoon leader slots, most were reassigned to staff or advisor tasks. George L. MacGarrigle telephone conversation with author, 27 November 1996, and letter to author 24 February 1999.

2. Baynes, *Morale: A Study of Men and Courage*, 178–79.

3. Du Picq, *Battle Studies*, 97.

4. Dollard, *Fear in Battle*, 44.

5. John B. Gaither, "Galahad Redux: An Assessment of the Disintegration of Merrill's Marauders," master's thesis, United States Army Command and General Staff College, 1975, iv.

6. Copp and McAndrew, *Battle Exhaustion*, 100.

7. Driscoll, interview. The words are the interviewer's, but Driscoll agreed. It should be noted that Driscoll's leaders were flying scout helicopters rather than leading infantry units on the ground.

8. United States Army Military History Institute, Company Commander in Vietnam Collection, Carlisle Barracks, Pa., William J. Scudder interview.

9. McKenna, Vietnam Interview Tape collection.

10. Charles R. Smith, United States Marine Corps historian, e-mail to author, 26 February 1999.

11. Thayer, "Systems Analysis View," 227. The same trend was true for company commanders if casualty statistics for those in the first four months of their commands were compared with those commanding four months or more, though the loss rate differences were not as pronounced. See page 228.

12. For example, see Anthony L. Wermuth, "A Critique of Savage and Gabriel," *Armed Forces and Society* 3 (spring 1977): 487.

13. Paul L. Savage and Richard A. Gabriel, "Cohesion and Disintegration in the American Army: An Alternative Perspective," *Armed Forces and Society* 2 (spring 1976): 358.

14. Thayer, "Systems Analysis View," 228.

15. Robbins, interview. Robbins served in the position from 27 September 1967 through mid-April 1968.

16. United States Army Military History Institute, Company Commander in Vietnam Collection, Carlisle Barracks, Pa., Lenard L. Shlenker interview.

17. Fritz interview.
18. Richard M. Swain interview with author, 20 December 1996.
19. Ibid.
20. Rhame, interview.
21. Moore and Galloway, *We Were Soldiers Once,* 343–44.
22. Thayer, "Systems Analysis View," 231.
23. Ebert, *Life in a Year,* 320.
24. Ibid., 328.
25. "Study of Strategic Lessons," 3-20 and 3-23.
26. For discussions regarding ticket-punching, see Kinnard, *War Managers,* 110–12; Lewy, *America in Vietnam,* 118; Anne Hoiberg, "Military Staying Power," in Sam C. Sarkesian, *Combat Effectiveness: Cohesion, Stress, and the Volunteer Military* (Beverly Hills, Calif.: Sage, 1980), 233; Paul L. Savage and Richard A. Gabriel, "Cohesion and Disintegration in the American Army, 353–63; and "Study of Strategic Lessons," 3-15.
27. Kinnard, *War Managers,* 110.
28. "Study of Strategic Lessons," 4-33.
29. First Cavalry Division respondent 90.
30. Combat medic, in e-mail to author, 26 December 1996. The soldier was not a member of the 1st Cavalry Division.
31. "Study of Strategic Lessons," 3-14.
32. First Cavalry Division respondent 194.
33. Ebert, *Life in a Year,* 122.
34. Garth Pratten, e-mail letter to author.
35. Bob Breen, e-mail letter to author.
36. Farley Mowat wrote of a Canadian regimental commander who, during the Second World War, "kept a keen eye on his company officers and when he saw the tell-tale signs—the vacant eyes, the slowed reactions, the heavily nicotine-stained fingers—he sent these men away to find some change of scene, some hope of rest." Mowat, *Regiment,* 233.

CHAPTER 7. Conclusion: Last Notes

1. Timothy Garton Ash, "Hungary's Revolution: Forty Years On," *The New York Review of Books* (14 November 1996): 22.
2. Sam R. Watkins, *Co. Aytch: A Side Show of the Big Show* (New York: Touchstone, 1997): 29–30.
3. Roger J. Spiller, "The Tenth Imperative," *Military Review* 69 (April 1989): 12.

APPENDIX 1: A Review of Military Surveys

1. A. R. Burn, "Introduction," in Herodotus, *The Histories,* trans. A. R. Burn (New York: Penguin, 1972), 34.
2. Thucydides, *History of the Peloponnesian War,* trans. Rex Warner (New York: Penguin, 1972), 48.
3. Ibid.
4. The events relating to Baron Larrey's disputation of soldiers' self-inflicted wounds were derived from three sources: D. J. Larrey, *Surgical Memoirs of the Campaigns of Russia, Germany, and France* (Philadelphia: Carey & Lea, 1832), 184–86; James Henry Dible, *Napoleon's Surgeon* (London: Heinemann Medical Books, 1970), 209–10; and Robert G. Richardson, *Larrey: Surgeon to Napoleon's Imperial Guard* (London: John Murray, 1974), 195–97.
5. Larrey, *Surgical Memoirs,* 184.
6. Richardson, *Larrey: Surgeon to Napoleon's Imperial Guard,* 195–96.

7. Larrey, *Surgical Memoirs*, 186.
8. Dible, *Napoleon's Surgeon*, 209. The "three days" comes from Dible (209). On page 196, Richardson states the examinations took place "from the sixteenth to the nineteenth of June," or four days. Larrey's memoirs are silent on the subject.
9. Larrey, *Surgical Memoirs*, 187.
10. Dible, *Napoleon's Surgeon*, 209–10.
11. The information pertaining to Siborne's efforts was drawn from the following four sources: David G. Chandler, "Captain William Siborne and His Waterloo Models," in Alan J. Guy, *The Road to Waterloo: The British Army and the Struggle Against Revolutionary and Napoleonic France, 1793–1815* (London: National Army Museum, 1990); David Hamilton-Williams, *Waterloo: New Perspectives, The Great Battle Reappraised* (New York: John Wiley & Sons, 1993); H. T. Siborne, *Waterloo Letters* (Mechanicsburg, Pa.: Stackpole Books, 1993); and W. Siborne, *History of the Waterloo Campaign* (Novato, Calif.: Presidio Press, 1990; originally published as *History of the War in France and Flanders in 1815*).
12. At the time of his initial research, the name was spelled "Siborn," the "e" being added in 1834. See Chandler, "Captain William Siborne and His Waterloo Models," 184.
13. Quotations and information regarding the questionnaire are from H. T. Siborne, *Waterloo Letters*, xvii–xix.
14. Hamilton-Williams, *Waterloo: New Perspectives*, 20. William Siborne wrote: "I was induced by the success of this experiment to embrace a wider field, and to extend my inquiries over the entire battle, and ultimately, throughout the campaign itself, from its commencement to its close." William Siborne, *History of the Waterloo Campaign*, iv.
15. Hamilton-Williams, *Waterloo: New Perspectives*, 21. Siborne's correspondence is currently held by the British Library.
16. Du Picq, *Battle Studies*, 94.
17. Ibid., 40.
18. Ibid., 209, and Ernest Judet in the introduction to Du Picq's *Battle Studies*, xvi–xvii. Du Picq was either being modest or he was expressing his belief in the inability of any one man to have sufficient experience to understand the totality of combat. Before his death at the front of his regiment during the Franco-Prussian War in 1870, Du Picq had seen service during the Crimean War and in Syria and Algeria.
19. Possony and Mantoux, "Du Picq and Foch: The French School," 209.
20. Du Picq, *Battle Studies*, 95–96.
21. Ibid., 110 and 139–40.
22. Baynes, *Morale: A Study of Men and Courage*, 3.
23. Ibid., 10–11.
24. Ibid.
25. Ibid., 6.
26. Baynes cites Liddell Hart also recognizing the significance of the regiment in Hart's *History of the First World War.*
27. Baynes, *Morale: A Study of Men and Courage*, 253–54.
28. The Abraham Lincoln Brigade was a completely volunteer unit comprised of Americans who fought Franco's fascist forces.
29. Dollard, *Fear in Battle*, 60.
30. Ibid., 58. Dollard noted that the questionnaire took "at least five hours" to complete, vii.
31. Ibid., 8 and 11.
32. Ibid., 22–23.
33. Ibid., 18–19.
34. Dollard, *Fear in Battle*, 12–15. The fears listed here are in decreasing order, that is, the greatest number of soldiers noted wounds to the abdomen, fewer wounds to the eyes, still fewer those to the brain.

35. Ibid., 24–27.
36. Ibid., 42–45, 54–55.
37. Ibid., 60.
38. Ibid., 60–61.
39. Ibid., 61.
40. S. L. A. Marshall, *Island Victory: The Battle for Kwajalein* (Washington, D.C.: Zenger, 1982), 1.
41. Ibid. For another description of post-combat interview technique in World War II, see Roger J. Spiller, "S. L. A. Marshall at Leavenworth: Five Lectures at the U.S. Army Command and General Staff College" (Fort Leavenworth, Kans.: Combined Arms Center, 1980), 18–20. For descriptions of its use by Marshall in Vietnam, see Marshall, "Vietnam Primer," 1; and Hackworth and Sherman, *About Face,* 554. See also F. D. G. Williams, *SLAM: The Influence of S. L. A. Marshall on the United States Army* (Fort Monroe, Va.: Office of the Command Historian, Training and Doctrine Command, 1990), Appendices A and B.
42. Marshall, *Island Victory,* 114–15.
43. Moore, "Shoot, Soldier," 21. "Small arms" was a term used to refer to weapons that could generally be carried by a man. Rifles, machine guns, and pistols were small arms as contrasted to artillery, tanks, and larger weapons systems.
44. Marshall, *Men Against Fire,* 57. As has been noted previously, Marshall did discriminate between men firing crew-served weapons and their counterparts armed with individual weapons. Writing of soldiers manning crew-served weapons, he found "usually the men with heavier weapons . . . gave a pretty good account of themselves."
45. Anthony Standish, "Crisis in Courage: Part One: Fighters and Nonfighters," *Combat Forces Journal* 2 (April 1952): 15.
46. Ibid., 23.
47. David Rowland, "Assessments of Combat Degradation," *Journal of the Royal United Service Institution* 131 (June 1986): 33.
48. Ibid., 43.
49. See Spiller, "S. L. A. Marshall and the Ratio of Fire," 68, and Smoler, "Secret of the Soldiers," 42–43.
50. Spiller, "S. L. A. Marshall and the Ratio of Fire," 68.
51. Author interview with Roger J. Spiller, 14 August 1987, Fort Leavenworth, Kans.; and Roger J. Spiller, "S. L. A. Marshall and the Ratio of Fire," 69.
52. John Douglas Marshall, *Reconciliation Road: A Family Odyssey of War and Honor* (Syracuse, N.Y.: Syracuse University Press, 1993), 186–87.
53. Hugh Cole, telephone interview with author, 6 February 1997.
54. Langtry, "Tactical Implications of the Human Factors in Warfare," 14.
55. Kissel, "Panic in Battle," 97.
56. Marshall, "Commentary on Infantry Operations and Weapons Usage in Korea," 4–5.
57. Marshall, "Vietnam Primer," 15.
58. Stouffer was the director of the professional staff. The studies were conducted under the auspices of the U.S. Army's Research Branch over a four-year period beginning on 8 December 1941.
59. Moskos, *American Enlisted Man,* 6.
60. Stouffer et al., *The American Soldier: Adjustment during Army Life,* vol. 1 (Princeton, N.J.: Princeton University Press, 1949), 12 and vii.
61. "Japanese Army Discipline and Morale: Special Translation Number 76," United States Pacific Fleet and Pacific Ocean Areas, Bulletin No. 171-45, 7 July 1945.
62. Edward A. Shils and Morris Janowitz, "Cohesion and Disintegration in the Wehrmacht in World War II," *Public Opinion Quarterly* 12 (summer 1948): 280 and 282.
63. Ibid., 280 and 285.
64. Ibid., 288.

65. Ibid., 303.
66. Donovan, "Use of Infantry Weapons and Equipment in Korea," 28. Donovan did not ask every man the same battery of questions.
67. Ibid., 3 and 11.
68. Ibid., 3.
69. Ibid., 6.
70. Ibid., 30.
71. Ibid., 31–32.
72. Ibid., 75 and 84.
73. Robert L. Weislogel and John C. Flanagan, "The Job of the Combat Infantryman," revised and rewritten by Suzanne G. Billingsley; prepared by the Operations Research Office, The Johns Hopkins University, for the Department of the Army, 18 September 1953, 1.
74. Ibid., 1. Weislogel and Flanagan described a critical incident as "an observer's report of an action or behavior on the part of an individual which resulted in that individual's performing an important aspect of the job either notably well or notably poorly," 7.
75. Ibid., 2. Emphasis in original.
76. Robert L. Egbert et al., "Fighter I: An Analysis of Combat Fighters and Non-fighters." Report prepared by the Human Resources Research Office, The George Washington University, for the Department of the Army, December 1957, 3.
77. Ibid., 4 and 7.
78. Ibid., 4.
79. Roger W. Little, "Buddy Relations and Combat Performance," in *The New Military*, ed. Morris Janowitz (New York: Russell Sage Foundation, 1964), 195–224.
80. Ibid., 196.
81. Ibid., 196–97. The "duration of membership in the organization" was the result of the U.S. rotation policy. Korean soldiers fought as members of U.S. Army units under the KATUSA (Korean Augmentation to the U.S. Army) program.
82. Ibid., 198 and 201.
83. Ibid., 221.
84. Ibid., 198.
85. Stanley W. Davis, "A Study of Combat Stress, Korea 1952 (Preliminary Report)," prepared by the Operations Research Office, The Johns Hopkins University, for the Department of the Army, 5 December 1952, 4 and 1.
86. Ibid., 152.
87. Ibid., 152. With respect to leadership, "all men interviewed said they were less afraid and had more confidence when they had good leaders."
88. Severin et al., "Measures of Combat Performance in Korea, I" and "Measures of Combat Performance in Korea, II."
89. Ibid., 2. Generally all men in a platoon were rated by the platoon sergeant and his three squad leaders. The raters were generally sergeants, but corporals and privates sometimes held these positions. Only men whom the leaders "had observed long enough to give a rating on combat performance" were evaluated.
90. Ibid., 5.
91. Lessing A. Kahn, "A Preliminary Investigation of Chinese and North Korean Soldier–Reactions to UN Weapons in the Korean War," prepared by the Operations Research Office, The Johns Hopkins University, for the Department of the Army, 1 February 1952, 5.
92. Ibid., 3.
93. Harley O. Preston et al., "A Study of Ineffective Soldier Performance Under Fire in Korea, 1951," revised by Lessing A. Kahn. Prepared by the Operations Research Office, The Johns Hopkins University, for the Department of the Army, 8 October 1954, 1. The enemy prisoners of war included 393 Chinese and 463 North Koreans.

94. Ibid., 1.

95. Ibid., 2.

96. William C. Bradbury, *Mass Behavior in Battle and Captivity: The Communist Soldier in the Korean War* (Chicago: University of Chicago Press, 1968), xxiii–xxix.

97. Ibid., xxvi.

98. Ibid., xxv.

99. Ibid., xvii.

100. Ibid., xxx.

101. Ibid.

102. Ibid.

103. Moskos, *American Enlisted Man,* 41.

104. Ibid., 190.

105. Ibid., 143.

106. Ibid., 155.

107. Ibid., 156.

108. George A. Clum and Jack L. Mahan, "Attitudes Predictive of Marine Combat Effectiveness," *Journal of Social Psychology* 83 (February 1971): 55–56.

109. Ibid., 56.

110. Ibid., 62.

111. Marshall, "Vietnam Primer."

112. George A. Magner et al., "Interviews on Small Unit Action in Vietnam," prepared by the Human Resources Research Office, The George Washington University, 1967, 1.

113. Ibid., 4–5.

114. Peter R. Prunkl and Wiley R. Boyles, "A Preliminary Application of the Critical Incident Technique to Combat Performance of Army Aviators," Human Resources Research Office Professional Paper No. 24-68, 1968, 1. The authors noted that the application of the critical incident technique differed from Flanagan's because Flanagan recorded incidents immediately after events in his initial studies, whereas Prunkl and Boyles were obtaining data several months after cited incidents.

115. Ibid., 1–2.

116. Ibid., 9.

117. Du Picq, *Battle Studies,* 41.

Bibliography

BOOKS

Ahrenfeldt, Robert H. *Psychiatry in the British Army in the Second World War.* New York: Columbia University Press, 1958.

Baynes, John. *Morale: A Study of Men and Courage, The Second Scottish Rifles at the Battle of Neuve Chapelle, 1915.* New York: Frederick A. Praeger, 1967.

Bourne, Peter G. *Men, Stress, and Vietnam.* Boston: Little, Brown and Company, 1970.

Bradbury, William C. *Mass Behavior in Battle and Captivity: The Communist Soldier in the Korean War.* Chicago: University of Chicago Press, 1968.

Brett-James, Antony, ed. *Wellington at War, 1794–1815.* New York: Macmillan, 1961.

Broadfoot, Barry. *Six War Years, 1939–1945: Memories of Canadians at Home and Abroad.* New York: Doubleday Company, 1974.

Bruce, Robert V. *Lincoln and the Tools of War.* Urbana: University of Illinois Press, 1989.

Buell, Thomas B. *The Warrior Generals: Combat Leadership in the Civil War.* New York: Three Rivers, 1997.

Burn, A R. "Introduction." In Herodotus. *The Histories.* Translated by A. R. Burn. New York: Penguin, 1972.

Cameron, Craig M. *American Samurai: Myth, Imagination, and the Conduct of Battle in the First Marine Division, 1941–1951.* New York: Cambridge University Press, 1994.

Chandler, David G. "Captain William Siborne and His Waterloo Models." In *The Road to Waterloo: The British Army and the Struggle against Revolutionary and Napoleonic France, 1793–1815,* edited by Alan J. Guy. London: National Army Museum, 1990.

Clausewitz, Carl von. *On War.* Translated and edited by Michael Howard and Peter Paret. Princeton, N.J.: Princeton University Press, 1976.

Coleman, J. D., ed. *1st Air Cavalry Division: Memoirs of the First Team, Vietnam, August 1965–December 1969.* Undated. This version was apparently published under the auspices of the division itself. A later edition was published in 1995 by Turner (Paducah, KY).

———. *Pleiku: The Dawn of Helicopter Warfare in Vietnam.* New York: St. Martin's Press, 1988.

Committee on Veterans' Affairs, United States Senate. *Medal of Honor Recipients, 1863–1978.* Washington, D.C.: GPO, 1979.

Cooke, James. "The American Soldier in France, 1917–1919." In *Facing Armageddon: The First World War Experienced,* edited by Hugh Cecil and Peter Liddle. London: Leo Cooper, 1996.

Copp, Terry, and Bill McAndrew. *Battle Exhaustion: Soldiers and Psychiatrists in the Canadian Army, 1939–1945.* Montreal: McGill–Queen's University Press, 1990.

Correlli, Barnett. *Britain and Her Army.* London: Allen Lane, 1970.

Davidson, Phillip B. *Vietnam at War: The History 1946–1975.* Novato, Calif.: Presidio Press, 1988.

de Saxe, Maurice. "My Reveries upon the Art of War." In *Roots of Strategy: The Five Greatest Military Classics of All Time,* edited and translated by Thomas R. Phillips. Harrisburg, Pa.: Stackpole, 1985.

Dible, James Henry. *Napoleon's Surgeon.* London: Heinemann Medical Books, 1970.

Dinter, Elmar. *Hero or Coward: Pressures Facing the Soldier in Battle.* Totowa, N.J.: Frank Cass, 1985.

Dollard, John. *Fear in Battle.* Washington, D.C.: The Infantry Journal, 1944.

Doubler, Michael D. *Closing with the Enemy: How GIs Fought the War in Europe, 1944–1945.* Lawrence: University Press of Kansas, 1994.

Dunn, J. C. *The War the Infantry Knew, 1914–1919.* London: Cardinal, 1989.

Du Picq, Ardant. *Battle Studies: Ancient and Modern Battle.* Translated by John N. Greely and Robert C. Cotton. Fort Leavenworth, Kans.: Combat Studies Institute, 1985.

Ebert, James R. *A Life in a Year: The American Infantryman in Vietnam, 1965–1972.* Novato, Calif.: Presidio Press, 1995.

Egger, Bruce E., and Lee MacMillan Otts. *G Company's War: Two Personal Accounts of the Campaigns in Europe, 1944–1945.* Edited by Paul Roley. Tuscaloosa: The University of Alabama Press, 1992.

Ellis, John. *Eye Deep in Hell: Trench Warfare in World War I.* Baltimore: The Johns Hopkins University Press, 1989.

———. *The Sharp End: The Fighting Man in World War II.* New York: Charles Scribner's Sons, 1980.

English, John. *On Infantry.* New York: Praeger, 1984.

Farcau, Bruce W. *The Chaco War: Bolivia and Paraguay, 1932–1935.* Westport, Conn.: Praeger, 1996.

Forman, Denis. *To Reason Why.* London: Andre Deutsch, 1991.

Fraser, George MacDonald. *Quartered Safe Out Here: A Recollection of the War in Burma.* London: Harvill, 1993.

Fuller, J. F. C. *The Foundations of the Science of War.* Fort Leavenworth, Kans.: Command and General Staff College Press, 1993.

Ginzberg, Eli. *The Ineffective Soldier: Lessons for Management and the Nation: Patterns of Performance.* Westport, Conn.: Greenwood, 1975.

Glass, Albert J., and Robert J. Bernucci, eds. *Neuropsychiatry in World War II,* vol. 1: *Zone of Interior.* Washington, D.C.: Office of the Surgeon General, 1966.

———. *Neuropsychiatry in World War II,* vol. 2: *Overseas Theaters.* Washington, D.C.: Office of the Surgeon General, 1973.

Gray, J. Glenn. *The Warriors: Reflections on Men in Battle.* New York: Harper & Row, 1970.

Griffith, Paddy. *Forward into Battle: Fighting Tactics from Waterloo to Vietnam.* Chichester, U.K.: Antony Bird, 1981.

Grossman, Dave. *On Killing: The Psychological Cost of Learning to Kill in War and Society.* New York: Little, Brown, 1995.

Hackworth, David H., and Julie Sherman. *About Face: The Odyssey of an American Warrior.* New York: Touchstone, 1989.

Hamilton-Williams, David. *Waterloo: New Perspectives, The Great Battle Reappraised.* New York: John Wiley & Sons, 1993.

Hastings, Max. *The Korean War.* New York: Simon & Schuster, 1987.

Hauser, William L. "The Will to Fight." In *Combat Effectiveness: Cohesion, Stress, and the Volunteer Military,* edited by Sam C. Sarkesian. Beverly Hills, Calif.: Sage, 1980.

Hess, Earl J. *The Union Soldier in Battle: Enduring the Ordeal of Combat.* Lawrence: University Press of Kansas, 1997.

Hoiberg, Anne. "Military Staying Power." In *Combat Effectiveness: Cohesion, Stress, and the Volunteer Military,* edited by Sam C. Sarkesian. Beverly Hills: Sage, 1980.

Holmes, Richard. *Firing Line.* London: Jonathan Cape, 1985 (uncorrected proof).

Hunt, Ray C. and Bernard Norling. *Behind Japanese Lines: An American Guerrilla in the Philippines.* New York: Pocket Books, 1988.

Jamieson, Perry D. *Crossing the Deadly Ground: United States Army Tactics, 1865–1899.* Tuscaloosa: The University of Alabama Press, 1994.

Johnston, James W. *The Long Road of War: A Marine's Story of Pacific Combat.* Lincoln: University of Nebraska Press, 1998.

Jones, Franklin D., et al., eds. *Military Psychiatry: Preparing in Peace for War.* Washington, D.C.: Office of the Surgeon General, 1994.

———. *War Psychiatry.* Washington, D.C.: Office of the Surgeon General, 1995.

Jünger, Ernst. *Copse 125.* Zimmermann & Zimmermann, 1985.

Keegan, John, and Richard Holmes. *Soldiers: A History of Men in Battle.* New York: Viking, 1986.

Kellet, Anthony. *Combat Motivation: The Behavior of Soldiers in Battle.* Boston: Kluwer-Nijhoff, 1982.

Kennedy, David M. *Over Here: The First World War and American Society.* New York: Oxford University Press, 1980.

Kinnard, Douglas. *The War Managers.* Hanover, N.H.: University Press of New England, 1977.

Kitson, Frank. *Warfare as a Whole.* London: Faber and Faber, 1987.

Larrey, D. J. *Surgical Memoirs of the Campaigns of Russia, Germany, and France.* Philadelphia: Carey & Lea, 1832.

Lehrack, Otto J. *No Shining Armor: The Marines at War in Vietnam.* Lawrence: University Press of Kansas, 1992.

Lewy, Guenter. *America in Vietnam.* New York: Oxford University Press, 1978.

Liddell Hart, B. H. *Thoughts on War.* London: Faber and Faber, 1944.

Little, Roger W. "Buddy Relations and Combat Performance." In *The New Military: Changing Patterns of Performance,* edited by Morris Janowitz. New York: Russell Sage Foundation, 1964.

Lord, Herbert Gardiner. *The Psychology of Courage.* Boston: John W. Luce & Company, 1918.

Luttwak, Edward N. *The Pentagon and the Art of War.* New York: Simon & Schuster, 1984.

Marshall, John Douglas. *Reconciliation Road: A Family Odyssey of War and Honor.* Syracuse, N.Y.: Syracuse University Press, 1993.

Marshall, S. L. A. *Island Victory: The Battle for Kwajalein.* Washington, D.C.: Zenger, 1982.

———. *Men Against Fire: The Problem of Battle Command in Future War.* Gloucester, Mass.: Peter Smith, 1978.

———. *Vietnam Primer.* Sims, Arkansas: Lancer Militaria, undated.

Mason, Robert. *Chickenhawk.* London: Corgi, 1984.

McNaugher, Thomas L. *The M16 Controversies: Military Organizations and Weapons Acquisition.* New York: Praeger, 1984.

McPherson, James M. *For Cause and Comrades: Why Men Fought the Civil War.* New York: Oxford University Press, 1997.

Miller, Franklin D. *Reflections of a Warrior.* Novato, Calif.: Presidio, 1991.

Moore, Harold G., and Joseph L. Galloway. *We Were Soldiers Once . . . And Young: Ia Drang: The Battle that Changed the War in Vietnam.* New York: Random House, 1992.

Moran, Lord. *The Anatomy of Courage.* Garden City Park, N.Y.: Avery, 1987.

Moskos, Charles C. *The American Enlisted Man: The Rank and File in Today's Military.* New York: Russell Sage Foundation, 1970.

Mowat, Farley. *The Regiment.* Toronto: McClelland and Stewart, 1973.

Neel, Spurgeon. *Medical Support of the U.S. Army in Vietnam, 1965–1970.* Washington, D.C.: Department of the Army, 1973.

Nevin, Thomas. "Ernst Jünger: German Stormtrooper Chronicler." In *Facing Armageddon: The First World War Experienced*, edited by Hugh Cecil and Peter Liddle. London: Leo Cooper, 1996.

Nolan, Keith William. *The Magnificent Bastards: The Joint Army–Marine Defense of Dong Ha, 1968*. New York: Dell, 1994.

Palmer, Bruce. *The 25-Year War: American's Military Role in Vietnam*. New York: Touchstone, 1984.

Patton, George S. *War As I Knew It*. New York: Bantam, 1981.

Possony, Stefan T., and Etienne Mantoux. "Du Picq and Foch: The French School." In *Makers of Modern Strategy*, edited by Edward Mead Earle. Princeton, N.J.: Princeton University Press, 1973.

Pyle, Ernie. *Brave Men*. New York: Henry Holt, 1944.

Quinn, Patrick. "The Experience of War in American Patriotic Literature." In *Facing Armageddon: The First World War Experienced*, edited by Hugh Cecil and Peter H. Liddle. London: Leo Cooper, 1996.

Richardson, F. M. *Fighting Spirit: A Study of Psychological Factors in War*. New York: Crane, Russak & Company, 1978.

Richardson, Robert G. *Larrey: Surgeon to Napoleon's Imperial Guard*. London: John Murray, 1974.

Savage, Paul L., and Richard A. Gabriel. "Cohesion and Disintegration in the American Army: An Alternative Perspective." In *The Military in America: From the Colonial Era to the Present*, edited by Peter Karsten. New York: The Free Press, 1980.

Shalit, Ben. *The Psychology of Conflict and Combat*. New York: Praeger, 1988.

Shay, Jonathan. *Achilles in Vietnam: Combat Trauma and the Undoing of Character*. New York: Atheneum, 1994.

Sheffield, Gary. "Officer-Man Relations, Discipline and Morale in the British Army of the Great War." In *Facing Armageddon: The First World War Experienced*, edited by Hugh Cecil and Peter H. Liddle. London: Leo Cooper, 1996.

Shils, Edward M. "Primary Groups in the American Army." In *Continuities in Social Research: Studies in the Scope and Method of "The American Soldier,"* edited by Robert K. Merten and Paul F. Lazarfeld. Glencoe, Ill.: The Free Press, 1950.

Shulimson, Jack. *U.S. Marines in Vietnam: An Expanding War, 1966*. History and Museums Division, Headquarters, U.S. Marine Corps, 1982.

Shulimson, Jack, Leonard A. Blasiol, Charles R. Smith, and David A. Dawson. *U.S. Marines in Vietnam: The Defining Year, 1968*. Washington, D.C.: Headquarters, U.S. Marine Corps, 1997.

Siborne, H. T. *Waterloo Letters*. Mechanicsburg, Pa.: Stackpole Books, 1993.

Siborne, W. *History of the Waterloo Campaign*. Novato, Calif.: Presidio Press, 1990.

Simpkin, Richard E. *Race to the Swift: Thoughts on Twenty-First Century Warfare*. London: Brassey's Defence, 1985.

Simpson, Keith. "Dr. James Dunn and Shell-shock." In *Facing Armageddon: The First World War Experienced*, edited by Hugh Cecil and Peter H. Liddle. London: Leo Cooper, 1996.

Sledge, E. B. *With the Old Breed at Peleliu and Okinawa*. New York: Bantam, 1983.

Slim, William. *Defeat into Victory*. London: The Reprint Society, 1957.

Stallworthy, John, ed. *The Oxford Book of War Poetry*. Oxford: Oxford University Press, 1984.

Stanton, Shelby L. *Anatomy of a Division: The 1st Cav in Vietnam*. Novato, Calif.: Presidio Press, 1982.

Stouffer, Samuel A., Edward A. Suchman, Leland C. DeVinney, Shirley A. Star, and Robin M. Williams, Jr. *The American Soldier: Adjustment During Army Life*, vol. 1. Princeton, N.J.: Princeton University Press, 1949.

Stouffer, Samuel A., Arthur A. Lumsdaine, Marion Harper Lumsdaine, Robin M. Williams, Jr., M. Brewster Smith, Irving L. Janis, Shirley A. Star, and Leonard S. Cottrell, Jr. *The American Soldier: Combat and its Aftermath*, vol. 2. Princeton, N.J.: Princeton University Press, 1949.

Straub, Christopher C. *The Unit First: Keeping the Promise of Cohesion.* Washington, D.C.: National Defense University Press, 1988.

Thayer, Thomas C. *War Without Fronts: The American Experience in Vietnam.* Boulder, Colo.: Westview Press, 1985.

Thompson, Robert. *No Exit From Vietnam.* New York: David McKay, 1969.

Thucydides. *History of the Peloponnesian War.* Translated by Rex Warner. New York: Penguin Books, 1972.

Truscott, Lucian K. *Command Missions: A Personal Story.* Novato, Calif.: Presidio, 1990.

Vetter, Lawrence C., Jr. *Never Without Heroes: Marine Third Reconnaissance Battalion in Vietnam, 1965–70.* New York: Ivy, 1996.

Watkins, Sam R. *Co. Aytch: A Side Show of the Big Show.* New York: Touchstone, 1997.

Weigley, Russell F. *Eisenhower's Lieutenants: The Campaign of France and Germany, 1944–1945.* Bloomington: Indiana University Press, 1981.

Westmoreland, William C. *A Soldier Reports.* New York: Dell, 1980.

Wiley, Bell Irvin. *The Life of Billy Yank: The Common Soldier of the Union.* Baton Rouge: Louisiana State University Press, 1989.

Williams, F. D. G. *SLAM: The Influence of S. L. A. Marshall on the United States Army.* Fort Monroe, Va.: Office of the Command Historian, Training and Doctrine Command, 1990.

Xenophon. *Anabasis: The March Up Country.* Translated by W. H. D. Rouse. Ann Arbor: The University of Michigan Press, 1991.

ARTICLES

Abrams, Creighton W. "Basic Facts on Basic Training." *Army Digest* 21 (July 1966): 7–11.

Ash, Timothy Garton. "Hungary's Revolution: Forty Years On." *The New York Review of Books* (November 14, 1996): 18–22.

Blumenson, Martin. "Did 'Slam' Guess at Fire Ratios? Probably: A Legend Remembered." *Army* 39 (June 1989): 16–21.

Bonsper, D. E. "The LP Doesn't Answer." *Marine Corps Gazette* 69 (August 1985): 57.

Chester, D. J., and N. J. von Steenberg. "Effect on Morale of Infantry Team Replacement." *Sociometry* 18 (1955): 587–612.

Clum, George A. and Jack L. Mahan. "Attitudes Predictive of Marine Combat Effectiveness." *Journal of Social Psychology* 83 (February 1971): 55–62.

Colby, Elbridge. "Replacements for a Field Army in Combat." *Infantry Journal* (March 1947): 15–16.

Dowling, Jerome. "Psychologic Aspects of the Year in Vietnam." *United States Army, Republic of Vietnam Medical Bulletin* (May–June 1967): 45–48.

Faris, John H. "An Alternative Perspective to Savage and Gabriel." *Armed Forces and Society* 3 (spring 1977): 457–62.

Flanagan, John C. "The Critical Incident Technique." *Psychological Bulletin* 51 (July 1954): 327–58.

Galloway, Joseph L. "Vietnam Story." *U.S. News & World Report* 109 (October 29, 1990): 36–51.

Glenn, Russell W. "Men and Fire in Vietnam." *Army* 39 (April 1989): 18–27.

———. "Men and Fire in Vietnam: Why They Didn't Shoot." *Army* 39 (May 1989): 38–45.

Grant, M. P. "Fighting Power: The German Army of WWII and the British Army of Today." *British Army Review* (December 1996): 59–72.

Gray, David W. "Is Unit Replacement *Really* the Way to Go?" *Army* 32 (June 1982): 55–57.

Gregory, John S. "Returnees Put Experience to Work." *Army Digest* 24 (July 1969): 45–47.

Hamrick, Tom. "Compared to Today's Sophisticated Basic Trainees `Dad Was a Dud.'" *Army* 21 (September 1971): 34–39.

Johnson, Thomas M. "The Contenders." *Infantry* 56 (July–August 1966): 43–46.

Kelly, John E. "Shoot, Soldier, Shoot." *Infantry Journal* 58 (January, 1946): 47.

Kern, Richard and Howard McFann. "The Trumpet Sounds: Can Our Troops Be 'Battleproofed?'" *Army Information Digest* 20 (December 1965): 24–27.

Kirkland, Faris R., et al. "The Human Dimension in Force Projection: Discipline under Fire." *Military Review* 76 (March–April 1996): 57–64.

Kissel, Hans. "Panic in Battle." Translated and digested in *Military Review* 36 (July 1956): 96–107.

Langtry J. O. "Tactical Implications of the Human Factors in Warfare." *Australian Army Journal* 107 (April 1958): 5–24. Also appears in digest form in *Military Review* 38 (February 1959): 84–93.

Le Mon, Warren J. "This Is Basic!" *Army Digest* 21 (June 1966): 42–44.

Livingston, David R. "Jungle Reaction Course." *Infantry* 56 (September–October 1966): 44–48.

Mater, Milton H. "If Shooting Is a Problem, Forces Should Find Out Why." *Army* 39 (September 1989): 17–18.

Moore, Roy E. "Shoot, Soldier." *Infantry Journal* 56 (December 1945): 21.

Perkins, Bradford. "Impressions of Wartime." *Journal of American History* 77 (September 1990): 563–68.

Ranson, Stephen W. "The Normal Battle Reaction: Its Relation to the Pathologic Battle Reaction." *The Bulletin of the U.S. Army Medical Department* 9 (November 1949, Supplemental Issue): 3–11.

Reusse, E. O. "Quick Kill vs. Marksmanship." *Marine Corps Gazette* 53 (December 1969): 38–40.

Richard, Paul D. "Realism Into Readiness." *Army Digest* 24 (January 1969): 57.

Rowland, David. "Assessments of Combat Degradation." *Journal of the Royal United Service Institution* 131 (June, 1986): 33–43.

Savage, Paul L., and Richard A. Gabriel. "Cohesion and Disintegration in the American Army: An Alternative Perspective." *Armed Forces and Society* 2 (spring 1976): 340–76.

Schneider, James J. "The Theory of the Empty Battlefield." *Journal of the Royal United Service Institution* 132 (September 1987): 37–44.

Scott, Anne Firor. "One Woman's Experience of World War II." *Journal of American History* 77 (September 1990): 556–62.

Shils, Edward A., and Morris Janowitz. "Cohesion and Disintegration in the Wehrmacht in World War II." *Public Opinion Quarterly* 12 (summer 1948): 280–315.

Smoler, Fredric. "The Secret of the Soldiers Who Didn't Shoot." *American Heritage* 40 (March 1989): 36–45.

Sobel, Raymond. "Anxiety-Depressive Reactions after Prolonged Combat—the 'Old Sergeant Syndrome.'" In "Combat Psychiatry: Experiences in the North African and Mediterranean Theaters of Operation, American Ground Forces, World War II," edited by Frederick R. Hanson. *The Bulletin of the U.S. Army Medical Department* (November 1949): 137–46.

Spiller, Roger J. "S. L. A. Marshall and the Ratio of Fire." *Journal of the Royal United Service Institution* 133 (December 1988): 63–71.

———. "The Tenth Imperative." *Military Review* 69 (April 1989): 2–13.

Standish, Anthony. "Crisis in Courage. Part One: Fighters and Nonfighters." *Combat Forces Journal* 2 (April 1952): 13–24.

Swank, Roy L., and Walter E. Marchand. "Combat Neuroses: Development of Combat Exhaustion." In *Archives of Neurology and Psychiatry*. Chicago: American Medical Association, 1946.

Weapons Department, United States Army Infantry School. "The M79." *Infantry* 53 (March–April 1963): 31–40.

Weinstein, Edwin A., and Calvin S. Drayer. "A Dynamic Approach to the Problem of Combat-Induced Anxiety." In "Combat Psychiatry: Experiences in the North African and Mediterranean Theaters of Operation, American Ground Forces, World War II," edited by Frederick R. Hanson. *The Bulletin of the U.S. Army Medical Department* (November 1949): 12–25.

Weitz, Mark A. "Drill, Training, and the Combat Performance of the Civil War Soldier: Dispelling the Myth of the Poor Soldier, Great Fighter." *The Journal of Military History* 62 (April 1998): 263–89.

Weller, Jac. "Good and Bad Weapons for Vietnam." *Military Review* 48 (October 1968): 56–64.

Wermuth, Anthony L. "A Critique of Savage and Gabriel." *Armed Forces and Society* 3 (spring 1977): 448–90.

Williams, U. P. "They May Not Die—But They Wither Fast." *Military Review* 30 (July 1950): 16–23.

Willis, Grant. "Chaplains Fired Weapons, Researchers Report: Despite Prohibitions against Doing So, 8 Percent of Those in Vietnam Report Using Weapons." *Army Times* (April 25, 1988): 17.

GOVERNMENT DOCUMENTS, REPORTS, MONOGRAPHS, AND DISSERTATIONS

"After Action Report—Keystone Robin Charlie." Headquarters, 1st Cavalry Division (Airmobile), 15 April 1971.

"Analytical Studies: The Army Replacement System." Command and Staff College, Fort Leavenworth, Kans., 21 June 1946.

"Army Rotation Study, 20 February 1953." Assistant Chief of Staff, G-1, Department of the Army, 23 March 1953.

"Battle Casualties of the United States Army." Office of the Assistant Chief of Staff, G-1, Department of the Army, 31 March 1954.

Beebe, Gilbert W. and John W. Appel. "Variables in Psychological Tolerance to Ground Combat in World War II." National Academy of Sciences for Medical Research and Development Board, Office of the Surgeon General, Department of the Army, 10 April 1958.

Cleaver, Charles G. "Personnel Problems." In "History of the Korean War, Volume III, Part 2." Office of the Chief of Military History, Department of the Army, 15 August 1952.

Davis, Stanley W. "A Study of Combat Stress, Korea 1952 (Preliminary Report)." Prepared by the Operations Research Office, The Johns Hopkins University, for the Department of the Army, 5 December 1952.

Dawson, David A. "The Impact of Project 100,000 on the Marine Corps." Occasional Paper, History and Museums Division, Headquarters, U.S. Marine Corps, 1995.

"Department of the Army Approved Small Development Requirement for a 40mm Detachable Grenade Launcher for Individual Weapons." United States Army Combat Developments Command, Fort Belvoir, Va., 13 June 1967.

Department of State response to Question 7, National Security Study Memorandum 1, 21 January 1969.

"Doctrine for Personnel Assignment and Rotation." United States Army Office of the Deputy Chief of Staff for Personnel, 8 March 1971.

Donovan, G. N. "Use of Infantry Weapons and Equipment in Korea." Prepared by the Operations Research Office, The Johns Hopkins University, for the Department of the Army, 13 May 1952.

Drucker, Eugene H. "The Effects of Basic Combat Training on the Attitudes of the Soldier." Prepared by the Human Resources Research Organization for the Office of the Chief of Research and Development (Army), June 1974.

Egbert, Robert L., et al., "Fighter I: An Analysis of Combat Fighters and Non-fighters." Prepared by the Human Resources Research Office, The George Washington University, for the Department of the Army, December 1957.

Egbert, Robert L., Robert V. Katter, and George D. Greer. "Incidental Observations Gathered During Research in Combat Units." Army Field Forces Human Research Unit No. 2, 22 October 1953.

"Feasibility of Individual Personnel Rotation, AGCTAG 62-7, Final Draft." The Adjutant General's Combat Development Group, Fort Benjamin Harrison, Ind., 30 March 1962.

"Final Report: XM-148 Grenade Launcher." Department of the Army, Army Concept Team in Vietnam, 8 May 1967.

Gaither, John B. "Galahad Redux: An Assessment of the Disintegration of Merrill's Marauders." Master's thesis, United States Army Command and General Staff College, 1975.

Glenn, Russell W. "Combat in Hell: A Consideration of Constrained Urban Warfare." Prepared by RAND for the United States Army and the Defense Advanced Research Projects Agency, 1996.

———. "Men Against Fire in Vietnam." Monograph, School of Advanced Military Studies, Fort Leavenworth, Kans., 1987.

"Headquarters, 7th Infantry Division." Office of the Assistant Chief of Staff, G-1, 22 June 1951, Tab B (Rotation).

Hughes, William M. "Rotation of Combat Personnel." Monograph, United States Army Command and General Staff College, Fort Leavenworth, Kans., January 1973.

"Interviews on Small Unit Combat Actions in Vietnam, Annex G: Interviews with Members of Cavalry Battalion No. 7." Prepared by the Human Resources Research Office, The George Washington University, for the Department of the Army, fall 1966.

"Interviews on Small Unit Combat Actions in Vietnam, Annex H: Interviews with Members of Cavalry Battalion No. 8." Prepared by the Human Resources Research Office, The George Washington University, for the Department of the Army, fall 1966.

"Interviews on Small Unit Combat Actions in Vietnam, Annex I: Interviews with Members of Cavalry Battalion No. 9." Prepared by the Human Resources Research Office, The George Washington University, for the Department of the Army, fall 1966.

"Japanese Army Discipline and Morale: Special Translation Number 76." United States Pacific Fleet and Pacific Ocean Areas. Bulletin No. 171-45, 7 July 1945.

Kahn, Lessing A. "A Preliminary Investigation of Chinese and North Korean Soldier-Reactions to UN Weapons in the Korean War." Prepared by the Operations Research Office, The Johns Hopkins University, for the Department of the Army, 1 February 1952.

Lerwill, Leonard L. *Department of the Army Pamphlet No. 20-211: The Personnel Replacement System in the United States Army.* Washington, D.C.: Department of the Army, 30 August 1954.

Little, Roger W. "Social and Psychological Differentials in Combat Survival." Prepared by the University of Illinois at Chicago for the U.S. Army Research Institute for the Behavioral and Social Sciences, July 1981.

"Logistics in the Korean Operations, Volume I." Headquarters, United States Army Forces, Far East, and Eighth United States Army (Rear), 1 December 1955.

Magner, George A., George R. Hoak, and T. O. Jacobs. "Interviews on Small-Unit Action in Vietnam." Prepared by the Human Resources Research Office, The George Washington University, for the Department of the Army, July 1967.

Marshall, S. L. A. "Commentary on Infantry Operations and Weapons Usage in Korea, Winter of 1950–51." Prepared by the Operations Research Office, The Johns Hopkins University, for the Department of the Army, 27 October 1951.

McNaugher, Thomas L. "Marksmanship, McNamara and the M16 Rifle: Organizations, Analysis and Weapons Acquisition." The RAND Corporation, March 1979.

"Officer and Enlisted Rotation." Headquarters, 1st Cavalry Division, 10 April 1951.

"Operational Report on Lessons Learned, Headquarters, 1st Cavalry Division (Airmobile) for period ending 31 Oct 66." 22 November 1966.

"Operational Report—Lessons Learned, 1st Cavalry Division (Airmobile)." 28 November 1966.

"Operational Report—Lessons Learned, HQ, 1st Cavalry Division (Airmobile)." 20 April 1967.

"Operational Report—Lessons Learned, Headquarters, 1st Cavalry Division (Airmobile), for period ending 31 January 1969." 6 June 1969.

"Operational Report—Lessons Learned, Headquarters, 1st Cavalry Division (Airmobile), for period ending 31 January 1970." 12 June 1970.

"An Oral History of Fort Polk, Louisiana with Mr. T. L. 'Sonny' Berry, Civilian Aide to the Secretary of the Army, 1940–1990." Military History Institute, Carlisle Barracks, Pa., undated.

Palinkas, Lawrence A. and Patricia Coben. "Psychiatric Casualties among U.S. Marines in Vietnam." Prepared by the Naval Health Research Center for the Naval Medical Research and Development Command, October 1985.

Preston, Harley O., et al. "A Study of Ineffective Soldier Performance under Fire in Korea, 1951." Revised by Lessing A. Kahn. Prepared by the Operations Research Office, The Johns Hopkins University, for the Department of the Army, 8 October 1954.

Prunkl, Peter R. and Wiley R. Boyles. "A Preliminary Application of the Critical Incident Technique to Combat Performance of Army Aviators." HumRRO Professional Paper No. 24-68, 1968.

"Relationship of Unit Training and Personnel Factors to Combat Performance." U.S. Army Research Institute for the Behavioral and Social Sciences, December 1995.

"Report of the M16 Rifle Review Panel: History of the M16 Weapon System." Office of the Director of Weapons Systems Analysis, Office of the Chief of Staff of the Army, 1 June 1968.

"Report of the Special Subcommittee on the M-16 Rifle Program." Committee on Armed Services, House of Representatives, Ninetieth Congress, 19 October 1967.

"Rifle Co, Inf Bn, Airmobile Div or Rifle Co, Airborne Inf Bn, Airmobile Div (TOE 7-57T)," undated.

"Rifle Evaluation Study." United States Army Infantry Combat Developments Agency, Fort Benning, Georgia, 8 December 1962.

"Rotation for period 1–15 July 1951." Headquarters, 2nd Infantry Division, 28 June 1951.

"Rotation Policy." Surgeon General, United States Army, 12 July 1949.

Sedberry, George R. "Army Replacements." United States Army War College, Carlisle Barracks, Pa., 25 January 1960.

"Senior Officer Debriefing Program: Major General John J. Tolson." Office of the Adjutant General, 15 July 1968.

"Senior Officer Debriefing Report: MG George I. Forsythe, CG, 1st Cavalry Division (Airmobile)." Period 19 August 1968 to 23 April 1969; 15 May 1969.

"Senior Officer Debriefing Report: 3d Brigade (Separate), 1st Cavalry Division (Airmobile)." Period 10 April 1971 to 13 December 1971; 3 May 1972.

"Seven Month History and Briefing Data (September [1965]–March 1966)." Headquarters, 1st Air Cavalry Division, June 9, 1967.

Severin, Daryl G., et al. "Measures of Combat Performance in Korea, I. Criterion Measures for Enlisted Men." Washington, D.C.: The Adjutant General's office, 7 April 1952.

———. "Measures of Combat Performance in Korea, II. Criterion Measures for Officers and Squad Leaders." Washington, D.C.: The Adjutant General's Office, 10 June 1952.

Shelton, Henry R. "The M-16 Rifle: Decade of Evolution 1957–1967." U.S. Army War College Research Element, 3 March 1969.

"South Vietnam Provincial Maps." Office of Basic and Geographic Intelligence, Directorate of Intelligence, Central Intelligence Agency, September 1967.

Spiller, Roger J. "S. L. A. Marshall at Leavenworth: Five Lectures at the U.S. Army Command and General Staff College." Fort Leavenworth, Kans.: Combined Arms Center, 1980.

"Staff Study: Team Replacement." Originating organization unknown, undated.

Steckel, Francis C. "Morale and Men: A Study of the American Soldier in World War II." Dissertation, Temple University, Philadelphia, 1990.

"Study of AGF Battle Casualties." Headquarters, Army Ground Forces Plans Section, Washington, D.C., 25 September 1946.

"A Study of Strategic Lessons Learned in Vietnam: Volume VII—The Soldier." Prepared by the BDM Corporation, 11 April 1980.

"Study of the 12-month Vietnam Tour." Office of the Deputy Chief of Staff for Personnel, Washington, D.C., 29 June 1970.

"Tactical Employment of the M79 Grenade Launcher." Developmental Bulletin No. 2-62, United States Marine Corps Schools, undated.

Thayer, Thomas C., ed. "A Systems Analysis View of the Vietnam War, 1965–1972, Volume 8: Casualties and Losses." OASD(SA)RP Southeast Asia Intelligence Division, Washington, D.C., 18 February 1975.

Toro-Quiñones y Silva, Francisco. "Rotation of Combat Personnel within the United States Army." Thesis, United States Army Command and General Staff College, Fort Leavenworth, Kans., 1972.

"Unit Historical Reports." Headquarters, 1st Cavalry Division (Airmobile), Republic of Vietnam, 7 June 1967.

"Unit Historical Reports." Headquarters, 1st Cavalry Division (Airmobile), 15 August 1967.

Weislogel, Robert L., and John C. Flanagan. "The Job of the Combat Infantryman." Revised and rewritten by Suzanne G. Billingsley. Prepared by the Operations Research Office, The Johns Hopkins University, for the Department of the Army, 18 September 1953.

West, F. J. "U.S. Fatalities During Vietnamization: Part I, Overview." Prepared by the RAND Corporation for the Advanced Research Projects Agency, June 1970.

"Winning in the Jungle for Squad through Battalion Operations." Center for Army Lessons Learned, Fort Leavenworth, Kans., May 1995.

INTERVIEWS AND PERSONAL CORRESPONDENCE

Bowers, Curtis. Chaplain with 1/327 Airborne Battalion in 1965–66 Vietnam. Author telephone interview, 12 November 1996.

Breen, Bob. Australian Army Land Headquarters Combat Historian. E-mail to author, 13 January 1997.

Cole, Hugh. Military historian with S. L. A. Marshall in WWII Europe. Author telephone interview, 6 February 1997.

Coleman, J. D. Commander, B Company, 2/8 Cavalry, and 1st Cavalry Division Information Officer. Author telephone interview, 7 October 1996.

Gavin, Laurence W. Ground liaison officer with the 3rd Tactical Fighter Wing, June–December 1967; troop advisor to 6th ARVN Cavalry Squadron, January–June 1968; senior operations advisor for Dinh Tuong Province, January–December 1971. Author interview, 10 April 1997.

Glenn, Russell A. Author interview, Atlanta, Georgia, 24 January 1998.

Gurany, Ernie. Author interview, Santa Monica, California, 16 October 1997.

Jones, William J. Respondent to 1st Cavalry Division survey who served with both B and C Companies, 1/8 Cavalry in 1968–69 Vietnam. Author telephone interview, 6 December 1996.

Junot, Arthur J. Executive Director, 1st Cavalry Division. Author telephone interview, 17 July 1995.

MacGarrigle, George L. United States Army Center of Military History. Author telephone interview, 27 November 1996.

Newman, Stephen. New Zealand Army. Author telephone interview, 21 November 1996.

Pratten, Garth. Historian, Australian Army Doctrine Centre. E-mail to author, 20 December 1996.

Purdy, John. Director of the Patton Museum, Fort Knox, Kentucky. Author telephone interview, 3 December 1996.

Raines, John Wayne. Scout dog platoon leader and officer assignments officer, 1st Cavalry Division, November 1966–December 1967. Author interview, Fort Leavenworth, Kans., 8 April 1997.

Siegel, Steve. Rifleman with 2/7 Cavalry in 1965. Author telephone interview, 17 December 1996.

Smith, Charles R., U.S. Marine Corps historian, e-mail to author, 25 and 26 February 1999.

Sommers, Richard J. United States Army Military History Institute; letter to author, 12 November 1996.

Spiller, Roger. George C. Marshall Chair, Command and General Staff College, Fort Leavenworth, Kans. Author interview, 14 August 1987.

Swain, Richard M. Forward observer with 1/5 Cavalry and battery commander with 1/77 Artillery in 1967–68 Vietnam; assistant S3 and battery commander with 1/21 Artillery in 1969–70 Vietnam. Author interview, 20 December 1996.

United States Army Military History Institute Senior Officer Oral History Program and Company Commander in Vietnam collection, Carlisle Barracks, Pa.

SEMINARS

Fussell, Paul. School of Advanced Military Studies, Command and General Staff College, Fort Leavenworth, Kans., 7 April 1995.

de Leon, Benjamin. Seminar Four, School of Advanced Military Studies, Command and General Staff College, Fort Leavenworth, Kans., 29 April 1996. Mr. de Leon was a second lieutenant in the Hukbalahaps who initially fought the Japanese during World War II. In 1943 he rebelled against the Huks to fight both their forces and the Japanese after Huk leadership promoted resistance against the United States.

NEWSPAPER AND TELEVISION NEWS REPORTS, NEWS RELEASES

"FMFPa.C Tours." News Release, United States Marine Corps, 28 June 1973.

"Tour for Marines with Far East Combat Units Cut to 13 Months." News Release, Department of Defense Office of Public Affairs, 3 October 1960.

SURVEYS

Survey of 1st Cavalry Division Vietnam veterans, conducted by Russell W. Glenn, autumn, 1987.

Survey of officer Vietnam veterans stationed at Fort Leavenworth, Kans., conducted by Russell W. Glenn, autumn, 1987.

Index

Note: Page references followed by *t* indicate tables or charts.

About the Author

Russell W. Glenn, son of a West Point graduate and career army officer, graduated from the United States Military Academy in 1975 and began his military career with the United States Army Corps of Engineers, serving at Fort Riley, Kansas and later in Seoul, Korea. After completing Command and General Staff College and the School of Advanced Military Studies, Glenn joined the 3rd Armored Division (Spearhead). His three-year tour with the Spearheaders included assignments during the Persian Gulf War in Operations Desert Shield and Desert Storm. Since his retirement after twenty-two years of military service, he has been a Senior Defense and Political Analyst with RAND in Santa Monica, California.

Dr. Glenn holds four master's degrees and earned his doctorate in American history from the University of Kansas with secondary concentrations in military history and political science. His military education included Airborne, Ranger, and Pathfinder schools. Though this is Dr. Glenn's first book, he has been published in American, British, and Australian military journals and is the author of several RAND documents, including a number of studies on military urban operations.

Russell W. Glenn is married to the former Deirdre Ann Burns. The couple have two sons, Russell and Andrew. They make their home in Moorpark, California. Dr. Glenn continues to write and is currently at work on a novel set during the American Civil War.

The Naval Institute Press is the book-publishing arm of the U.S. Naval Institute, a private, nonprofit, membership society for sea service professionals and others who share an interest in naval and maritime affairs. Established in 1873 at the U.S. Naval Academy in Annapolis, Maryland, where its offices remain today, the Naval Institute has members worldwide.

Members of the Naval Institute support the education programs of the society and receive the influential monthly magazine *Proceedings* and discounts on fine nautical prints and on ship and aircraft photos. They also have access to the transcripts of the Institute's Oral History Program and get discounted admission to any of the Institute-sponsored seminars offered around the country.

The Naval Institute also publishes *Naval History* magazine. This colorful bimonthly is filled with entertaining and thought-provoking articles, first-person reminiscences, and dramatic art and photography. Members receive a discount on *Naval History* subscriptions.

The Naval Institute's book-publishing program, begun in 1898 with basic guides to naval practices, has broadened its scope in recent years to include books of more general interest. Now the Naval Institute Press publishes about one hundred titles each year, ranging from how-to books on boating and navigation to battle histories, biographies, ship and aircraft guides, and novels. Institute members receive discounts of 20 to 50 percent on the Press's more than eight hundred books in print.

Full-time students are eligible for special half-price membership rates. Life memberships are also available.

For a free catalog describing Naval Institute Press books currently available, and for further information about subscribing to *Naval History* magazine or about joining the U.S. Naval Institute, please write to:

Membership Department
U.S. Naval Institute
291 Wood Road
Annapolis, MD 21402-5034
Telephone: (800) 233-8764
Fax: (410) 269-7940
Web address: www.usni.org